# Choice *of* Honor

RANDY A. GREEN

Copyright © 2019

Randy A. Green

Choice of Honor

All rights reserved
No part of this book may be reproduced, transmitted, or stored in any form or by any means, mechanical or electronic, without permission from the publisher.

Contact: Ragreen731@icloud.com

Cover and interior design by Deborah Perdue,
Illumination Graphics

Softcover ISBN 978-0-9997724-4-7
Ebook ISBN 978-0-9997724-5-4

# Dedication

To my amazing friends at Soldiers Angels; your work is noble, necessary, true, and respected. Your incredible efforts to assist our service men and women and their families, day in and day out, are so very difficult to articulate in a few short words. The amazing selfless contributions that Amy Palmer and her army of angels deliver every day is awe-inspiring. I am so very proud to be a part of your organization and I am very proud to call all of you my friends. May God continue to bless you and bless all that you serve!

Visit their site at: https://soldiersangels.org/

# Chapter 1

HE HEARD THE WORDS THAT were being spoken, but then he really didn't. His body was numb, not from the cold wind blowing that had everyone shivering, but from the pain of losing his wife. He knew the preacher, but not very well. After what he had seen men to do to each other in the war, he hadn't found a way to reconcile with the Man upstairs yet; truth be known, he held a grudge. Was that why he was being treated this way now? He didn't know the answer and he knew he wouldn't find it today as he stood there at the gravesite, watching men lower his wife into a six-foot hole in the ground on this cold Christmas day. He found that fact alone to be another ironic twist to his reconciliation with the Almighty.

Janie had her arm wrapped tightly around his left leg and Jimmy had his arm wrapped tightly around his right leg. He could feel the vibrations of their little heaves as both Jimmy and Janie tried not to cry, but both failed. He held them both as tightly as he could, but unlike his kids, he actually tried to cry and got nothing. He just wasn't a crying man; life was tough, and it wasn't always fair, and he certainly felt like he had been dealt a hand of cards from the bottom of the deck on this one. She was the best thing in his life and now she was gone.

"Lord, we relinquish our mortal embrace of this good Christian woman so that she may be comforted in yours. Protect her while she sleeps and provide us comfort while we grieve, Ashes to Ashes, Dust to Dust, we return all things to you. Amen." The preacher was a tall skinny man who would stop by the Patton Farm every so often. He always thought that he only stopped by when he wanted a free meal or maybe Doris had forgotten to pay the family tithes. He didn't have a lot of room for religion in his life. He and Doris would get into some pretty heated arguments about that ten percent that she would carve out of their yearly income and give to the Littlefield Baptist Church. He tried to argue that they needed the money more than God some years, but she never broke. Even during the toughest times, she would ante up and give their ten percent.

So many times, he wanted to illustrate to her what God allows to happen by sharing a few stories about what he had seen on Iwo Jima. He knew of no God that would allow that to happen to anyone. Was he supposed to feel blessed right now? He would never feel blessed; the sarcasm and pain would bubble to the surface as he heard the skinny preacher talk about her sleeping and releasing her embrace. He just didn't see it; she wasn't sleeping, she was dead, and now he would have to live life without her. Their children would have to grow up without a mother. The thought of how he would farm his land while raising two children entered his mind, but he forced it back down.

It was winter; he would worry about farming in the spring. Right now, James Robert Patton just needed to be left alone. Agnes would provide milk for him and the kids and he had dropped a huge 12-point buck just North of Lamesa, so they had plenty of meat. They would be just fine. Agnes was a Holstein cow that produced all the milk they needed. She was as reliable as gravity, but she really didn't like anyone but Doris to yank on her teats. That was another thing he couldn't worry about now. "I will be by this evening around 5:00 to fix you and the kids a good hot meal. I made some pies this morning and I will bring them by so that ya'll can have a hot supper."

## Chapter 1

He was still staring at the rectangle carved out of the ground that now cradled his wife. Janie and Jimmy were still clinging to his legs. He looked up to see Mavis Aldridge looking at him. He didn't realize that she had put her hand on his hand that was still resting on Janie's head. It was the hand that was missing part of his pinky. It throbbed when it was cold, but today it just made his whole hand numb; he figured that's why he didn't feel her hand on his or he would have pulled it back. "Thank you, Mrs. Aldridge, but me and the kids need to sort things out tonight." He might have taken her up on the offer as Mavis Aldridge was a nice enough woman, but it was well-known that she was a lousy cook. She was the only person in all of West Texas that didn't know she couldn't cook. She would make two pies almost daily and would just give them to people.

The joke around town was that nobody in her own home would eat them, so she had to give them away. Nobody had the heart to tell her, including her husband. He was a good man who Buddy had always respected because Buddy thought he was a square dealer, a term he stole from his dad. He didn't know exactly what his own dad qualified as a "square dealer" but in his time fighting a war in the South Pacific and now trying to scratch out a living in the flat lands of West Texas, he had his own definition for a "square dealer." In Buddy Patton's world, you were either a "square dealer" or a "phony" and if you were a phony, he had no patience or time for you. "Now, Buddy Patton! I will not take no for an answer. What in the world are you going to feed these precious babies tonight? Deer soup? Nonsense! I won't have any more talk of it." Even though his name was James Robert, everyone called him Buddy.

It was a product of being James Robert Patton, Jr. He was named after his father, and keeping with tradition, his son was James Robert Patton the third, but everyone called him Jimmy. Doris used to joke that they would save a fortune in monogrammed shirts if they ever had any. She actually bought him a really nice handkerchief for Christmas two years ago. She made him drive them all the way to Lubbock one day to pick it up, but she said she just needed to pick up some fabric for a new dress for Janie to wear to school. She saw it in the Sears catalog and ordered it way ahead of time so they would hold it for her until she got there. They didn't make many trips into Lubbock, so she had to plan things out really well. He knew he would miss that about her for sure because the only planning he did was when to plant; Doris Elaine Patton did all the rest.

"Thank you, Mrs. Aldridge, we appreciate that." He was not in the mood to argue and by the look her husband was giving him, he knew it was best to choke it back and argue a different day. He just hoped he and the kids could choke back whatever she brought. "Buddy, I'm real sorry. If there is anything you need, just holler. We are all gonna miss her." Mavis moved down to the kids and managed dislodge them from his legs. She was making a fuss over the kids. "Thank you, Shipley. I will come by tomorrow and square up the bills."

Shipley Aldridge owned the feed store where Buddy bought all the scratch, grain, oats, cotton seed, and just about anything else he needed. He kept a tab with Shipley and squared up on the 26$^{th}$ of every month. Shipley grabbed Buddy by the arm and pulled him a little distance from Mavis and her fussing over Janie and Jimmy. "Buddy, you were pretty square going into December and besides a little scratch and the oats, you don't hardly owe a thing; a few dollars at best. I'm calling it square." Buddy gently pulled his arm away from Shipley, looked up at the sky, took in a deep breath of the biting cold West Texas air, then looked back at Shipley and said, "I ain't no charity case, Shipley, don't try and make me feel like one." Shipley realized he may have insulted Buddy and tried to take it back as quickly as he could. If there was one thing that everyone knew about James Robert Patton, it was that he would starve before he would take a hand-out, and even worse, they all thought he might even let the kids starve before he would take a hand-out.

Buddy Patton had done pretty well for his family. He bought the land they were on when he returned from the war. At the

## Chapter 1

time, he felt like he paid too much but as it turned out, it was a pretty good deal. He got nearly 200 acres of flat land that hadn't been busted in nearly two years. The previous owner was a man named Eustace Langford. Eustace was planning on his son coming back from the war to help him with the farming, but his son never came back.

The story goes that Eustace was driving his tractor one day and someone happened to see him slumped over the tractor. The tractor was driving itself around in circles. His wife obviously couldn't manage the farm after losing her son to a war and a husband to a heart attack, so she packed up the house and sold it all to Buddy. That's why Buddy didn't mind at the time that he thought he paid too much. She used the money to move to Dallas to live with her sister. As far as Buddy knew, she was doing pretty well and had even remarried. "Buddy, I know that. I didn't mean anything by it. I'm sorry, I just wasn't thinking." He stammered around trying to figure out how to get out of this conversation when he saw the preacher coming their way; he leaned in close so no one could hear but he and Buddy. "The preacher is coming over. I suggest that you figure out a way to get him to come by your house tonight; he will eat anything." He patted Buddy on the arm and walked away. Buddy appreciated the recovery, and if it hadn't been such an awful time with so much rolling around in his head, he would have laughed at Shipley's jab at his own wife's cooking. Instead, on Christmas day 1954, he was trying to find a way to say goodbye to his wife, forever.

"Buddy, I hope I did her justice with my sermon. She was a fine woman and she will be missed by everyone, especially me; and I know it's early, but I've spoken to some of our ladies in the church and they are more than willing to come help you when it comes time to plant." Buddy looked up at the preacher, who, at that moment, didn't seem as tall as he actually was. He had a messy head of hair that even when the wind wasn't blowing, like it was today, it looked like he had just rolled out of bed, and for a man who made his living talking to people, he had terrible breath. Every time he spoke, he had to take a step back or turn his head and gulp some air. Today, he didn't notice it as much because of the way they were standing and the direction the wind was blowing. "Thank you, Reverend." Buddy shook his hand and was careful not to get down-wind of the preacher. He turned away from the preacher and saw that several of the ladies had joined Mavis in her fussing over the kids. He was happy that the kids were being fussed over, at least they weren't thinking about the death of their mother.

He took a couple steps toward the kids when he felt another hand on his arm. He wished people would stop touching him. He turned to see Arthur Lee Henry standing there. Arthur Lee was the wealthiest man in all of Littlefield, probably all of West Texas, as far as Buddy knew. He first made his money in cotton, but he switched over to oil and made a fortune. He was buying everything he could get his hands on in West Texas, but as far as Buddy knew, he was still a pretty down-to-earth man. He hadn't made up his mind yet whether Arthur Lee was a phony or not; he was leaning towards the side of "square dealer" though. "Buddy, I am sure sorry. She was a good woman. If there is anything I can do to help make it easier on you and the kids, just let me know." One thing that led Buddy to believe that Arthur Lee was a "square dealer" was that he didn't linger; he got to the point and then moved on. Buddy barely had time to say *thank you* before Arthur Lee had already put his trademark white fedora back on his head and walked away. As long as Buddy had known Arthur Lee, he had worn a white fedora.

He waded into the crowd of ladies that were each fussing over Jimmy and Janie in their own ways. "Ladies, I need to get the kids out of this cold." He smiled at each one of them and thanked them for being there. There was a lot of chatter back and forth about bringing food out to their place and being available to help with the kids. Jimmy and Janie wasted no time resuming their previous positions with each attached to his legs. Jimmy and Janie were a year apart to the day. Both were born

## Chapter 1

on December 18th. They hadn't planned it that way, but it just worked out that way. He actually liked it because he was terrible at remembering dates. Doris always took care of the details.

He managed to shake hands with everyone who offered up a consoling gesture, but it was excruciating for him to handle each one with the genuineness that Doris would expect him to have, especially when he came across the phonies; he knew them all. He grew up in this part of the country and knew them before the war and he knew them after. With them, he simply said *thank you* and moved on as quickly as he could. He loaded Janie and Jimmy into the truck, one of Buddy's most prized possessions. It was a 1941 Ford flatbed that did more than its fair share of work around the farm. It had a single seat and as the kids got older and bigger, things got a little tight, but they managed. He was proud of that truck and kept it running like a top. He handmade some side rails for the bed so that he could haul feed and supplies from Shipley's without things sliding off, and they came in handy if things got too tight in the cab; the kids could ride in the back and hang on to the rails. They enjoyed that quite a bit during the summer.

He climbed into the driver's seat, shut the door, and started her up. Just as he was about to shift it into gear, he heard someone call his name. "Mr. Patton, wait up just a second, I have something for you." Buddy turned to see Clancy Biggars, the local postmaster, mason, and all-around repairman. He owned a small fix-it store downtown. He could fix just about anything as long as you gave him plenty of time. He ran the post office out of his repair shop, so he got distracted easily. Sometimes he would forget where stuff was, and it would take a few months to get a fan or a clock back to the customer. He always claimed he was waiting on parts, but most people just figured he had forgotten where he put the item to be fixed or he had already lost the part he ordered.

The strangest thing about his inability to remember where stuff was is that he never screwed up the mail. He got the mail to folks in the rain, shine, sleet, and snow. "I grabbed your mail; I am real sorry about the missus. She was a good woman. I hate to give it to you here, like here, I mean. I mean, I wanted to make sure. I mean, I just figured you might not get back into town for a while." Buddy knew that Clancy Biggars meant well, and he was definitely not a phony. He couldn't be; when he was nervous, he stuttered really badly, so when he said *I'm sorry about the missus*, it came out as *muh muh muh mis sis*. Just about any word that started with an M he really struggled with, like when he said he wanted to make sure that they got their mail, it came out as *may may may may kuh*.

To Buddy, Clancy was the most genuine person in Littlefield. Clancy was with him when he shot that 12-point buck last month. When they were out hunting together and Clancy was comfortable in his environment, he spoke without any trace of a stutter. "Thank you, Clancy." He took the mail and put it in Janie's lap, and she had slid as close to her daddy as she could. He stuck his hand out the window and shook Clancy's hand. It was the only handshake that James Robert Patton offered that day. He liked Clancy because he knew he was sincere in his words no matter how much he had to struggle to get them out.

He jammed Ole Blue into first and let off the clutch. It was time to go home.

# Chapter 2

HE TURNED OLE BLUE DOWN the long gravel road that led to the house; it's what he liked to call his truck, because of the dark but faded blue color and the fact that the truck was thirteen years old. Even though it was bitter cold this Christmas day, the truck kicked up plenty of dust. The heater in the truck had broken long ago and he never found the time or the need to fix it. The kids wrapped the blanket around themselves that he kept in the front seat for that very reason. The blanket was another reminder of who would not be at home when they got there. Doris made that blanket eight years ago when they first got married. She spent all year on it because it was her first attempt at one by herself. After that, she could crank out a blanket about every three months. She sold most of them for some really good money.

Their house was nothing special, but he loved it the minute he saw it. It was tucked way back off the main road, if you could call it that; even the main road was gravel, but when you turned on to their property, it was probably three or four hundred yards down a winding road, which was really a wheel-worn trail. If it rained any longer than three days straight, which it hardly ever did, they would be stuck until the mud dried. When he and

Doris first drove down the trail to the house with the salesman, they crested the slight hill that was hiding the house from their view, and they both knew this was the home they would settle in. It needed a ton of work because it had been neglected for the last two years, but he loved the oversized porch that wrapped all the way around the house. The biggest issues were that it needed a new roof and some of the floors needed to be repaired.

The rain, when it rained, would leak right down the middle of the living room and a bunch of opossums had managed their way up through some holes in the floor. He fixed the holes in the floor first because Doris nearly came out of her skin when she opened a cupboard and one of the critters hissed at her. It had a wood stove in the main room and a fireplace in the kitchen. It had three bedrooms, but since Janie and Jimmy still slept in the same room on bunk beds that he made himself, they used the third bedroom for Doris's quilt frame and all her sewing stuff. The quilt frame was another example of his handy work. He spent a week putting it together out in the barn so she couldn't see; he loved to surprise her with gifts. He was quite proud of the way he made it adjustable in height and width. She absolutely loved it when he gave it to her. As best as he could remember, she was so happy that day that Janie might have been a result of her happiness that night.

The truck rolled up to the front steps of the house. He set the brake and turned the truck off. All three sat there without moving. He knew Jimmy and Janie were thinking about the same thing he was, she wouldn't be in there anymore. She wouldn't meet them with a kiss and hug as she always did. They wouldn't smell any food cooking or cakes baking. The only thing they would walk into would be an empty house. Even Betty-Jean could sense something wasn't right because she just sat there on the porch. She didn't come running up to the truck like she always did. She was a blue tick hound but wasn't full-blood. He thought maybe she had a little heeler in her because her ears weren't as big as a blue tick, but she was the best hunting dog he had ever

*Chapter 2*

had. She was a fierce fighter, too. He once saw her tangle with Bob Boatright's German shepherd, and she whipped him good. Bob kept telling him to put Betty-Jean away because he was in town and she was on the back of the truck like she always was. Bob's shepherd kept barking and carrying on, acting like he was gonna jump up on the back of the flat bed where Betty-Jean was minding her own business. He told Bob that Betty-Jean wasn't the problem and he needed to put his shepherd away. He asked Bob why he would buy Hitler's ugly dog anyway, especially after they had whipped the Germans.

Bob was a phony and Buddy didn't like him anyway. He always acted like he was better than everyone else when everyone knew he wasn't. Bob decided to be cute and act like his shepherd got loose from the leash and he jumped up on the flatbed where Betty-Jean was still minding her business, but the minute his four paws hit the bed of that truck, she took exception to it and the two tangled up quickly. The noise was incredible; the growling and biting and a little later the yelps of pain. The battle on the flatbed drew a crowd and a couple fellas walking by stopped and took the opportunity to wager a bet. Betty-Jean wasn't nearly as big as the shepherd, but by God she was smart. She got a hold of that shepherd's nads and that dog howled with pain like nobody had ever heard. The noise was hard to stomach.

The shepherd tried to jump off the back of that truck, but Betty-Jean still had a firm grip on his privates. It was a horrifying sight for every man who stopped to watch it. There was that shepherd, dangling off the side of the truck, squirming and screeching, clearly begging for mercy, but Betty-Jean had her front paws firmly planted on that truck. She was dug in with her backside down and wasn't in a hurry to let go of that poor German shepherd's weenie. Buddy could see every man standing there begin to cross his legs to mimic the pain they were seeing that dog endure, so he hollered for Betty-Jean to let go and she obeyed. The shepherd dropped to the ground right on its head, rolled over a few times, jumped up clearly disoriented, let out another long yelp, and took off running. His leash was trailing right behind him. Nobody ever saw that dog again. He was pretty sure that Bob found it and shot it. That was the kind of guy Bob Boatright was.

"You kids run in and get changed into your work clothes, we still got some chores to do. Jimmy, grab some wood off the back porch and start the stove. I imagine it's gone down by now. Janie, you start the fire in the kitchen." Both kids sat there quietly and didn't move. Normally, he would have had no patience for such behavior, but today he understood. Janie looked up at him with the tears running down her face, "I don't want to go in, daddy, I want mommy back." She said it so quietly and so softly; he expected his heart was about to break in two. He felt the tear run down his own cheek, "I do, too, baby. I do, too." He put his arm around both of them and huddled in the truck for just a few minutes.

He could again feel the little heaves of their chests rise and fall with each sob and he wasn't sure he could handle this all alone. "Betty-Jean is sad, too, honey, ya'll make sure she is ok, and I will take care of starting the fires." It must have worked, both the kids jumped out of the truck and started to fuss over Betty-Jean on the front porch. The two smothered that dog with hugs. He could barely see Betty-Jean through the tangled-up mess of hugs she was getting, but he could see her tail wagging under the pile. She obviously enjoyed the attention. He wished his pain would go away as easily as Betty-Jean's had. He looked down at the seat and saw the pile of mail that Clancy Biggars had handed him at the funeral. He grabbed it all, smacked it into a neat little pile in his hand, then got out of the truck.

When he walked into the house, he could still smell her, it wasn't really her perfume, but it was definitely her. It was a mix of everything from her toothpaste, facial cream, soap, and perfume. Her scent was on everything in this house, so much so that it overpowered the Christmas tree that still stood in the corner with several packages yet to be unwrapped still under it. Minus the Christmas tree, he hoped it would stay that way forever, but

## Chapter 2

he knew it wouldn't. Since she day she caught that cold, he had been doing most of the cooking and chores. It seemed like she sneezed and a few days later he was standing at her graveside.

As he stood there in the living room looking at the potbelly stove and the furniture that surrounded it, he wondered if life would ever get easy again, then he laughed. He didn't mean to laugh, it just came out. He felt guilty for laughing, but he was laughing at his own sarcasm. Life was never easy, he knew that for sure, but his life with Doris was as easy as he had ever known it. He walked into the kitchen and tossed the mail on the kitchen counter where they always threw the mail. She would open it later, he thought, then he caught himself. He shook his head, fought back another wave of tears, and pulled an armload of wood from the back porch.

Janie and Jimmy had consoled Betty-Jean on the porch to the point where their little hands were frozen. Both immediately went right to the stove where they could hear the fire begin to crackle where their daddy had already stoked the fire back up. They warmed their hands for minute, but decided that their butts were colder, and both turned in near unison. They pressed so tightly against the stove that he thought maybe they would singe their little backsides, but they didn't. Once they had warmed themselves enough, they both ran back to the bedroom to change clothes. He could hear their shoes loudly as they rumbled across the wood floors.

He was already changing out of his suit but took the time to smell some of her clothes that still hung in the closet. His thoughts took him to simple places and times until he lost track of time. He wasn't sure how long he had smelled her clothes when he realized he still hadn't started the fire in the kitchen. He would need to do that so that the kitchen would warm up. Mavis and Shipley would be coming for sure, and knowing Mavis, she would round up a bunch more people to show up at the house. He really wished they would just leave them alone, but he knew they meant well and decided that Doris would smack him a good one if she could hear his thoughts now.

He put on his jeans, a work shirt, and found some thick socks in the drawer. His work boots were on the back porch where he always left them. If he even tried to walk through the house with this work boots on, Doris would be on him like nobody's business. He wondered if he tried to walk in the house with the work boots now would his feet get stuck to the ground, would she intervene from heaven and smack him with a broom? He smiled at the thought; he would do just about anything to have her yell at him again. He walked down the hallway and peeked in the kid's room; both had climbed on the bottom bunk and were fast asleep. Jimmy had his arm over his sister and the covers were pulled up close to their heads. He thought about waking them because it was too early for a nap, but what the hell, if they slept, at least they weren't thinking about it.

## Chapter 3

THE KIDS TOOK A GOOD NAP and woke up a little hungry, so he cut some slices of a ham that was given to them the day that Doris died and made some small sandwiches. He had them fed before Mavis and her crew arrived. He didn't want the kids to have to suffer through any of Mavis's cooking if they didn't have to. He heard the cars coming down the wheel-worn trail and, by the sound of it, there were quite a few. The sun was going down and it was getting colder, but the house was much warmer now. He let Betty-Jean in the house because he figured it was getting down into the single-digit temperatures tonight. The thermostat on the front porch already said it was below freezing and the sun hadn't quite gone down yet.

While the kids were napping, he gave Agnes a try, but she wouldn't have any of it. She kicked and fussed every time he touched an utter. Oh, he got a few squirts out of her, but that was by luck. He didn't even bother trying to bring the bucket into the house. He figured he would have to spend some time with her so she could get used to the idea of someone other than Doris milking her.

He turned on the radio that was against the front wall in the living room. It was an Admiral that he bought in Lubbock two years after he and Doris were married. It was her Christmas gift that year. Doris thought it was a wonderful addition to the home and so did he. The kids loved it and he enjoyed it the most when the he could listen to the Burns and Allen radio show, but they quit doing radio and were now on TV. He thought about buying a TV last year when they had a few extra dollars; both the fall and spring cotton came in extremely well and the price of cotton went up in the fall, so they managed to pay all the bills and ended up with quite a bit more than he had anticipated. They decided to put the money in the bank instead, besides, they were too expensive, and he wasn't sure that Clancy could fix one if it broke.

Just as expected, Mavis came walking through the front door holding two pies. The folks that came with her all had some kind of food with them. There was fried chicken, another ham, turkey legs, a huge bowl of mashed potatoes, and Ms. Ellen Conner brought a pan of stuffing. He was surprised when he saw Shipley walk in with an armload of gift-wrapped packages; it seemed like they just kept coming, even Clancy brought in some packages. Pretty soon, there was no more room under the tree and the packages were starting to spill into the living room floor.

The house was small, and it got a lot smaller with all these people there now. Mavis took charge of the kitchen and started fixing plates and setting things out properly, as she called it. She separated the dessert from the main courses and the side dishes. The kitchen counter and the table were covered up in food, so much so that there was no place left to sit and eat. He had to admit that the smell of the food hit him pretty hard and he realized that he hadn't eaten much in the last few days. His stomach started growling and he was afraid it was so loud that someone might hear it, but it was so noisy in the Patton home now.

Among all the fuss in the house, he could see that Janie and Jimmy had heard the noise, awoke from their slumber, and were now eying all the packages under the tree and realized that the additional packages under the tree had their names written on them. They could not believe how many packages were under

## Chapter 3

their tree now. "Ya'll hush up for a second so we can get started eating and these babies can tear into all these packages that Santa Claus told us to drop off to Janie and Jimmy!" Mavis had a booming voice when she wanted to, and her pronouncement stopped everyone in their tracks. The house got quiet enough to hear the crackle of the wood stove. He would not put any more wood in the stove, the addition of all these people in the house made him sweat. He could see that Shipley was sweating too.

"Reverend, would you say the blessing so we can dig in?" The tall, skinny reverend seemed to appear in the middle of the room. Buddy thought that the reverend loved to be the center of attention, but he saw that Jimmy and Janie were still wide-eyed as they rummaged around the packages under the tree, so he decided he could tolerate his presence for the evening. "Lord, we know you are with us every day, but especially today. We celebrate the birth of your only son and ask that you watch over all of us, but especially the Patton family. Oh, and thank you for all this wonderful food and the good folks that prepared it." There was a long pause because everyone knew he was long-winded with his prayers, so they waited to see if he was done. He must have realized this, and he said, "Let's eat! I'm starving!" There was some laughter in the room, and everyone started stirring with Mavis as the food wrangler and meal Sheppard. She barked orders to everyone on where to go, how to form a line, she even smacked the preacher's hand when he tried to pick up a slice of ham before she was ready.

Buddy did the best he could with small talk, as it really wasn't his strong point, however, he was genuine every time he said *thank you* to someone. He was especially grateful for all the gifts they had brought to Jimmy and Janie. He and Doris had picked out their Christmas presents long ago; some were practical, like much needed school clothes, and he knew from his own childhood that clothes were always appreciated, but children had more fun if there was a toy or something that caught their attention more than a new pair of socks. He bought both

*Choice of Honor*

Jimmy and Janie new baseball gloves. They were top-of-the-line Stan Musial mitts. Doris fussed at him for getting Janie one, too, since she was a girl, but he wouldn't have any of it. He had seen her use his glove from when he was a kid to play catch with Jimmy. It was pretty worn, but Jimmy would let her use it and he would catch bare-handed. Fact was, Janie wanted to do everything that Jimmy did. She wasn't much on dolls and girl toys. She was always trying to keep up with Jimmy.

Make no mistake, she had her mother's looks and was as pretty as a shiny new penny, but she would scream bloody murder when she was forced to wear a dress. He managed to get her into a dress for Doris's funeral, but only when he told her that Doris would be upset in heaven if her little girl wore blue jeans to say goodbye to her.

Mavis clapped her hands together for attention. Some of the folks were standing around the living room with a plate in their hands, but you could hear the forks clank against the plates as they all stopped to hear what she had to say. "Now, all of you saw Santa Claus stop us on the way in, but you didn't hear him tell me specifically what to do with all these gifts." Janie and Jimmy were sitting in front of the tree with their legs crossed staring at Mavis with excited looks. Buddy was so grateful that they were not thinking about Doris at the moment and Janie had temporarily stopped crying. "He told me that he was way behind, and he had two very special kids he needed help with. He said that if I could help him get all the presents to Janie and Jimmy Patton, he would make sure that he made Christmas special for me. Since I agreed, he gave me this."

She stuck out her ring finger on her left hand and revealed to everyone that Shipley had sprung for another diamond ring. Buddy had to admit that it was the biggest diamond he had ever seen, but he thought it was a little self-serving for her to take the stage for such a show, but that was Mavis, she liked being the center of attention as much as the skinny preacher did. There were some gasps that bounced off the walls of the small house,

Chapter 3

but he couldn't tell if the gasps were from the ladies that admired the ring or from Shipley, whose face had turned beat read and was trying to melt in somewhere behind the crowd.

The preacher, not to be upstaged, walked over to her as she still had her hand stuck out for everyone to see, grabbed her hand, and kissed the ring like she was a queen. He made a little bow and a swooping motion with his arm. "M'Lady, may we assist you in the presentation of these charming gifts to prince and princess of the house?" Mavis pulled her hand back and pretended to be embarrassed, but she managed to cover her mouth with the hand that still sported the huge diamond ring in case someone had missed the showing. "Oh stop, Reverend!" She did manage a blush but gathered herself and told the preacher to help separate out the gifts.

Jimmy and Janie were mesmerized by everything that was happening. Buddy felt good about it and for the first time since Doris said goodbye to him and closed her eyes, he felt like everything was going to be all right. Janie and Jimmy tore into every package and, for just a brief time, Buddy thought that the Stan Musial baseball gloves would be an afterthought, but as it turned out, it was their most favorite present of all. He laughed when Janie opened hers and she got this giant smile on her face. She could not believe that she had her own baseball mitt now. She slid it on her hand and smacked the inside of it with her right hand just like a big leaguer would. All the ladies watching were a little confused by the gift, he even caught Mavis crinkling up her nose and raising her eyebrows as if Janie had just opened a box of cow dung.

Pretty soon the grown-ups went back to small talk and had shifted from the main course to dessert. Buddy thought it was amusing to watch Shipley try to choke down some of Mavis's pecan pie. Shipley and the preacher were the only ones that actually sliced into her pie. Shipley ate it because he needed to keep the peace at home, and the preacher because Shipley was right at the funeral, her pies were terrible. One by one, they started to leave. Buddy walked each one to their cars and thanked them again.

He got hardy handshakes and pats from all the men who left, and he got a gentle kiss on the cheek and slight hug from every one of the ladies who left. He wasn't much on hugging, but these folks had given up part of their Christmas night to make sure his children had as good of a Christmas as possible under the circumstances. The preacher, Mavis and Shipley, and Ellen Conner were the last ones to leave. Ellen and Mavis put things away in the kitchen while the three men re-organized the living room and chatted a little. He didn't realize it, but somewhere in all the cleaning, when he went to go check on the kids, someone had managed to get them into their pajama's, got them into bed, and had tucked them in. They were both sleeping on the bottom bunk and just like the afternoon nap, Jimmy had his protective arm over his sister. He fought back a tear and wiped it on his sleeve. He made sure he had himself together when he re-entered the kitchen where they were all sitting at the table having a cup of coffee. Besides some plates that were still out on the counter and had been covered in tin foil, the kitchen was spotless.

"I can't thank ya'll enough for what you have done for my kids. It's been a tough couple of days for them." He paused and looked around the room as if he was distracted, but the pause was to give him time to fight off the lump that was trying to make its way up his throat. "And me." He finished. Mavis jumped up from the table, put her arms around him and hugged him. She held the hug a little longer than Buddy was comfortable with, but he wanted to keep the peace, so he just went with it. When she finally let him go, he looked at the clock on the wall; it was nearly 9:00 p.m. and he had to get up early. His chore load had doubled in the last three days with having to get the kids up, feed them, and get them going. He felt very lucky that they were out of school for Christmas, but he wasn't sure how he would handle all of it when they went back in a little over a week.

Mavis looked around the room, too, like she was looking for something and then she said, "I'm gonna look in on those precious children and then we will leave you be. I am sure you

*Chapter 3*

are wore out." He was worn out, but he wanted a drink more than anything. He was determined to have a glass of whiskey like he did every night before he went to bed. He told Doris that it helped him sleep, which was somewhat true; from time to time, he would have some pretty bad nightmares, but the further away he got from Iwo Jima, the less he had them, but nevertheless, he still had them. He still couldn't believe he had seen what men are capable of doing when you stripped away all versions of humanity. She still didn't approve of it and made him keep his bottle way out of sight from the kids, which he did, so she tolerated it.

Mavis made her way through the living room and down the hallway to the kids' room. At the same time, Shipley stood up and said he was going to take some of the empty dishes to the car while she checked on the kids. Buddy was more than happy to help; the quicker he could get them on their way, the quicker he could have his drink. He and Shipley started hauling stuff to their car, he was amused that the preacher helped himself to another piece of pecan pie while they hauled things to the car. Buddy put some big plates in the trunk while Shipley started the car. It was bitter cold now and when he cranked the Oldsmobile, it put up a little fight before she decided to start. Shipley stayed in the car so he could pump the accelerator a little to help it warm up while Buddy went back inside to pick up what was left.

He passed by Ms. Ellen Connor on the front porch and she grabbed his arm. He really wished people would stop grabbing his arm. He stopped and the two stood on the front porch looking at each other. "Mr. Patton, I am very sorry about the loss of your wife. I don't know if I got a chance to tell you that. She was such a sweet lady. If you ever need anything, please don't wait to ask." She took her hand off his forearm and turned for the car. She seemed embarrassed a little, but at least he thought it was genuine. He hadn't really started the process of labeling women like he did men. He thought she must be a "square dealer."

He went through the living room and glanced down the hall and immediately wished he could un-see what he was seeing,

Mavis and the preacher were wrapped tight, the preacher had her pressed against the wall and there was no mistaking that they were kissing. Luckily, they didn't see him, so he increased his speed into the kitchen where he proceeded to make as much noise as he could by taking perfectly clean dishes and dropping them in the sink. It must have worked because the preacher came into the kitchen, first proclaiming that he needed to use the facility before they made the long drive back into town, and it wasn't long before Mavis came back into the kitchen. "Why those children are just precious little angels!" He was at a loss for words. It wasn't any of his business what people did, and he could care less about Mavis, especially that preacher, but good grief. That was all he could say inside his head was *good grief.*

Shipley came back in and they all exchanged pleasantries one more time before the front door shut and the house became quiet again. He stood there in the middle of his living room and let out a deep breath. He still had the image of Mavis and the preacher kissing right in this hallway. He tried to shake that image out of his head, it wasn't a good image; Mavis wasn't much to look at and neither was the preacher and when you put the two together, it just looked ugly.

He made it to the kitchen and fished his bottle of Old Fitzgerald whiskey from the top cabinet over the sink. He grabbed a glass from the cupboard and poured it about a quarter full. That was his version of two fingers. He normally liked to drop a chip or two of ice from the ice box, but he was in somewhat of a hurry to have this drink, so he just tilted the glass and downed it all; no sipping tonight, that drink was going to go down fast. He set the empty glass on the table and decided after what he had just seen, the day he had and life he was about to lead, he was sure a second two fingers was not overdoing it. He wouldn't down this one though, he sat there and sipped on it for a while, thinking about going to bed and not having her warm body against him when the pile of mail Clancy had given him earlier that day caught his eye. He stood up and walked over

*Chapter 3*

to the counter where the mail was. Someone had spilled what looked like mustard on the top envelope, which was nothing more than a newsletter from the church, but the next envelope really caught his attention, so much so that he threw the remaining envelopes back on the counter without even looking at them.

It was a plain white envelope with a red and blue striped border that was addressed to Sergeant Major Patton. He hadn't been addressed with that title in a long time. He tore the envelope open and began to read; the more he read, the more his hands started to shake. It was from Corporal Alvin Jerome Mack, A.J. for short. He downed the second glass of Old Fitzgerald and poured another. When he finished the letter, he folded it back up, slid it in the envelope, and stuck it in the top cabinet alongside the bottle of Old Fitzgerald that he had now returned to its hiding place.

He flipped off the lights, walked down the hall, and stuck his head in the kids' room where he could see that Jimmy still had his arm draped over his sister. He stood there wondering how in the world he could do all that he needed to do on the farm, raise his cotton and his kids, and now this. Not to mention that he had just caught a supposed man of God making out with a married woman in his own house. He wished he could forget this Christmas, but he knew he never would.

When he got to his and Doris's room, he stood and stared at the bed. It was a nice feather bed that the two had made themselves. He collected all the feathers, Doris bought the mattress fabric and did all the sewing. It was a good bed, but it was not calling to him that night, in fact, he didn't want to lay down in it. He hadn't slept in it since she passed. He grabbed a pile of blankets that were laying on top of the bed and made his bed on the floor, just like he had done the last three nights. He just couldn't stand the thought of not feeling her warmth anymore. Now, after reading that letter, the grotesque images of war filled his head, which meant that he was sure to have nightmares again.

# Chapter 4

ALVIN JEROME MACK, JR. WAS born in Andalusia, Alabama, the first son of Alvin Jerome Mack, Sr. His daddy was a sharecropper, but had a tough time making it work, so he moved the family to Montgomery when Alvin was just a small boy, so he didn't remember anything about Andalusia. Whenever someone would ask him where he was from, he always told them that he was from Andalusia, though, not for any other reason than he just liked the sound of Andalusia better than Montgomery. It was a conversation piece and even though he couldn't remember anything about the town, he would make up details about it to the guys he met while he was in the war. His daddy took a job at a concrete plant in Montgomery and worked there until the day he died.

When the Japanese bombed Pearl Harbor, Alvin, Jr., or A.J. as all his friends and family called him, went to downtown Montgomery with what seemed like everybody he knew and enlisted. His daddy was as patriotic as they come, and he didn't try to stop his oldest boy. Since he was only 16 at the time, his daddy had to sign papers saying that he had no objection to his son entering the war. Alvin, Sr. was very proud of the fact that his son was a Marine and he let everyone he knew know about it.

## Chapter 4

When A.J. enlisted, he was certain that there was so much hatred for the Germans and the Japanese that the military would forget about Jim Crow and let men fight for their country, but that wasn't the case. He went through basic training segregated and pretty much stayed that way until he got to Iwo Jima. He was assigned to the 36th depot company, which meant that they were supposed to stay back, load cargo, handle ammunition, and any other manual labor job that needed to be done, but the island was small and the battles so fierce, there was no way anyone could "lay back." That's how he met Sergeant Major Patton. The Japanese tricked them all into thinking that when they landed on Yellow Beach that there was no resistance. He remembered everyone laughing and joking and saying things like, "They are running now. The Marines are here and there ain't nowhere to hide!" The Japanese waited until they had as many men on the beach, standing around in that thick black sand, all laughing and joking, and then they unleashed hell on everybody. As far as he could tell, the Japanese didn't care what color the soldiers were, they just wanted to kill them all.

When they opened up the machine guns, the soldiers around them started dropping like flies. If the rounds fired by the Japanese that were dug in on the hillsides didn't hit them, they were hit by exploding ammo that had been hit by the Japanese. He had never in his life been that scared. Everyone tried to scramble inland so at least they could find some kind of cover, but the thick black sand was so hard to move on that it was like being stuck in the mud. A.J. was one of the very few who made it to the tree line. He had done so without a rifle. He remembered lying there thinking that this was it, he had no weapon, and men were trying to kill him. He stayed on his stomach and crawled as far inland as he could. He knew based off the briefings that the other divisions would be making their way inland, advancing toward the two airfields. He knew he couldn't go back to the beach because there he would be a sitting duck. His only hope was to run into some other soldiers before he ran into the Japanese. He figured if he ran into the enemy first, his goose was cooked.

Before long, the sun went down and before he knew it, it was pitch black. He could barely see anything. He continued to crawl to where he thought was the airstrips when he heard the voices. It was definitely not English, so he froze. He tried his best not to breathe, but he heard the voices getting closer. The only thing he had on him was a pocket knife and a bayonet for a rifle that he didn't have. He could hear them, and by the sound of it, they were digging. They would take a few steps closer to him and then they would dig. As he lay there, they got so close he could feel the vibrations from their footsteps, and he could also smell them. He then wondered if they could smell him and that's when he realized what the digging sound was. They were stabbing their own bayonets in the ground in hopes of spearing an enemy that might just be lying around waiting for them to stab them.

He was unsure of whether to stay still and die or get up and fight and surely die or get up and try to outrun them back to the beach. He had concluded that he had a better chance if he just stayed perfectly still, but when he felt the blade enter into the back of his hand, he couldn't help but jump; they had found him. He tried not to, but he let out a muffled whimper because the pain was intense, and then all hell broke loose. He heard rifles firing, both M-1's and Thompson Subs, so he knew he was not alone. Those were U.S. issued weapons and he knew their sound well. He didn't move for fear that if he stood, his own guys might shoot him, and then it stopped. Just as quickly as it started, it stopped. He felt a hand grab him by the back of his collar and heard a voice say, "Let's go, Marine!" He scrambled to his feet, but he still couldn't see much and wondered who the hell the man was that was still holding the back of his shirt and was now practically dragging him through the dense part of the island jungle. After the two men had slogged through what seemed like a mile of thick foliage, they stopped, and the man holding the back

## Chapter 4

of his shirt forced them both to the ground. "Keep quiet." They both lay there side-by-side not saying a word. A.J. managed to wrap his hand. He couldn't feel the pain anymore and wondered if maybe he had lost some fingers.

As soon as the sun started to come up, the man beside him became clearer. That was when he first met Sergeant Major James Robert Patton. "They weren't digging; bastards were bayoneting Marines." It was like this guy was reading his mind, but when he said it, he could hear that his voice was raspy. When the sun was completely up, he could see blood all around the sergeant's mouth and he was struggling to breathe. "You're hit!" His excitement came out a little too loudly and the man lying there reached up and put his hand over A.J.'s mouth as if to say *be quiet*. It was a weak gesture and now A.J. wondered how this man had dragged him out of that mess to that point. He ripped open the Marine's jacket and saw a hole on the left side of his chest just below his shoulder. He took his canteen and cleaned the wound as much as he could.

Every time he cleaned the hole, it would fill back up with blood and then it would bubble like a little volcano. He knew from what little medic training he had that this guy had been shot in the lung and air was leaking out. He would die for sure if he didn't do anything. The only logical thing he could think to do was to stick his finger in the hole and hopefully plug the leak. The thought repulsed him a little, but he decided he had no choice. As soon as he plugged the hole in the man's chest with his finger, he could see that the sergeant would breathe much better. This was quite a dilemma now; he could either stay here with his finger in this man's chest, or he could go try and find some help, or they both could get up and try and get help, but he had no idea which way to go.

As if the sergeant was reading his mind again, "We can't move, 3rd Marine hasn't advanced yet, we are surrounded." A.J. processed that information as best he could then looked down at his finger in this man's chest, and once again the sergeant was reading his thoughts, but he threw some humor in there when he wasn't expecting it. "Make sure that's the only hole you stick that finger in." A.J. almost laughed out loud, but he thought better of it. "I don't want my finger in this hole, what makes you think I want it in another one you got?" The man lying on the ground chuckled, which caused his finger to slip out of the hole and he could immediately see the difference in his breathing. "Because I'm pretty and you are out of options right now." A.J. could not believe that this man laying here with a hole in his lungs was making jokes.

    He was about to laugh when he heard the thunder of footsteps and some kind of scream. Before he could turn and look, he saw the sergeant's hand come up behind his head and knock a bayonet away from what was meant to be A.J.'s head. He caught a glimpse of either the man's pinky finger or a part of his pinky finger go flying up in the air. The Japanese man stumbled over the both of them and rolled away. For not one second did A.J. take his finger out of the man's chest. In hindsight, he thought he probably should, but as he calculated what he was supposed to do, he decided on keeping his finger in Sergeant Major Patton's chest. As it turns out, Sergeant Major pulled his .45 from his holster and just as casual as swatting a fly, put two rounds into the Japanese man. Everything got really quiet again and the sergeant slid his .45 into A.J.'s jacket pocket. "Your turn next time." A.J. was speechless. He had never in his life seen anyone behave so calmly in a crazy situation like this. "Man, that is the third time you saved my ass." The sergeant looked up at him and with another calm reassuring voice he said, "We stay even as long as you have your finger in my chest, Corporal. The minute I lose your finger, I am dead. Maybe you can find what's left of my pinky and stick it in the hole." He laughed when he said that, and he held his severed stump of a finger up for dramatic effect. The two stayed in that spot for an entire day.

    A member of the 147th infantry came across them on the way to the fighting. Before the medics took Sergeant Major away, he

## Chapter 4

looked at Corporal Alvin Jerome Mack and said, "You're a good Marine. If you ever need me, I will be there." The syrette the medics popped in him took its effect and that was the last time he ever saw Sergeant Major James Robert Patton. It certainly wasn't the last time he thought of him, but he was sure thinking of him as he sat there in that cold, dank, smelly, jail cell in Montgomery, Alabama. He gave one of his last two dollars to a jailer and asked for some paper and a pencil. Right there in that jail cell, he pinned a letter to the Marine that had said if he ever needed him, he would be there. He hoped *Semper Fi* really meant something.

# Chapter 5

~

WHEN ALVIN RETURNED FROM THE war, he was ready to be done with war, but he wasn't ready to settle down. He spent nearly three years in San Diego renting a room from a crusty old man on the beach who liked to walk around his house naked. That fact alone kept A.J. away from him as much as he could, but every Friday when it was time for payday, A.J. would show up to collect his pay to pay his rent, and there the old fart would be, standing there in nothing, wrinkled from head to toe, and as far as A.J. could tell, nothing to be really proud of. The rent was cheap, though, and he didn't need much. He did odd jobs all over San Diego, but mainly he worked close to the beach for the old crusty man; everything from maintenance to cabana boy.

He knew he would eventually move on, but he simply wanted to be left alone and hopefully, get his head cleared of what he had seen while he was in the war. He had seen enough of ugliness to last him the rest of his life. He wanted badly to find a nice girl, marry her, and start a family, but he didn't think he could do that just right away, but the dream was still there. It was the same dream that every soldier returning from Europe and the South Pacific had.

After he thought he had his mind cleared, which really wasn't true because no matter what he tried, he still had nightmares

## Chapter 5

every night, and every time someone stabbed an umbrella in the sand on the beach, he would get a knot in his stomach. He woke up in his little rental room on the beach in San Diego one night and decided he had lingered long enough. The very next morning, he packed his bags and he bought a greyhound bus ticket bound for Montgomery. It was time for him to go home. He was surprised to find out that he still had to sit in the back of the bus, and nobody seemed to care that he was wearing his dress blues all the way to Montgomery. He figured if he wore his dress blues, he would get treated better, but he found out very quickly that people only saw the uniform for a second and then they just saw a black man.

He handled all of that as best he could, but he really struggled when the bus would stop and he would have to use something different than the "white's only" restrooms, which sometimes meant that he was forced to go into the woods behind the bus station. It was an eye-opening ride all the way to Montgomery. He had been struck in the leg and the hip by sniper fire, received two Purple Hearts because of it, and he still couldn't use the same toilet as a white man. Despite all that, he managed to stay focused on what he wanted to do once he got to Montgomery. He first wanted to start his own cab company and then he wanted to finish school if he could. The he wanted to find a wife, but he wasn't in a big hurry for that because women scared him badly. He just could not get comfortable around them, so he decided to hard charge his way to getting the first two things on his list done. So, with his determination and almost four years of service pay still tucked away, when he arrived in Montgomery, he took his money and bought a 1939 four door Packard to start his own cab company. He made all sorts of deals with old friends from his days in school to get his cab up and running. He didn't have any family left other than an uncle that lived in Montgomery. His mother and father had passed away within two days of each other while he was in the South Pacific. He had no siblings and could have settled down anywhere, but he felt like Montgomery was home.

*Choice of Honor*

    The Packard he bought was a solid car, but it needed a lot of mechanical work. It needed a new carburetor, starter, and transmission, all of which he bartered for. His uncle on his mother's side was an auto mechanic and agreed to do all of the transmission work if he promised him free taxi service to anywhere in Montgomery for the next two years. He knew his uncle didn't really go places that often, so he thought it was a bargain. He made another deal with a second cousin that worked at a body shop in Selma that was about an hour West of Montgomery. He really didn't even know that he had a second cousin until his uncle told him about him. He figured the engine work had to be first and when the car was ready to drive, he would drive over to Selma and have his cousin do the paint and body work.

    He knew exactly how he wanted the cab painted; he wanted it painted in marine scarlet red and with flashy gold. He wanted people to see the cab from far away. The main body of the car would be marine scarlet red with the doors and the roof painted gold. It was so vivid in his mind that he would get excited just thinking about it. He had drawn the cab several times on a piece of paper, but he just wasn't good at it. It always turned out looking like something a child would draw, but he knew what his dream was, and he wasn't going to let his inability to translate his thoughts into paper drawings stop him. He didn't know anything about transmissions, but he sure learned a lot helping his uncle fix it.

    The garage his uncle worked at was in downtown Montgomery and was owned by a man named Orville Gibson. Orville Gibson was a successful businessman in Montgomery. He made most of his money in real estate but had recently started buying all kinds of little businesses in downtown Montgomery. When he asked his uncle for help, he said he wouldn't do a thing until A.J. had gone and talked to Mr. Gibson. He said that he doubted Mr. Gibson would let them work on his car without something in return. He told A.J. that if he could get Mr. Gibson to let them work on the car, he would do it, but that A.J. would have to

## Chapter 5

make that deal first, so A.J. showed up at the garage the very next day and asked to speak to Mr. Gibson. A.J. was not keen on procrastinating now that he had spent nearly three years on the beaches of San Diego. He was ready to get started. The man at the front desk wasn't very polite. He told A.J. that Mr. Gibson didn't see his kind and that their garage didn't work on black folks' cars anyway. A.J. let the man's insolent tone go and was undeterred; his ambition to get his cab going was greater than that man's stupidity.

Through a little investigative work, He figured out where Mr. Gibson's real estate office was and waited nearly half the day for Mr. Gibson to emerge. He knew he would never get past the secretary, so his opportunity would have to come from a meeting on the street. He knew it would be tricky; Mr. Gibson would certainly have his guard up considering the difference in their race and he would not appreciate the unexpected encounter on the street. He decided the best way to approach him would be in his Marine uniform. Even if he didn't meet with "their kind" like the ignorant man at the garage said, maybe he could appeal to his patriotism. The respect for the GI's returning was immense at the moment, even though he hadn't seen much of it on his bus trip. No matter what he felt inside, he thought that the uniform had a positive effect on people, even if it was temporary.

His office was in a two-story building in downtown Montgomery. He walked along the opposite side of the street for nearly an hour before he spotted him leaving for lunch. He ran across the street and was so focused on catching up to Mr. Gibson in a nonchalant way that he was nearly hit by a city bus. The bus screeched its tires and honked at him, which caused everyone on the street that day to stop and look at him. So much for nonchalant. After he thanked his lucky stars that that bus didn't squash him, he stepped up on the sidewalk and realized he was face-to-face with Mr. Gibson. The two made eye contact, but his mouth managed to become as dry as a cotton ball and his tongue felt like it had swollen to twice its size. The two men

*Choice of Honor*

passed each other without saying a word. Alvin stood there trying to gather himself when he finally just blurted his name out. "Mr. Gibson!"

Alvin hadn't turned around yet, but figured since he said it out loud, he better quickly face the man, so he spun on his heels just like he had been taught in basic training. He stood straight up and pulled the sides of his jacket down in an act to make him feel more pressed and presentable, as they say in the military. Mr. Gibson stopped and turned to see who was calling his name just in time to see an impressive turn by a soldier in uniform. He stepped toward the soldier more out of curiosity than courtesy. "Do we know each other, Corporal?" Alvin thought, *great!* He knew the uniform, so maybe he was former military. "Uh, no, sir, but my uncle works for you in your garage. I was wondering if I might have a word with you?" Orville Gibson looked the soldier up and down, took another step toward him, then stopped. Alvin froze and was about to say something, but Mr. Gibson beat him to it. "You just get back?" Alvin felt a little better by this point, at least the man hadn't told him to go jump in a lake. That was always good, plus, he wasn't going to ask for anything other than the use of his garage. He didn't think that was too much and he would offer to pay if necessary. "No, sir, I got back three years ago, but I got hung up in San Diego." Orville Gibson stood there for a few more seconds staring at Corporal Alvin Jerome Mack, Jr. until both men felt a little uncomfortable, so Mr. Gibson broke the silence. "You know my name so what is yours?" He didn't extend his hand to shake, but that didn't matter to Alvin, what mattered was his cab and this man could help him with that, he just didn't know it yet. "My name is Alvin Jerome Mack, Jr., sir, and I would like to use your garage to help me fix my cab."

There it was, Alvin was never one to waste a bunch of words. He liked to get right to the point on everything. He thought maybe he should have small-talked this man a little more, but a black man and a white man standing on the street in Montgomery

## Chapter 5

was not a common thing. He wanted to move on as fast as he could. "I'm sorry, son, we don't work on your cars. I hear there is a real good mechanic East of town that specializes in your folk's type of cars. Maybe they can help you." He patted Alvin on the shoulder, which Alvin took as a friendly gesture, but he also took it as an end to the conversation, which he knew he couldn't let end. "Yes, sir, I am aware, but I intend to do all the work with my uncle. He knows transmissions and I don't. I just want to use your garage to help me fix it. I won't cause any trouble; I will work overnight and be gone before anyone sees my uncle or me. I promise if I break anything, I will fix it." Orville Gibson cocked his head to the side in sort of an amused way and was about to say something, but Alvin felt like he needed to sweeten the pot a little. "I will even work for you for free, no charge. I just need to get my car ready to go." Orville Gibson stood there on the sidewalk looking amused. He was unsure of what to think about this Marine standing here negotiating business right on the sidewalk of downtown Montgomery, Alabama. "You'll work for free, huh? That's an intriguing proposal. Why don't you take the bus? Why do you even need a car?"

Alvin told him the entire story and what he intended to do with the car. He explained that if he could get the car rolling and start picking up fares, he would be profitable in less than 6 months. He had it all figured out. Orville crossed his arms and listened. Alvin wasn't sure if he was really paying attention or if he was just enjoying this show he was putting on, either way, Alvin felt awkward, like he was begging for something and he hated to ask for anything of anyone, but this was different. "Ten percent." Alvin was not sure what he heard and meant to say *sir* in question form, but it came out as "huh." It wasn't intended and he immediately corrected the response. "I'm sorry, sir, I don't think I caught that. Did you say ten percent?" Mr. Gibson looked around the street, then up in the sky. He took his handkerchief out of his back pocket and blew his nose. While he was blowing his nose, he said, "You can use the garage, overnight only. I can't let anyone see you doing it; you have to be done in one week from start to finish and I get ten percent of your business for as long as the business operates, and you drive for me on the weekends, Friday, Saturday, and Sunday for three years, whether the business makes it or not."

Alvin wasn't expecting to negotiate terms here on the sidewalk and was caught off-guard, but he recovered quickly. "Ten days use of the garage, I work Saturday and Sunday for you doing whatever you need me to do for one year, and three percent of the business profits, not revenue." Mr. Gibson burst out laughing at what he had just heard Alvin say. He hadn't expected him to bargain so quickly, either. Alvin didn't know if he should interrupt him or ask him what was so funny, but he stood firm. "You work Saturday and Sunday for me as my driver for one year, you have to get the work done in 8 days, and I get three percent of revenue, not profits. I have no idea if you know how to run a business and I am not going to wait on you to figure out a proper balance sheet. Take it or leave it."

Alvin wasted no time making the decision and stuck out his hand to illustrate that they had a deal and even said, "Deal" as he stuck out his hand, but Mr. Orville Gibson did not take it. Instead, he fiddled with putting the hankie back in his pocket and simply said, "Start next Friday." He gave Alvin his address that was on a business card, handed it to him, and said, "6:00 a.m. sharp, don't be late." He turned back in the direction he was originally headed. Alvin let out a deep breath. Who cares whether he shook his hand or didn't, he had just struck a deal; he was on his way to starting his cab company and he had just learned that he was a pretty good negotiator and could think on his feet extremely well. He was not thrilled that Mr. Gibson didn't have to do a thing to help him in his daily operations and he would still get three percent of sales. That was just business, he figured.

# Chapter 6

ALVIN WENT RIGHT TO WORK on his car. He showed up at his uncle's house right after his meeting with Mr. Gibson to inform his uncle that they had the run of the shop for almost two weeks. His uncle didn't believe him, so he had to explain the deal, but he left out the percentage of the sales part. He didn't want his uncle to get any ideas about cutting into the business. He was already out three percent of his revenue and he hadn't had a single fare yet. Then it occurred to him that maybe Mr. Gibson knew that, too. Maybe he thought the brash young black Marine would fall flat on his face and he would be out nothing other than the use of his garage, and overnight at that. It was almost 8:00 p.m. when A.J. brought the news to his uncle and was a bit surprised when his uncle stood up off the couch, grabbed his hat, and said, "Let's get to work, boy."

A.J. was not expecting to work that night and had actually planned on kicking up his heels in celebration of the deal he made today. He was feeling pretty darn good about his dream becoming a reality and figured he deserved to celebrate. "I wasn't planning on starting tonight. I was thinking about going to Old Town for a bit then getting started tomorrow." Old Town was a part of town that was full of honky-tonks, gin joints, and what his uncle called flop houses. It was a place where a young man could have a good time, relax, enjoy some good music, and dance with as many ladies as he could stand. He was feeling so good about his first deal as a businessman that he was ready to tackle that fear of women he had.

He was actually looking forward to kicking up his heels, cutting a rug with a woman, and waking up with a hangover if possible. He still had a lot of money and he hadn't cut loose since he arrived back in Montgomery. He had a smile on his face and was certain that his uncle would understand, he didn't even mind if his uncle wanted to tag along; they could both celebrate and get to know each other better. But the smile went away when his uncle replied with, "Boy, you ain't sold a nickel yet and you already want to celebrate? Besides, ain't nothing good gonna happen for you in Old Town. I swear on everything Holy I don't understand you kids. We start tonight or you fix that jalopy on your own, take it or leave it." A.J. had heard that very same deal-ender that day; he knew he would have to skip Old Town.

Alvin sat quietly in the passenger seat of his uncle's old Desoto, he knew he had unintentionally pressed the wrong button with his uncle; he wanted to repair it, but wasn't sure how to do that, so he decided the best way was to just be quiet and let his uncle speak first. They headed straight North on Perry, making their way downtown. Mr. Gibson's garage was just off of Washington and Dexter. It was tucked back just a little, so it was difficult to see from the street. His uncle eased the Desoto into the back of the building where he parked it in the spot he normally parked it. Because he had been an employee of the garage for several years, he had been trusted with the keys to the building, a responsibility he did not take lightly, but even as a trusted employee, he was never allowed to enter the front door. He was always required to enter from the back. He flipped the lights on to the shop and there it was, the '39 Packard. It was still ugly, but to A.J., it was the most beautiful car he had ever seen. He had already driven the car earlier that day under the ruse of it being brought in for a white customer who was too frail to

## Chapter 6

bring the car in, so he was hired to bring it in. Mr. Gibson had left specific instructions that the only person allowed to work on the car would be Marvin Moore. That way, the other mechanics would leave it alone.

Marvin was the best mechanic in the shop and often, customers would request that he and he alone be the only person to work on their cars, so it wasn't uncommon. "A car is like a woman, boy, you gotta take care of her, listen to her, give her what she wants, and be gentle when you are handling her." A.J. smiled as he heard his uncle talk for the first time since they left his house. He was in his uncle's world right now and he was going to learn as much as he could. He would still rather be dancing in Old Town, but he was also happy that he was getting started on his future. "You see, someone has mistreated this lady somewhere along the line and now she is feeling ugly and damaged. It's up to us to make her feel good about herself again. It's as simple as that."

A.J. started to ask a question, but he realized that school was in session and it was best if he just listened and did what he was told, which is exactly what he did. His uncle popped the hood and for the next five days for three hours a night, the two men worked on repairing the transmission and since they had the means and location, they tuned it, lubed it, replaced the brakes, and aligned the front end. The car was immaculate as far as A.J. was concerned; all he needed now was a paint job and he would get that from his cousin next week. They left the last day in separate cars. His uncle had asked him to lead the way home so he could watch the beauty queen, as he called it, and see how she strutted. A.J. always got a kick out of the way his uncle described his cars. He was truly in love with the automobile. It started to make sense to A.J. because it was all his uncle really had left. He lost his wife to the fever 10 years earlier and only had the one brother who was A.J.'s father, and he had passed away while A.J. was at war from a heart attack. A.J.'s mother and Marvin's sister-in-law passed away two days later of unknown causes. Marvin told A.J. it was a broken heart and that he had never seen a man and woman love each other like his mom and daddy did. *They were two peas in a pod*, he said.

A.J. was leading the way; he had crossed the Norman bridge going South with his uncle right behind him, he thought, when he saw the lights flash in his rear-view mirror. He tensed up, his hands gripped the steering wheel tightly, he could feel all of the saliva leave his mouth. He pulled over to the side of the road wondering what he could have done wrong. He wasn't speeding; he hadn't run any stop signs. He tried to think, but his mind went through a series of "what if's" that he didn't have answers to; the main question was, what if he got thrown in jail? He saw his uncle's car pass by and continue heading South. Why didn't his uncle stop his car and stay with him? It was 3:00 a.m. in the morning; getting stopped by the police was not a good thing.

He was still running through all the questions when he heard the tap on the window, and he saw the flashlight come through the passenger side of the car. He slowly rolled the window down, sure to keep his right hand on the steering wheel. Once the window was all the way down, he heard the voice say, "Step out of the car." He made sure that his motions were slow and deliberate; he didn't want the police to have any irrational thoughts about how quickly he exited the car. Once he was out of the car, he stood up straight and faced the officer. "What's your name and where are you going?" Even though his mouth was dry, he answered the question and couldn't remember the exact address of his uncle's house but offered to take the officer to the house to prove he wasn't lying. The officer that was looking through the passenger window had now joined Alvin and the other officer.

He heard him say he didn't find anything. "Did I do something wrong, officer?" The officer he had been speaking to asked to see his ID without answering his question. He reached into his wallet and started to pull his ID from the wallet, but the officer took the wallet out of his hands. He fumbled through the wallet and found the nine dollars A.J. was going to use to help pay

*Chapter 6*

for the paint job he would be getting next week. "Alvin Jerome Mack, Jr., huh? Says here you are a Corporal in the United Stated Marines. Is that right?" Except when he said, "Is that right" it came out more like "ZAT RIGHT?" He looked at his partner as he held the ID up for his partner to see. He put the ID back in the wallet, but still had the nine dollars in his left hand. "Yes, sir, I was in the Marines. I've been discharged now that the war is over." The cop with the flashlight shined the light in his face, "I don't give a shit if you Harry Truman boy. You can't drive on my highway with a busted taillight." He didn't think he had a busted taillight, but he sure wasn't going to argue the fact.

The officer holding his wallet handed the wallet back to him, but still had the nine dollars in his hand. "Come here and I will show you." He grabbed Alvin by the arm and shoved him to the back of the car. Alvin had turned the car off when he pulled over and he had shut the lights off, so he didn't know what he was going to see, but when the three got to the back of the car, the officer with the flashlight smashed the driver side taillight with his flashlight. Alvin flinched a little when he saw it happen but thought better of saying anything. "Boy, you know what the fine is for driving around in a piece of shit Packard with a busted taillight?" Alvin tensed up, he could feel the anger building inside him, but forced it back down. "No, sir, I don't." The one still holding his money laughed and said, "Well, good thing for you that we know every rule and regulation there is in the great state of Alabama and the fine for such arrogant stupidity is four dollars and fifty cents." His partner laughed at the stupid joke then walked to the passenger side taillight and smashed it with his flashlight. "Well, God Almighty, would you look at that, boy. You got two busted taillights on this jalopy." The two men laughed while Alvin took a deep breath; he clenched his fists, but he let them loose as soon as the realized he was taking an aggressive posture.

He tried with everything he had to control the muscles in his jaw, but he couldn't. His teeth were clinched tightly, and he could feel the muscles in his face twitch uncontrollably. "Looks like you owe the great state of Alabama and the proud city of Montgomery the sum total of nine dollars, boy." He didn't say anything. He tried to force his stare beyond them; he wanted to see through them. He had fought for his country, been wounded, and these two morons were shaking him down for money at 3:00 a.m. on a Montgomery highway. He knew this was a battle he could not win, however, he was no longer nervous. His mind became as sharp as it ever was, he became focused, not on this moment, but how he would change it for others.

He would have to be more careful in the future and he would certainly begin taking steps, however small, to change the harassment and inequality that he was suffering at this very moment along this dark highway. "Yes, sir, can you make sure the great state of Alabama and the proud city of Montgomery gets the money and I will get those taillights fixed first thing tomorrow?" The two men laughed and the one with the flashlight said, "We'd be proud to take care of it for you, but you mind your tone, boy." Just as he said that, he slammed the flashlight into Alvin's stomach. He was not prepared for the punch and immediately lost his breath. He crumpled over and felt the flashlight hit him in the small of the back, which sent him sprawling on the ground. The officer holding Alvin's money bent down close to Alvin's head, patted him on the back, and with a sarcastically friendly voice said, "Get those lights fixed real soon, boy."

The town cops went back to their car and drove around Alvin as he lay there on the ground still trying to force air back into his lungs. He rolled over on his back and took a few deep gasps and he started to breathe again. He heard the sound of a car roll up behind his and thought that the police had come back to finish him off. He tried to sit up, but his lower back would not cooperate. "You hurt bad, boy?" He was relieved to hear the sound of his uncle's voice. "I don't think so, knocked the wind out of me and my back is sore." His uncle put his hands under his shoulders and helped get him in to a sitting position. "Why

## Chapter 6

did you drive off? Why didn't you stop and help me!" It wasn't a question as much as it was a frustrated scream, but he didn't want an answer. "Get up and get in your car. We need to get outta here before they come back." His uncle, once again, locked his arms under Alvin's arm pits and pulled him up to his feet.

By now, Alvin was frustrated and mad, very mad. "Get your damn hands off me, you old coward! You just let me get robbed and beat by two damn cops!" He wiggled free of his uncle's backwards embrace as he said it. "Cause if I hadn't, you'd be dead instead of just getting your ass kicked. Now get in your car and let's go home!" His uncle turned and walked back to his car. He got in and sat and waited for his nephew to get in his car. He could see that Alvin was still standing there looking at him. He got out of the car and came back to him. "Damn fool, kid, you ready to change things now are you, ready to just kick that dream to the curb and go fix all the injustice in the world, huh?" Alvin was staring at him with extreme anger in his eyes. His uncle continued, "All because two white morons cracked your taillights, took your money, and smacked you around a little?" Alvin didn't blink, he continued to stare at his uncle, he was hurt and felt betrayed. "Boy, you need to understand something, they is boys around here, same age as you and younger, not makin' it back home at night at all because of fools like those two!" His uncle looked around and could see a car coming, "Get in your car and let's go, we ain't gonna solve all of Alabama's problems right here on the side of this road."

Alvin processed what he had just heard and finally blinked, shook his head, and got to the real issue of what was bothering him and said, "You left me alone, old man!" Marvin continued to watch the car lights coming and was relieved to see that the car passed them, and it was not a police car. "All right, you think I am a coward, huh, you think I should have come back and helped you do what?" He paused, "Knock heads with those fools?" He threw up his arms and spun around in a dramatic boxing style move. "Oh, yeah, they would have fought us fair and square and we both would have been hangin' from a tree come sun up!"

He put his hand under his nephew's chin and forced him to look him in the eyes because his head was down now. "They would have seen me as a threat. If I was to pull in front of them, behind them, or any which way, they would have thought I was there to cause trouble and I swear on everything Holy, the world would never find your car or my car, all they'd find is a couple old loud mouth fools hangin' from a tree. This is Alabama, son, those fools don't play by any rules you are familiar with and you ain't been here long enough to learn them, but if you listen to me, you can live long enough to get this old bucket of bolts working."

His uncle didn't say anything else until he was walking away leaving him standing there on the side of the road, "I will follow you close so nobody stops you for those busted taillights, now let's go." Alvin didn't put it all together until much later that his uncle returned to him after the police were through shaking him down because he had gone down far enough to keep his eye on the road, pulled off on a side street, and waited. He knew of boys that got pulled over and ended up in the back of their police cars, taken away, and never heard from again. He was prepared to follow the police car with his lights off so that if he had to, he would stay close enough to them to know where they were taking him and then be in a position to keep his nephew alive. He wasn't a coward at all, but he understood the current rules, and he knew his nephew did not.

# Chapter 7

HE TOOK THE LESSON FROM the police and vowed never to get caught off-guard again, but he took the lesson from his uncle even more seriously. He had openly called his uncle a coward, when in fact, he was anything but that. He hadn't left him behind as he thought, he had simply applied experience and logic to the situation, and they were better for it. He was down nine bucks but was thanking the Lord Almighty that earlier that day he had stashed the rest of his money at his uncle's house. Up until then, he had been carrying it around in his wallet. He took that as another life lesson.

He made arrangements to drive over to see his cousin in Selma, after he got the taillights fixed. His uncle ordered the parts and had it fixed in a few days. He grew very fond of his uncle after that encounter that night, fonder than he ever thought he would. He was a good man and he could learn a lot from him if he was just patient and listened.

When he got to Selma, he found his cousins house. It was a shotgun house with an oversized porch that turned out to always have some kids playing on it. The house was on the Southeast side of town tucked into a row of other houses that looked just like it.

He spent a week with his second cousin and, as it turned out, they were both the same age, and both enjoyed the same things.

Alvin liked baseball and so did his cousin. His cousin was from his mother's side, his name was Douglas Jerome Johnson, and everyone called him D.J. They laughed when they talked about how everybody in their family liked to shorten the names down to just a couple letters if possible. D.J. talked A.J. into going to a party out in the country one night while, as he liked to say, *they were letting the paint dry*, as in the paint job his Packard had gone through. Alvin helped D.J. though the whole process and learned a great deal about painting a car, especially the amount of tear-down and prep work that had to be done to do it right. Neither had seen the completed work yet as the final pieces, which were the right and left front fenders, were still drying.

His cousin had already said that it was time to celebrate because the work was done. All that was left to do was put the fenders back on and he would have himself a cab. He also told him that he did not want Alvin to help him do that part because he wanted Alvin to be able to see the finished work when he pulled the cover off. He called it the "Debut." He found out while working with his cousin that he was a good man. A man that had tried to enlist like Alvin had right after Pearl Harbor but was denied because he had a club foot. It was slight and hardly noticeable, but he said the military would have none of it.

His cousin would joke that he didn't need his foot to kill Germans; he could do that with his bare hands. He was clearly bothered by the fact that he didn't go to war. Alvin would try to assuage his anxiety by telling him that he didn't miss much, and he told him about the Marine he ended up spending 24 hours with, with his index finger stuck in his chest. The conversations ended up having the opposite effect because D.J. couldn't get enough of his stories about war, even the ones that A.J. thought were boring and mundane. D.J. would ask a ton of questions, almost to the point where A.J. would get annoyed, but he never let his cousin know.

Alvin knew lots of guys that didn't get to go serve and they all seemed to have something missing in them. He wished he

*Chapter 7*

could tell them all that war was no place to be and that they were lucky they missed it. He wished they would really listen to him when he would tell them that he still had bad dreams and that he still had a hard time understanding the evil that men could do to each other. No matter how much he tried to emphasize that point, he always got the same response, "Yeah, well, if I would have been there, the war would have been over sooner."

"I'm gonna take you out to Millers, you gonna see some dancin' and, oh, my God, you are gonna see some of the prettiest girls in all of Alabama!" D.J. was so excited to be going out to Millers that it was all he talked about the final day of painting. Millers was nothing more than a huge barn on the Southwest part of Selma. You had to bring your own liquor if you wanted it and everyone got all dressed up for the occasion. "Man, this is the biggest dance of the year. Everybody that is anybody is gonna be there."

Alvin could hear the excitement in D.J.'s voice and felt some of that enthusiasm rub off but had a problem. "D.J., I didn't bring any dress-up duds to wear. I thought I was gonna be painting a car, not going to a ball." D.J. laughed at the thought of going to a ball; although everyone got dressed up, it was certainly not a swanky place, it was simply a big breezy barn that, for one night every month, was cleared of all its contents and the whole place was turned into a dance hall. The excitement for this one was especially heightened because rumor had it that a kid from Mississippi that was crazy good with a guitar was going to play that night.

Millers always had a band, but this was different. There was all kind of talk about this fellow because folks would say he could make that guitar sing all by itself. D.J. couldn't remember his name, but the gossip about it was so heavy it had everyone talking about it. Besides, Millers was one of the few places in Selma that they could go without running into the police. It was a place where they all could have fun and relax. "Don't worry 'bout it. I got you covered."

*Choice of Honor*

    D.J. cobbled together a respectable ensemble for Alvin to wear. He had a nice navy jacket and a nice navy pair of slacks, but the colors were slightly off. D.J. said it didn't matter because the place was always a little dark and nobody would notice. Alvin and Douglas were close to the same size, but the suit fit A.J. just a little tight.

    The barn was bigger than A.J. imagined. There were cars everywhere, the lights were strung across every rafter, and the place was hopping. The normal band was playing, and folks were already dancing. D.J. picked a spot in the far back, but close enough where they could see the dance floor, and they had a good view of everyone in the place. A.J. had seen a lot in his day, but he sure never expected to see this. Everyone was dressed to hilt, finest hats, finest dresses, finest shoes; there seemed to be nothing spared for this night.

    Some of the dancing was so good that it didn't look real. He couldn't dance and couldn't imagine ever learning how to do some of the things that they were doing on that dance floor. The music was just as he had been led to believe by his cousin - it was loud, it was fast, and he liked it. He caught himself tapping his foot on the floor, completely out of rhythm with the music, but it was so loud that nobody even noticed. "Man, I have to go find me a lady to cut a rug with! Come on, man, let's go grab some tail."

    A.J. could barely hear his cousin and he leaned closer to him so he could hear him. He only caught the part about "grabbing some tail" and he pieced the other parts together. He shook his head emphatically so that D.J. could see him saying no. He knew he couldn't talk loud enough to be heard, so he simply shook his and mouthed the words "No way, man." A.J. shaped his hand to simulate a drink, as if to inform his cousin that he needed a drink first. He really wanted a drink, and with the music making him feel the way he was feeling now, the thought actually crossed his mind that he might try to dance tonight, but even if the mood struck him, he would not make the attempt without a few drinks

## Chapter 7

in his system to help him overcome the fear of making a complete boob of himself.

Before he could even blink, D.J. was gone. He had evaporated into the crowd of folks dancing on the floor, swinging each other like he had never seen anybody dance. He left the tall table they were both standing beside to go find a drink. He circled the entire back wall from one side of the barn to the other. He didn't see anywhere to get a drink, but he saw people with drinks in their hands. Actually, he saw lots of people with drinks in their hands, some of them even dancing with the drink in their hand.

He watched as one woman downed her drink in the middle of a dance and left the dance floor. He decided he would follow her to see if maybe she was going for a refill, and as luck would have it, she was. She exited the back of the barn where he followed her. He was immediately hit with a nice cool breeze; even in the short time he had been inside, he could now see how the air was stifling in there. He continued to follow her as she made her way down a winding path that was pretty well worn. He saw a couple coming in his direction, both were laughing, and both had drinks in their hands. He smiled as he was quite proud of his ability to improvise and adapt, something he learned while he was in the Marines.

"You're following the wrong broad, dipshit." He heard the voice behind him, but at first it didn't register that the voice was directed at him, so he continued down the path behind the woman he chose to follow to find the drinks. "Hey, fool, I am talking to you, you're following the wrong broad." This time, there was no mistaking that the voice was meant for him, so he stopped and turned to see who it was. It was dark on the path, but he could tell that there were at least four guys standing a few feet behind him. "I'm sorry? You talking to me?" He raised his hands and showed his palms to give off the signal that he was confused and meant no harm.

"She's taken, dumbass." He could feel the tenseness in the air, as he wasn't sure where this was going. It finally hit him that perhaps they had the wrong idea about what his motives were and although he didn't think he owed anyone an explanation, he also didn't feel like getting into a fight; he was still sore in the ribs from the introduction to the Montgomery Police Department's version of the Welcome Wagon. "Brother, I'm not following that lady. Well, I am kinda following her, but only because I wanted a drink and I didn't know where to get one."

All of the men who were now standing a few feet in front of him looked at each other. He couldn't make out the expressions on their faces, but he could tell by the way their heads were turning that they were confused. The man who yelled at him from behind stepped even closer to him. "Why didn't you bring some hooch with you, boy?" He shook his head, shrugged his shoulders, showed the palms of his hands again, and said, "Cause I'm not from around here, sir. I'm just here visiting my cousin. I'm sorry if you thought I was following her, but since I can't dance for shit, I decided I needed a drink."

A.J. could smell the alcohol on the man's breath, he knew he needed to tread lightly. He wasn't afraid of the fight, but he simply wasn't in the mood for one. "Well, in that case, it cost you a dollar just to walk down this path and get your drink." A.J. reached into his pocket where he knew he had a crumpled-up dollar, took it out, and handed it to the man. "Now, where do I go to get a drink?" He could see the man open up the crumpled bill to see if it was really a dollar. "Keep headin' down that path until you see the tent. They will fix you up but mind me when I say keep your distance from Abigail." He didn't wait around to ask who Abigail was and he didn't care.

He spun around and went down the path away from these guys. He passed two more sets of couples before he found the tent. It wasn't much of a tent, that was for sure. It was more like four posts with a piece of canvas strung across the tops of each post. There were lanterns hanging off all four posts, so the place was pretty well-lit. He could see the tables set up underneath the canvas in a horseshoe shape with stacks of bottles in the middle

*Chapter 7*

of the horseshoe. He heard a voice from behind the table laugh. "Abigail, don't you think you done had enough, girl? You know you got a drinking problem, woman!"

He could hear other voices laugh around the table as there were several people all around the tent laughing it up. He heard a female voice laugh and reply, "Hell, yeah, she got a drinking problem, ya'll, every time she drinks, her legs spread apart!" The crowd around the table howled with laughter. He walked up to the table where he was surprised by the greeting, especially since it was still dark, and even though the lamps lit the site up decently, you still had trouble seeing clearly. "What'll ya have, Marine?"

It startled him just a little, had someone recognized him from the service? He looked at the man behind the horseshoe table that had made the comment, but decided he had no idea who he was. "Do we know each other?" was all A.J. could think to ask. "Nope, but I know a Marine when I see one." A.J. asked the man for a whiskey. The man reached behind the counter, actually, under the counter, looked around as if he didn't want to get caught, and poured A.J. a drink from a bottle he had under the counter. "This here is the good stuff, brother; you'll like this, made it myself. That'll be fifty cents, though." A.J. looked back at the path he had just come down and then looked back at the bartender.

He was confused as to why he paid a dollar already but had to pay another fifty cents. "I just paid a man a dollar to come down here to get a drink." The man behind the counter howled with laughter. "Young man, you just got snookered. It don't cost nothin' to use my path; it's my property we are on right now and it's my whiskey and gin. Anybody tell you it costs a dollar to walk down that path is full of shit and hell-bent for Shinola!" He howled with laughter again. A.J. realized he just got taken for a dollar and it didn't sit well with him. He had already lost nine dollars to the Montgomery police and now some local band of hucksters had just taken him for another one.

"I will pay for his drink, Tommy." The voice was soft and sultry. He felt a hand brush all the way up his backside. It was no accident, either. This hand fully intended to feel his backside. He turned to his right to see the same woman he had followed out of the barn to lead him to this drink tent. "That's very kind of you, ma'am, but no thank you." The bartender poured him a glass of whiskey and slid it to him. A.J. reached into his pocket and gave the man fifty cents. "My money not good enough for you? You don't like women?" Through deductive reasoning, A.J. concluded that this was Abigail. "No ma'am, I love women, just not ones that are spoken for or ones named Abigail." She laughed when she heard her name. "You must have run into Freehold already. Damn, that boy sure does make life tough for me."

He raised his whiskey glass to the woman who had just felt his backside, tilted his head back, and took the entire glass of whiskey down in one big gulp. He reached into his pocket and pulled another fifty cents out and set it on the table. The bartender understood the gesture and quickly refilled his now empty glass with the good stuff. "Freehold don't own me, I can do whatever I want to! No man owns me!" She started to make a scene when he heard a voice somewhere nearby. "I told ya'll she got a drinking problem, just watch, her legs are spreadin' right before our very eyes!" The crowd laughed again, which gave A.J. an excuse to throw this shot down the hatch and walk away. He had met girls like Abigail in the war; they were trouble, they knew it, and they liked to cause it. He wanted nothing to do with her, but he did want his dollar back and he intended to get it.

He made his way back up the path leading to the barn. Once back inside, he could hear the music, but not like he had when he first walked in. He was looking for Freehold and that was all he had on his mind. He circled the back wall again until he saw his cousin standing in the corner talking to three women. He wasn't completely sure what Freehold looked like since it was dark on the path when he was tricked into paying a toll, he needed to see if his cousin might know this Freehold fella. He walked up and tapped his cousin on the shoulder. D.J. turned to see who it was. "Hey, cuz! Look here, man, I want you to meet Donna, Joyce,

## Chapter 7

and Beverly." A.J. shook each one of their hands and was cordial to each because they seemed like very nice girls, one of them was actually pretty, but he thought the other two looked a little too homely for him.

It was still noisy, and he was having trouble hearing, so he leaned over and yelled into D.J.'s ear, "Who is Freehold?" D.J. quickly stepped back away from A.J., grabbed A.J. by the arm, and led him outside. "What do you want with Freehold, man? Ain't nothing good attached to that boy." D.J. was looking around to see if anyone heard him and he seemed very nervous. For no other reason than reflex, A.J. looked around as his cousin had done. "Man owes me a dollar and I want it back." D.J. Looked around again. "No, you don't, man. That fool is crazy." A.J. was in no mood for this, he wanted his dollar and he was going to get it back. In his mind, if a man got bullied and taken once, he would get bullied and taken again, and pretty soon all he would be doing was letting others take everything he had, including his dignity, and he was not having any of that.

He had gone off to fight in a war, seen and done terrible things, and he damn sure didn't come back to the states to be treated like a chump. There were certain things worth standing up for and this was one of them. "Fine, I will find him without you." He turned and started back towards the barn. "Hold up, man, I can't let you go up against him by yourself, that prick don't play fair and neither do any of the goons he runs with." D.J. took him back inside. After a few minutes of looking around the barn and all of the people in it, he nudged A.J. and pointed towards a man on the dance floor.

Even from the distance, A.J. could tell that was the guy he met on the path. Without saying anything, he made his way to the dance floor where the music had turned slow and soft and everyone was slow dancing; some of the couples were making out pretty heavy. When he reached Freehold, he tapped him on the shoulder. "May I cut in?" The look on Freehold's face was priceless, this was obviously a situation that he had never dealt with, and while he was searching for the proper response, A.J. had already somehow wiggled the woman out of Freehold's arms and was beginning a slow dance of which he knew nothing about. He just pretended to shuffle his feet.

The couples that were dancing nearest to them could tell something was not quite right, so they slowed down even further and almost stood motionless. Freehold was still standing there on the dance floor, not moving, while everyone watched him. He was the type of guy that was used to being the center of attention for his own actions, not for the actions of others. When he finally figured out he was being watched, he decided to act. "Boy, you better get your ass off my dance floor and let go of my woman!" A.J. heard Freehold perfectly clear, but never acted like he did, he just continued to dance. He swore to this day that he could feel the woman's heart beat as she was obviously scared. She smelled very nice to A.J. and thought he could actually get used to this dancing stuff.

He was about to make a slow spin move with the girl in his arms, so he could see Freehold a little better when he heard the click of the blade. A.J. knew that sound very well, Freehold had brought a switchblade to a dance with him. He smiled because he knew that this meant that Freehold was rattled. He knew that if for one minute Freehold thought he could simply beat A.J. with his fists, he wouldn't show his little friend. A.J. spun the woman out of his grip and with one fluid motion, grabbed Freehold by the wrist holding the blade, spun Freehold's arm to an awkward position, then bent the wrist backwards until he heard it snap. If the little ruckus on the dance floor didn't disrupt things, the scream that Freehold let out sure did. The music stopped, all the people that were on the dance floor stopped, and the barn was as quiet as a church now.

The crowd parted enough so that everyone could see that Freehold had dropped to one knee with his arm awkwardly to the side and a man in a navy colored suit had his wrist in his hand and was holding a switchblade knife in the other, but the

## Chapter 7

hand holding the knife was at his side. A.J. thought he better clear this up with the patrons as best he could, so he looked around the barn and said, "I'm here visiting my cousin. Earlier, this gentleman charged me a dollar just to use the path to get a drink. I later find out that the path is free, and I was just asking him to give me my dollar back."

He could hear the shuffle of feet coming thought he crowd. The other guys that were with Freehold on the path earlier had obviously now caught on to what was happening and were coming to aid their buddy. A.J. turned in their direction, and when he did, twisted Mr. Freehold's wrist enough to cause him to scream in pain again. "Gentlemen, nice to see you again, too. I assume you were with Mr. Freehold on the path tonight, so you will attest to my claim." One of the guys took a step toward A.J., but A.J. stopped him by twisting Mr. Freehold's wrist again. The scream got even louder. "His wrist dangles in my hand like a rag doll, he won't be using this wrist for quite some time. Should you take another step toward me, I will wring it like a chicken neck, and he will never use the damn thing ever again."

Everyone in the crowd froze, including the man who had taken an aggressive step towards A.J. The crowd was utterly quiet when A.J. heard a man's voice. "Come on now, folks. We get enough shit from white folks in town, this is our place, don't ruin it for everyone. Let that moron go, son, and toss that blade out the door. Ain't no place for any of that in here." A.J. could tell it was the man who had served him a drink in the tent. While he still had a grip on Freehold's wrist, he bent down and asked which pocket his dollar was in. Freehold grimaced and motioned to his jacket. After a few attempts at several pockets, A.J. pulled a wad of dollars out of Freehold's inside jacket pocket, let one of the dollar bills fall to the floor, and slid the wad of dollars back into Freehold's inside pocket. Then he whispered, "We can be friends or enemies after today, the choice is yours, but take caution, when I was in the Iwo Jima, I had some enemies over there, but over there, I killed ALL my enemies."

*Choice of Honor*

    He let loose of Freehold's wrist and when he did, Freehold let out another scream and crumpled to the floor. A.J. turned quickly to Freehold's buddies who were still trying to figure out what to do. He folded the switchblade back safely and tossed it to the one man who made the aggressive step towards him earlier. The music slowly came back to life as the band started back with a much livelier tune. The crowd closed in around Freehold as if it swallowed him up. Actually, his buddies helped him leave the barn where he could be heard screaming as the local saw bone, who luckily was at the dance that night, set Freehold's wrist back in place then rigged a splint to keep it in place until he could fix it properly on Monday.

    A.J. also got swallowed up by the crowd as he made his way back to where he could see his cousin standing with a very dumbfounded look on his face. Just as he was about to say something to D.J. just to break the ice, he was caught by the arm. He spun quickly because his first thought was that one of the idiots that hung with Freehold had decided to try and get even, but it wasn't, it was the bartender and the man who had just broken up the fight. "Son, you sure know how to make your presence known. Weren't no call to break that boy's arm like that." A.J. tilted his head back and took a long look up at the barn rafters, then looked back at the man still holding his arm. "Mr…" He paused for just a second when the man interrupted his pause and said, "Name's Curtis Freehold, that boy out there with the broken wrist is my son." A.J. let out a long breath, looked down at the hand still holding his arm, then back to the man's face. It was a worn and weathered face. A face that had seen a lot over its time, a face that was surrounded by what looked to be pure sugar colored hair, which included a very well-groomed beard.

    "No, sir, Mr. Freehold, that boy out there with the broken wrist is the huckster on his way to Shinola." Curtis Freehold turned A.J.'s arm loose and looked at him with some of the most intense eyes he had ever seen. Both men stood there looking at each other for what seemed like an eternity to D.J., who was

## Chapter 7

standing next to the men wishing this was all over. Just as he was about to grab A.J.'s arm and usher him out of the place, he saw a smile begin to slowly appear on Mr. Freehold's face. At first it was slow, but when it reached its full peak, both D.J. and A.J. could see the most beautiful set of perfectly white teeth either had ever seen. A.J. thought he looked like a movie star or something when he smiled. After his smile was full blown, he let out a howl of laughter.

A.J. didn't know what to make of this and was very cautious about joining in. It actually scared D.J. a little and he took a step back, looked around nervously. The band seemed to get louder with the belly laugh of one Mr. Curtis Freehold, the owner, promoter, and bartender. "Come on, son, let's go back to the tent and get to know one another. The drinks are on me and we've enough of this fightin' bullshit for one night; violence always gives me gas and then the missus won't let me have none tonight, and at my age, I need all the nights the missus will give me." He howled again and practically drug A.J. from the barn. The three men, Mr. Freehold, A.J., and D.J. walked down the dark path towards the tent. It crossed A.J.'s mind that perhaps Mr. Freehold was taking them away from the barn so he could extract some family revenge, but the longer they were on the path and the more that Mr. Freehold talked, the more relaxed A.J. became.

Mr. Freehold was loud, funny, and from what A.J. could tell, decent. "Your son pulls a blade on a lotta folks, does he?" Mr. Freehold laughed again and said, "That boy is a momma's boy if there ever was one. She babied him too much. I lost two boys over in Europe and he's all I got left. He thinks cause he didn't get to go be a war hero, he's got something to prove. He is harmless as you can see, after all, you just disarmed him and neutralized his roving band of idiots that hang out with him. Yes, sir, I love him dearly, but I swear on everything holy, he needed to get his ass kicked tonight. I just hope you didn't break his yankin' hand because that boy can't go a day without pulling his pud." He let out another howl and they kept walking.

Once they got to the tent, Mr. Freehold went behind the horseshoe table again, reached under the table, and pulled the good stuff out. He poured three drinks and raised his glass. He looked at D.J. and then back to A.J., raised his glass even higher and said, "*Semper Fi*!" A.J. felt the tension leave his shoulders. He clanked his glass against Mr. Freehold's and D.J.'s and said, "*Semper Fi*." D.J. played along, but after a little bit, he finally had to ask, "What the hell does that mean?" Mr. Freehold, always free with his laugh, let loose another belly laugh and said, "Gotta be a Marine, son. It means *always faithful*. You know, like when your cousin here was standing in the middle of that crown ready to take on everybody there, if you were a Marine, you would have been by his side instead of slinking back in the crowd like you did." D.J. didn't think he had "slinked" back into the crowd, he thought he was more in shock than anything else and couldn't figure out what to do. He didn't think he was alone in that regard, the rest of crowd was in shock, too.

A.J. felt the need to defend his cousin a little. "He doesn't know me very well, Mr. Freehold, I am sure he would have jumped in if he needed to." Mr. Freehold seemed to understand that and didn't argue the point. The three men stood and talked while Curtis Freehold told them all about his sons and his own military experience in the *Great One*, as he referred to it. Mr. freehold fascinated A.J. He told him all about his dream of owning his own cab company and tried to pick the man's brain for every piece of worldly experience and advice he could extract from him. Mr. Freehold had obviously built quite a farm and business from nothing and there was a lot to be learned from him.

As they were talking, A.J. noticed a woman walk behind the tables and begin to serve drinks to other folks coming up. A.J. lost his entire train of thought when he saw her. She was the most beautiful woman he had ever seen. She had a beautiful complexion and when she smiled at customers and talked to them, A.J.

## Chapter 7

thought she must be an angel from heaven. She was wearing a skirt that hung below her knees, but he could see that her legs were incredible. Mr. Freehold could tell that A.J. was not paying attention to him anymore and turned to see what had caught A.J.'s attention. He smiled when he saw what had stolen the young man's attention. He snapped his fingers in front of A.J.'s face; even that almost didn't work, but eventually, A.J. snapped his attention back to Mr. Freehold.

"Her name is Kari, Kari Harper. She's been working for me, going on a year now. Don't know much about her, but she sure is pretty, ain't she? Want to meet her?" The lightning bolt was still ringing in A.J.'s ears, but he managed to answer, "Uh, I don't think I'm, uh, ready to, uh, meet any, uh, woman's, uh, I mean women's, I, uh, mean ladies tonight." Mr. Freehold howled with laughter again, "Son, you sure went from bear to bunny mighty quick!" He laughed, and as he was laughing, he hollered, "Miss Kari, come her for a second, baby, I got somebody I want you to meet."

A.J. immediately felt his throat close and his tongue began to swell, and he wasn't sure, but he thought he might actually pass out. She was wearing an apron over her skirt, he could see her reach down and pull the apron up high enough for her to wipe her hands on it. When she raised the apron, it caught part of her skirt and it came up slightly, too, enough for A.J. to catch a glimpse of the bottom of the thigh and he thought for sure he would pass out. She caught the error and gently pushed the skirt back into place, then made her way over to them. "Miss. Kari Harper, this here is Mr. Alvin J. Mack. The J is for Johnson, as in "long one!" Mr. Freehold howled again and slammed his hand down on the table, he held his stomach like he was in pain and continued to laugh. A.J. was mortified. This crazy man had just referred to his private parts right in front of the most beautiful woman he had ever seen.

He actually looked around for a place to hide but couldn't find any. He could see her roll her eyes and shake her head, but he could also see the smile begin to form on her face as she extended her hand. Reflexively, he grabbed her hand, but realized he was grabbing it like a Marine would grab a rifle, and he slowed his actions down just enough to loosen his grip and gently return her shake. 'Uh, ma'am, it's Jerome, not, uh, John…" He caught himself about to repeat it and quickly changed it to, "uh, it's not the other. Uh, Alvin Jerome Mack, friends call me A.J." He smiled at her as best he could, but he was so nervous that he was sure his smile looked like some kind of circus clown. "Well, it is nice to meet you, A.J. I am Kari Rae Harper, friends call me Kari." He was still holding her hand when D.J. smacked him on the arm. "Oh, Mrs. Harper, this is my cousin, D.J." She gently pulled her hand that A.J. was still holding away from him so she could shake A.J.'s hand. "I am Douglas Jerome Johnson, ma'am, but friends call me D.J., and that is the truth on my last name and the other." D.J. started to laugh when his laugh was cut short by a punch to the side of the head. It wasn't a terribly hard punch, but one that stung and knocked him off balance a little. "Apologize to Mrs. Harper!" D.J. was rubbing the side of his head and managed to come up with, "I'm sorry, ma'am, just going along with Mr. Freehold's joke is all."

She shook her head but managed a curt little smile. Mr. Freehold was nearly on the ground laughing so hard. "It's okay, A.J., and it is not Mrs. Harper, it is Miss Harper. If you work around here long enough, you get used to the language and jokes." A.J. nodded his head and looked at D.J. like he was going to hit him again. Mr. Freehold finally got a grip on himself and stood up. "Kari, we've had enough whiskey and we'd like cold beer, go fetch one for us." She nodded her head and started to turn, but turned back to look at A.J. She looked directly at him, almost intentionally, as if she wanted no mistake as to who she was talking to and said, "Are we not friends?" A.J. looked around, but he knew she was talking to him. "Uh, yes, ma'am, I believe we are now. It was a pleasure to meet you."

She didn't move, nor did she change her stare. "Then call

## Chapter 7

me Kari as all my friends do, but if you insist on calling me Mrs. Harper, the correct address would be Miss Harper." She started to turn away, but then turned back quickly and said, "Hopefully, the next time we meet, you will have a matching suit." She smiled and left. A.J. felt the heat rise up to the top of his head. How in the hell, in this dimly-lit tent area, was she the only one that could tell he had two different colors of navy clothes on? Damn! She must have really looked at him!

He was too embarrassed to wait around for the beers, so he grabbed D.J. by the arm, thanked Mr. Freehold for his hospitality, apologized for hurting his son, and promised him free cab rides if he was ever in Montgomery and left. He whistled all the way back to his cousin's house. He had no idea if he would ever see her again, but he knew at that very moment, he had just met the most incredible woman on Earth.

## Chapter 8

"YOU READY FOR THIS, ALVIN? Cinderella is about to show up at the Ball." D.J. was pacing around the body shop. He had the car covered. He and A.J. had done most of the work, so he knew that A.J. had pretty much seen the paint job, but he hadn't seen the car after D.J. put the cab sign on the top and company name on both doors and the trunk so that everyone could see the cab company name. They all stood there in the body shop, A.J., D.J., and his Uncle Marvin, looking at a car that was shielded by a canvas cover that draped it nicely from the roof to the floor.

"Well, did anyone bring a bottle a wine to break over this thing like they do the ships? I mean, this a big deal and we want to launch this cab good and proper." His uncle looked at the two waiting for an answer, but he knew that they didn't have a bottle. "I knew you two knuckleheads would forget the most important detail, so I took care of it." His uncle went over to the counter and pulled out a bottle of champagne that he had stored under the counter. A.J. was impressed that he had thought of such a detail. "Now, normally, we would get a lady to say some fine words and then smash this here champagne bottle on the ship's hull, or in this case, the car's bumper, but we don't have that, so I will do the honors. But before I do that, I think we will sample

## Chapter 8

this here champagne before we smash it." He popped the cork on the champagne and poured three glasses. Actually, they were paper cups. He raised his cup and said, "To the owner of this here cab, may the cab always be filled with customers and his pockets filled with cash!" All three men laughed and drank the champagne. "All right, D.J., let's see Cinderella."

    A.J. actually got very nervous. He had not expected such pomp and circumstance to see his '39 Packard's new paint job, but for some reason, the reality of it had now set in. Being in business for himself, he had taken every step; he had applied for the cab operator's license, and although he thought he was forced to jump through some hoops that the white cab owners were not, he couldn't be sure because he had never been through the process.

    D.J. walked all the way around the car. To add to the suspense, he would rub his hands over the canvas like he was caressing a beautiful woman. "Boy, this is one fine looking automobile, but it is missing something." He rubbed his chin as he continued to walk around the car. "Uncle, what was it you said about a woman and bustin' that bottle on the hull?" He stopped and looked at his uncle. His uncle had this huge smile on his face. "Well, yeah, if we weren't such damn fools, we would have found us a lady to come help us with this here christening. Instead, we got three ugly fools all standing around this canvas looking like dopes." His uncle rubbed his chin for dramatic effect. "It's too late now, go on and yank that cover so we can see Cinderella and all of her beauty, D.J."

    D.J. started to grab the canvas but stopped. He turned to look at both A.J. and his uncle. "Ya'll hear that? I swear I hear somebody knocking on the door. Hang on and let me go check it out." He ran through the shop area towards the front door. There was a wall that hid the front door from the shop. When D.J. returned, A.J.'s mouth went dry again. There she was, Kari Rae Harper, standing there, more beautiful than A.J. could even remember from the tent. "Uncle, what was it you was saying about the lady and that bottle smashing thing?" A.J. froze. His excitement about the unveiling of his new paint job had been wiped away by the entrance of a woman who took away all of his words just with her presence. His uncle was smiling ear to ear, as was D.J.

He stood there next to his uncle, frozen in place and unable to move. He was brought back to reality by a hard slap on the back from his uncle. "Boy, ain't you gonna say hello to the lady? She got off work today in order to come over to help us christen this here automobile good and proper!" The slap on the back had dislodged A.J.'s feet from the place they had become frozen as he slowly made his way towards Miss Harper. Once he was standing in front of her, he stuck his hand out to shake it, but he still couldn't find any words to offer up at that moment. D.J. realized that A.J. was struggling with the occasion and decided to help it along. "Uh, cousin, I went back to see Miss Harper and told her what we was about to do. She was as happy as she could be to be included on this monumental occasion. Ain't you gonna say thank you?"

D.J. had to admit that she was absolutely beautiful. She wore a very pretty light blue dress that showed her shape at the hips and bust line but flared out a little when it got down around her knees. She was definitely out of place in this nasty old body shop, but she sure made things look better and smell better. "Your cousin was kind enough to ask if I would be here for this occasion and I was honored to be included in the launching of your new business." A.J. was still holding her hand but had yet to utter a word. It finally hit him that he needed to acknowledge her. "Thank you, Miss Harper for coming today. I had no idea. I, uh, am afraid I am not very presentable. I, uh, wish I had known. I, uh, would have cleaned up a little better, my apologies." She smiled; she almost blushed at the genuineness in his voice. "No need to apologize, A.J., it is quite an undertaking starting your own business. I just assume that getting dirty is a part of the process. I am very excited to see the car; do you think we can take the cover off now?" Her presence made A.J. completely forget why they were there.

*Chapter 8*

"Oh, yeah! D.J., the lady wants to see the work!" D.J. didn't wait around any longer, he yanked the cover off the car, and everyone stood silent for a few minutes. A.J. was speechless again. He could feel the emotion rising up in throat and he felt his eyes moisten to the point where a tear freely rolled down his cheek. Besides the woman standing next to him right now, he had never in his life seen anything so beautiful. The two-tone crimson and gold paint was exactly what he dreamed, but this was the first time he saw a dream materialize right in front of his eyes.

He was mesmerized by the beauty of the car and was at a loss for words, he felt his hand being touched when he looked down and saw her hand embrace his. She squeezed it ever so gently and to him, it was as if she had somehow pumped some strength back into him simply through her touch. He smiled and looked at his uncle. "Let's christen this car now, I am ready to go to work!" He continued to hold Kari's hand as he strolled over to the car. On the way to the car, he grabbed the bottle of champagne with his free hand. Once he and Kari were standing in front of the car, he let go of her hand and asked her if she would do the honors.

He was a little nervous about where she would smash the bottle, he didn't want her to damage the hood or the paint job, but he was not about to instruct her. As far as he was concerned, this woman could smash a hole in the hood, and he wouldn't care. She took the champagne bottle from him and said, "I would be honored, but what is the company name? I see it on the side, but what does KRC Company stand for?" Without even missing a beat, he said, "I hope you don't mind, but the name of the company came to me after I met you. I decided to call it KRC Cab Company, as in Kari Rae Cab Company, KRC." Now it was her turn to be speechless.

"I hope you don't mind, I just couldn't think of a more perfect name for my company." She smiled, looked at the bottle that she had gripped tightly around the neck of the bottle, looked around the room, and then back at the car. "May you deliver each occupant safely and expedite them on their journey, may you bring joy to each of your arrivals, and may you bring satisfaction and pride to its owner. I christen you the first of many of the KRC." With that, she smashed the bottle against the sturdy front bumper of the car, and it exploded, as it should have. They all clapped, and in the excitement of the moment, she hugged A.J. He was quite relieved that she did not smash it on the hood but found himself locked in an embrace with a woman who had completely and unexpectedly stolen his heart.

A.J. kept his left hand on the car as he circled it, his palm glided over the smooth beautiful paint job. He caressed the car like he was brushing out the mane of a beautiful racehorse. He could not believe he was standing in front of the car of his dreams. He had made it through a war and was about to be a business owner, but something else was on his mind now, too. He was not one to linger on decisions long. Just like starting the cab company, once the idea wormed its way into his head, there was no going back, no stopping him. He had been driven that way his whole life. He knew he would never meet another woman like Miss Kari Rae Harper, and he knew he wanted her to become Mrs. Kari Rae Mack.

He knew it was rushing it. After all, he hadn't even asked her out on a date, but this was simply the way he was wired, and he couldn't do anything about it. "Uh, hold on, everybody, I have something to say, or ask, and I know I won't sleep a wink the rest of my days if I don't say it, so I have to." He looked around and found the cup of champagne that they had used to toast earlier. He wasn't even sure if it was his, but it still had some champagne in it, so he grabbed the cup and drank what was left. "I don't have much, but I know what I want when I see it." He stopped and looked at the car, then he looked at Kari. "Since the minute I saw you, I knew that I would never in my sorry life meet anyone like you." He paused, gathered himself, bent down on one knee right in front of Miss Kari Rae Harper, and said, "I'd like you to marry me. I promise you will never find anyone that will treat you better than me." His uncle dropped the cup he had in his hand and went

Chapter 8

over to where A.J. was kneeling, grabbed him under the arms, and picked him up so that he was standing again. "Hold on there, boy, you ain't known this woman all of two days and you're already asking her to marry you! You are crazy as a shit house rat, boy!" He looked at Kari. He also saw that D.J. was just as dumbfounded as he was. "Miss Harper, I apologize for my language and I am sorry 'bout my nephew's rude behavior, please forgive us all for being just a bunch of love-sick fools, especially this one."

The surprising thing to all of it was that Kari didn't seem shocked or upset. To Uncle Marvin, it appeared that this kind of thing happened to her every day and she was used to it. "Mr. Moore, there is no need to apologize. I happen to like a man that doesn't waste time, so I will give you my answer. Mr. Alvin Jerome Mack, I will marry you, BUT..." She paused, looked around at the room and at the car, and continued, "You will court me proper for one year. That should give you time to get your business up and running and then, and only then, will I marry you." D.J. stood there with his mouth open. He couldn't believe she had just said yes! Even though she had laid down some rules to the game, the fact was, she had just said yes to his cousin.

D.J. couldn't hold it in any longer, "Damn! Is that how it works these days? Hell, I got to rethink my strategy on catching me a woman." Uncle Marvin didn't act as dumbfounded as D.J. For some reason, he knew that these two kids' hearts had collided in this world and sometimes that is just the way it was. Cupid let loose an arrow and pierced them both right square in the ass. "Well, Miss Harper, I reckon this is turned into an engagement party, too!" A.J. walked over to her, took both her hands in his and said, "I promise to court you proper, I promise to make you proud, and I promise to love you with the breath I take now until the very last." She smiled; they were nearly eye-to-eye as she was as tall as he was. In fact, with her heels on, she was just slightly taller than A.J., but he didn't care. He really hadn't even noticed, and he never would.

## Chapter 9

A.J. DID KEEP HIS WORD. He dated her properly, although, it was tough balancing all of it for a little while. The business was slow at first and he spent most of the days parked outside the Endicot Hotel in downtown Montgomery. The Endicot was one of the swankiest places there was and that was where most of the folks in from out of town stayed. Before he ever took his first fare, his uncle had warned him to never tell anyone that he owned the cab. He said to tell them that he was just an employee. Marvin Moore knew the rules of Alabama and rule number one was the white folks would not support a black business. They wouldn't set foot in a cab if they thought a black man owned the cab, but they would quickly jump in a cab if they thought the driver was just an employee.

Although A.J. found it insulting to be treated with such disrespect, he realized that his uncle was correct. He even made a game of it when he felt like it. He would throw out his worst Southern accent and was sure to toss in a bunch of *yessuh* and *noosuh*, instead of a clear *yes sir* and *no sir*, of which white folks seemed to enjoy immensely. He hated it very much, but he was truly fascinated by the fact that the more he acted like an uneducated black man from the "poe" side of Montgomery, the more tips he received. He could sometimes come home with as much

## Chapter 9

as thirty dollars in tips, and that was free and clear cash, that didn't include the cab fare.

He was very good with the customers, although some weren't so good to him. He was certain to never pick up a white woman alone and he was certain to never pick up a black person in the daylight. He hated that it had to be that way, but white folks had more money and they would not ride in a cab that was used by a black person. He never understood all these rules of racial engagement, but thanks to his uncle, he understood the consequences for not following the rules.

He spent an awful lot of time with his uncle and came to admire and respect him greatly. He continuously had a word of encouragement for him and he always seemed to know the pulse of not only Montgomery, Alabama, but he understood the pulse of the United States. It was a happy time, but it was also a scary time. Folks were coming back from the war, starting families, and things were good. There was talk that there would never be another war and the future of America was bright and A.J. was hell-bent on being a part of it. He was high-strung and unafraid; the Japanese had made him that way. He could barely sleep anymore; it used to be because he would have bad dreams, but now it was because he couldn't wait to get up and get busy with his business. Even though he was high-strung and tended to rush into decisions, like asking Kari to marry him just two days after meeting her, he had come to know that he needed the help of his uncle, his uncle's council and guidance. He would spend almost every Sunday at his uncle's house cleaning up the car for the next week's business. He tried running the cab on Sundays when he first got started, but there simply weren't any fares. He figured he wasted more gas and money than it was worth, so he started doing all the oil changes and lube work in his uncle's front yard. There was a nice huge oak tree in his uncle's yard, and if they weren't working on the car, they were sitting in the shade having a glass of lemonade or a cold beer. They only drank the beer when his uncle said his bones hurt and he needed to loosen up.

*Choice of Honor*

He had almost come to look forward to Sunday with his uncle as much as he looked forward to working and Kari.

"A.J., pass me that ½ inch." A.J. and his uncle were putting the finishing touches on a new carburetor for the Packard. A.J. reached into the toolbox and found the wrench his uncle was asking for, but he saw a box with a bow on it. He handed the wrench to his uncle and picked up the tiny box. "Uncle, what in the world is this little box doing in your nasty old tool tray?" He replied, "I figured it was about time you stopped being a dumbass and fix things up right with that girl." A.J. picked up the box and held it like it would bite him. He held it up towards the sun, but since they were in the shade of the massive oak tree, it didn't help him much.

"Well, go on and open it, boy." A.J. looked at his uncle and then back to the box, "I don't understand, what is it?" His uncle leaned up from under the hood, grabbed an oil rag that was laying across the front bumper and rubbed his hands on it, then stuck the rag back in his back pocket. "Boy, I swear, for someone that has as much juice in the tank and brains in the bank, I swear you are thick as a mule sometimes! Just open it and see!" A.J. slid the bow off the box; he almost let it drop to the ground and realized it was too pretty to get dirty, so he held it gently and placed it on the top of the Packard. He flipped the box open and was stunned to see a beautiful diamond ring; it sparkled against the dark black velvet that it was resting in.

"Uncle Marvin, this is beautiful, but we are related, and I don't swing that way." He laughed when he said it and so did Uncle Marvin. "Dumbass, it's for that girl you been seeing. She said you had to date her proper, you already asked her to marry you and you didn't even give her a ring!" A.J. felt a lump rise up in his throat. He really loved his uncle, but his uncle had just done something that he never would have dreamed of. "It was your mother's, boy. You was off at war when she and your daddy passed away. Wasn't nobody around to take it and I figured she would want you to have it and give it to your future wife. I sure

*Chapter 9*

wasn't gonna let the undertaker steal it because that fool sure would have. He was as crooked as they come. Trying to charge me for everything under the sun when your old man had already paid for everything and I had the papers to prove it. Damn cheat is what he was."

A.J. stood there in shock. He had no idea his mother even had a ring, since he returned from war and his uncle had given him what he thought was everything his parents had. He guessed he'd really never looked. He couldn't believe he was holding his mother's ring. The fact that it was his mother's made it even more beautiful. "Uncle Marvin, I don't know what to say, this is, uh, this is incredible. I, uh, don't know what to say."

"I hate to pump any more air into that big ole noggin of yours, it's big enough as it is, but you were smart to grab that girl real quick like you did. She has *special* written all over that face. I never seen anything like it. It was like you and her was cut from the same cloth. She deserves to have your mother's ring and if you don't hurry and give it to her, I damn sure will." A.J. looked down at the ring and then back up to his uncle. He shook his head and drew in a deep breath; he pretended like he was just trying to breathe in the fresh Alabama air, but in truth, he was trying not to cry. He took a couple steps towards his uncle and, before he knew it, he had his uncle in a bear hug and was bawling like a baby. There he was, a grown man in the front yard underneath that big ole shade tree, crying like a baby.

His uncle embraced him as tightly as he could. Uncle Marvin knew that every now and then a man had to *wring out the sponge*, as he liked to say. After he was comfortable that A.J. had wrung out his sponge, he let him go. A.J. kept his head down and seemed embarrassed to look up. "Look here, boy, ain't one ounce a shame in a man shedding a few tears. I say a man's a damn fool if he tries to keep them all inside. See, I think a man, a good man, is like a sponge; he soaks up a whole bunch a shit through his life and sometimes, well, the damn thing just gets too big and too full, he got to ring it out every now and then and start over."

A.J. didn't look up but shook his head as if he understood. "You been makin' an awful lot of trips over to Selma to see that girl. I pray every day that a year comes quick so you two can be together. I don't like that trip over to Selma one damn bit. It ain't no place for black man to be at the wrong time a day. You make sure you are careful." He knew he had to slightly change the subject because A.J. still wouldn't look up. "Anyway, that ring belongs on that girl's finger just as soon as you can swing it." He knew his uncle was right. He didn't have the extra funds to buy her a ring, just about everything he had and made was going back into the cab company. Things were going pretty well, and he had managed to show a profit after just eleven months of operations. He was a month ahead of schedule as he had planned to be profitable by the end of his first year, and he was one month away from being able to marry Miss Kari Rae Harper. He was even profitable after paying Mr. Montgomery his three percent cut of the revenue every month. It was also an inconvenience to have to be Mr. Montgomery's personal chauffeur on the weekends that he beckoned. He would be glad when the year was up on that arrangement.

Being the chauffeur for Mr. Montgomery carried weight, and he met some people in the process, but it also carried secrets. He sometimes wished he didn't see some of the things he saw or go to some of the places that he went, but a deal was a deal. He had thought about telling his uncle about some of the things he had seen and learned while in the employment of Mr. Montgomery, but he felt it was best to keep his uncle as far away from that stuff as he could. As far as he knew, the revenue sharing would last the rest of his life. He regretted not hammering out a better deal than that. But at least he knew the driving part would be over in a month. Yes, sir, with the exception of being Mr. Montgomery's driver, as his daddy used to say when he was a boy, he had the rhino by the horn.

His business was good, and he had begun to look for a house that he and Miss Kari could live in and have a bunch of kids.

## Chapter 9

A.J. held tightly to the box that held the ring. "Uncle Marvin, I can hardly wait until this month is over and I can marry Kari. Do you think mom and dad would like her?" Uncle Marvin put the ½ inch wrench back in the tool tray that he had been holding throughout the entire hug. A.J. could see the smile on his face as he spoke. "Listen here, anything you did, your parents was proud of. They would talk everybody's ear off about their son was a Marine and their son did this and their son did that. It would get so that folks would figure out ways to change the subject or go hide someplace. We all got sick of hearing about Sergeant Alvin Jerome Mack." A.J. felt embarrassed when he heard his uncle say all this stuff and was about to say so when his uncle continued, "I was pretty sure it was all bullshit until I actually got to know you." He looked at A.J. with the sincerest look A.J. had ever seen. "I am proud of you, so I know your mom and dad are too."

# Chapter 10

WITH THE RING IN HIS pocket, he drove to Selma that night. He couldn't wait another second to put that ring on her finger. She wouldn't be expecting him because usually Sunday night she went to prayer service and he didn't care much for prayer service. Even though she had been dealt some pretty bad cards in the game of life, she still insisted that God was looking out for her.

A.J. was fascinated with people and their belief in something they couldn't see. He had seen how ugly people could be to one another, hell, just a little over a year ago, there were men with bayonets and guns trying to kill him and any other man they could find that didn't look Japanese. Why in the world would any God allow men to do that? Why in the world would a God allow people to hate him just because of his skin color? None of it made sense to him, which is why he had no use for Sunday morning church or Sunday night prayer service. He would drive over to Selma every chance he could get to see Kari where he *courted her proper*, as she put it. He never even tried to sneak a kiss until they had been going out for almost six months. She lived in a tiny house on Mr. Curtis Freehold's property. He didn't charge any rent as long as she worked for him, which turned out to be pretty much seven days a week. She did all the cooking and

## Chapter 10

cleaning and she worked the barn dances every Saturday night. It wasn't overly hard work as Mrs. Freehold kept a pretty neat and orderly house, but she hated to cook. Kari loved to cook so that never seemed like work.

What was work was keeping Mr. Freehold's idiot son's hands off her. He would pester her all the time for a kiss and would actually try to take one, but she fought him off every single time. He wasn't overly aggressive and didn't try to do anything beyond stealing a kiss, but Kari thought he would eventually try if he got drunk enough. When he had been drinking and especially after he got into a fight, he wanted a woman to relieve that last little bit of steam he had left in him, and he usually found a suitor willing to take care of him at one of the barn dances. He once got caught in the loft with Grace Moore and he is very lucky he lived through it. If it hadn't been for his daddy, he'd be deader than a doornail.

Grace was the wife of pastor Jim Moore, and Pastor Moore was supposed to be away that weekend doing a summer tent revival as the guest pastor and she stayed behind with their two babies. Grace Moore was half the pastor's age. Folks figured she wasn't more than twenty-one and the pastor was approaching fifty, he may have even already topped it, nobody really knew. He just showed up one Sunday morning and introduced this young girl as his new wife and that he had met her over in Birmingham. Kari remembered everybody in church whispering that morning he introduced her because they had just buried his second wife only a month ago. Poor girl probably had nowhere else to go, otherwise she wouldn't have taken up with the pastor. He was a good man, but his wives kept dying off on him. There was always talk that she like to dilly dally around when the pastor wasn't looking, so it didn't surprise anyone at the dance when she showed up. As the story now goes, seems the tent show over in Birmingham caught fire and the tent they were supposed to be using to hold services in burned up. Nobody was hurt, but right after the tent was left in ashes, the rains came and they didn't have any place to have the revival, so he came back earlier than she expected.

Even though they weren't surprised to see her, nobody could really figure out why she went to the barn dance anyway because there wasn't a soul in Selma that could keep a secret and the pastor was sure to hear about his hussy wife going out dancing when he was gone. When the pastor got home that Saturday evening and she wasn't there, the little girl that she had brought over to watch their kids gave up the ghost and told the pastor where she was. He was as mad as a hornet that she had left their two babies with a girl that wasn't much more than a baby herself and that she had gone to a place where they drank liquor and did God knows what and all kinds of unspeakable acts.

He showed up at the dance with a .410 shotgun and waded into the crowd, he didn't say anything as walked and looked. He would make eye contact with every man he saw as if he was trying see into their souls and determine if they had been with his wife that night. When he didn't find her on the dance floor of the barn, he went down the path to the liquor tent, he didn't find her there either. He was about to give up looking and may have concluded that he had overreacted and perhaps was given some incorrect information when he overheard two ladies talking about Freehold being up in the loft with *that hussy*, as they put it. He knew right away who they were talking about. He made his way back to the barn at a much quicker pace and climbed the loft with the shotgun still in his hand. What was funny to Kari was that everyone knew where he was going, everyone knew that Freehold was in the loft, everyone knew that Grace Moore was up in the loft with him, and nobody made any attempt to warn young Mr. Freehold that he was about to meet his maker.

Luckily for young Mr. Freehold, someone had warned his daddy and Mr. Curtis Freehold and made his way from the main house to the barn just in time to hear the gun go off. Sure enough, the pastor climbed the loft to find his wife giving young Mr. Freehold everything a young man dreams about.

## Chapter 10

They were so busy that they didn't hear the pastor climb the ladder and so busy that they continued their activity while the pastor stood and watched. The anger welled up in him like he had never felt and would have killed them both if it hadn't been for Curtis Freehold.

Pastor Moore pulled the trigger on the shotgun that was squarely aimed at young Freehold's exposed backside but was knocked off its course by Mr. Curtis Freehold. The shotgun blast harmlessly hit the roof of the barn but managed to kill a pigeon that just happened to be in the wrong place at the wrong time, but the noise of the blast and the floating feathers was clearly enough to dislodge the two from their embrace. The noise was enough to stop the band for just a few minutes, long enough for everyone to stop what they were doing and see young Freehold come flying down the ladder of the loft, naked as a jay bird and tally-whacker still locked in its active position.

Young Mr. Freehold sprinted through the crowd without one ounce of shame. The crowd was standing there in stunned silence for just a few minutes, with only the sound of arguing could be heard above them in the loft, until a lady from the crowd yelled, "Somebody get that boy something to wear. Lord, from the looks of it, he is already freezing!" The crowd burst out laughing and the band kicked back up just as quickly as they had shut down. For a while, he was known as *Little Freehold*, but just a few weeks after, he had had his fill of the taunting and he nearly beat a kid to death over cracking an unwise joke.

When he hit the backside door to the barn that had the path that led back to the main house, he was not seen the rest of the night. While Curtis, Jr. made his way out the door in his birthday suit and the band started back up, Curtis Freehold, Sr. faced off with Pastor Moore in the upstairs loft. "I'm gonna kill that little son of a bitch Curtis Freehold, I swear on everything holy I will crush his spine with my bare hands!" The pastor had clicked the barrel latch open and since his .410 was a single shot, he was trying to load another shell. His hands were shaking so badly that he dropped the shell on the floor.

Mr. Freehold, Sr. had arrived just in time to change the trajectory of the shotgun blast, which clearly spared his son the agony of an ass full of birdshot. It wouldn't have killed him, but just going to the outhouse would have been a painful experience for a while. "Now, Pastor Moore, I ain't gonna excuse that boy or that girl's behavior, but there ain't no use in you going to jail over a loose woman and a horny boy." The pastor tried to pick up the shell, but Curtis, Sr. kicked it away and it rolled off the loft and on to someone's head below. "What are you calling my woman, old man!" Pastor Moore fumbled around in his coat pocket, obviously looking for another shell. Grace Moore had managed to get her drawers pulled back up and her skirt back down where it should have been. Mr. Freehold took a glance in her direction and nearly laughed when he saw that in her haste to put her clothes back on, her shirt was still unbuttoned and one of her boobs was still clearly on display, but decided the situation was still too volatile to make a joke of it. "I called her a loose woman, Jim Moore, and if you try to put another shell in that stupid little gun, I will toss your Bible-thumpin' ass right off my loft. Don't you think I won't do it either!" Mr. Freehold was quite a bit older than Pastor Moore and physically was no match for the pastor, but his sheer grit carried a lot of weight with folks and it was carrying some weight with Pastor Moore at the moment.

"Look over there at your woman, boy - barley dressed with her teat hanging out. What the hell do you call a married woman who takes a ride on another man's merry-go-round?" The pastor was clearly fuming, but at least he was listening now, and it was a good thing because Mr. Curtis Freehold, Sr. wasn't finished. "I will tell you another thing, too, since you are hell-bent on killing someone." He stepped toward the pastor and yanked the shotgun out of his hands. The gesture stunned the pastor and for the first time, he stood still and stopped looking for another shell. "You gone through a few wives already and ain't nobody sure

## Chapter 10

what happened to the other two, but if ANYTHING happens to this young girl after today, I swear on that Bible you poke in everybody's face that I will hunt you down and end your preaching days."

As he said all this, he had stepped nose-to-nose with the pastor and even though the pastor was taller than Mr. Freehold, Sr., the intimidation factor had set in for the good pastor and his shoulders slumped. He actually began to sob, which Mr. Freehold found amusing, but he really didn't have any sympathy for him. Well, he had a little, he had no idea how he would react if he caught his missus humping a young buck, but he knew he wouldn't let anybody stop him from doing whatever he wanted to do to rectify it. Mr. Freehold turned to Grace Moore, "Young lady, you better hear me, and you better hear me good. You married this man and that means something in my book. If you want to go around and let every horny pecker find its way up your skirt, then you deserve to be out on your boney ass, but you don't deserve to get dead." Mr. Freehold looked directly at the pastor when he said it so that the pastor would know he was serious about him not turning up with another dead wife. "Now, put your boob back in your shirt, fix yourself, and both of you idiots climb down out of my loft and get the hell off my farm!"

He took the shotgun he had taken from the pastor and shoved it back into Pastor Moore's chest. It knocked the pastor back a few steps and apparently knocked the pastor back into the moment. His rage was gone, his eyes were still watery, and he was hurt, but he would survive to preach his sermon the very next Sunday. Ironically, his sermon that Sunday was about forgiveness, and to everyone in the congregation's amusement, he used Mary Magdalene as the focal point of the story. Young Grace Moore sat in the first pew with her two babies rocking back and forth, just like she did every Sunday. Nobody thought she heard a word of it.

Young Freehold was a hell raiser of monumental proportions; he loved to party, chase women, get drunk, and get into fights. It was a pretty well-known fact that he had no control over his pocket pole. Folks would make jokes that the fence would close the holes in their knots when he would walk by. It was true that he would fight anybody though, especially people he didn't know, and if he couldn't find anyone to fight, he would pick a fight with his buddies he ran with, that is, until he met Alvin Jerome Mack. The doctor said that his mangled wrist that Alvin left him with would never heal up right and he would have a crooked hand from now on. He could use it just fine, but the way it was now cocked to one side, he couldn't ball up a fist just right and it actually hurt to hit anything. Alvin Jerome Mack had ended his fighting days just as quickly as they began. Mr. Freehold, Sr. was actually grateful for the turn of events, because the fight with Alvin Jerome Mack had taken the starch out of the boy's fists and he was now getting things done around their farm. He just wished that the confrontation with the pastor had taken the starch out his baby-maker, but it didn't.

As he drove to see Miss Kari Harper, he thought about how much he liked to just sit and listen to her stories about all she had seen while employed at the Freehold farm. She made it very clear that Mr. Freehold was one of the finest and noblest men she had ever met, but she stayed as far away from his son as she could. She told him that the Freeholds had taken her in when she was very young and had no place else to go. They could have easily taken advantage of her or treated her badly, but Mr. Freehold wouldn't stand for it. When he and his wife took her in, they treated her very well, not quite like a family member, but like a very trusted friend and neighbor.

Her own parents were killed when she was very little. She was never told how they were killed and every time she asked, she was told not to ask, so she just accepted things as they were and made a life for herself. The Freeholds made sure she had clothes on her back and food in her stomach. They sent her off to school and made sure she got educated all the way through high school. A.J. knew she was really smart because every time he tried to

## Chapter 10

figure out a math problem that was applicable to his work, like the three percent he owed Mr. Montgomery each month, she could figure it all out in her head in just a few seconds. He was impressed by her ability to do lots of things and the more he thought about it, the more he believed that he had surely made an impulsive but correct decision on asking her to marry him. He couldn't imagine taking on the challenges he faced without her. He couldn't wait to stand on the porch of her little home and ask her to marry him properly with a ring this time. First, he would stop by the main house and visit with Mr. Curtis Freehold, Sr. Not because he had to, Mr. Freehold already knew that he had asked her to marry him, so that wasn't the issue. The issue was showing the proper amount of respect for a man who helped his future bride when he didn't have to, and he never asked her for anything in return. Mr. Curtis Freehold was a good man.

# Chapter 11

AS HE DROVE THE HIGHWAY 80 as it stretched between Montgomery and Selma, he reflected on everything he had done to this point. How he had managed to not get killed in the war, the ugliness he had seen while he was at war, how a man, a white man no less, had seemingly materialized right out of the sands of Iwo Jima and saved him from a Japanese search party and he, in turn, had saved that same white man by sticking his finger in a hole in his chest.

He shook his head as he drove. He wished his own father and mother could be here to see what he was about to do. He was quite relieved when his uncle told him that he was proud of him and he was certain his parents would be, too. He didn't expect his uncle to say anything different really, his uncle was a straight shooter, but he didn't have a mean bone in his body. Even if his uncle weren't proud of him, he would have found a way to encourage him no matter what. That was just the kind of man his uncle was. He tried not to walk down memory lane because he knew it didn't do any good. He had a teacher in sixth grade that told him that he should always remember the past, but don't spend any time dwelling on it, and to keep his mind on the future and it would be there; it is in the future that his mind

## Chapter 11

should dwell on. He tried to focus on how he would present Miss Kari Rae Harper with the ring his mother used to wear and went through every scenario in his head.

Just as he had decided that the best approach would be just to get down on one knee and propose like a real gentleman should, he saw the lights flashing in his rear-view mirror. He remembered a sign on the highway that said Benton, so he wasn't sure exactly where he was. He looked down at his speedometer and he wasn't speeding. His heart began to race. He remembered what his uncle had said about playing the game; being humble, don't be seen as a threat. He tried to breathe, but his breathing became very labored. He slowed down; he even put his blinker on so that police car behind him would know he was pulling over. He pulled the car to a stop and set the brake. He turned the ignition off and rolled down the window. He sat there in silence for what seemed like an eternity.

It was dark, but he could see farmland on both sides of him. What he didn't like seeing was a huge maple tree that was nestled next to a pond. The only reason he knew there was a pond there was because he could see the reflection of the moon in the water. He went through every scenario in his head, how he would handle the broken taillight or headlight or all the personal questions about where he was going and what he was doing. He also remembered the seriousness in his uncle's voice when he had told him that he really wanted him to hurry up and get married so that he wouldn't have to make that drive over to Selma anymore.

He heard the doors close and two officers approached his car. The one that approached his window seemed quite old. It was hard to tell because the officer trained the flashlight directly in his face. He blinked as the light was blinding him, but he didn't dare look away. "You got a license to drive this hunk a junk on my highway?" A.J. swallowed what little saliva he had in his mouth and said, "Yes, sir, I will get it for you."

He reached back to pull his wallet out of his back pocket. "Whoa, whoa! Hold on there, boy! Don't you be reaching for no switch blade knife now!" A.J. was surprised to see that the policeman had stepped back and had actually drawn his gun and was now pointing it directly at A.J.'s face. "Uh, uh, I'm sorry, sir." He remembered his uncle's lesson to *learn to play the game* and it came out with a very thick Southern drawl. "I'm sorra, SUH," he continued, "I's jus reachin' foe my wallet is all. Sorra, SUH." He didn't move his hands anymore and wasn't going to until he was given permission. No way was he getting accidently shot on this cornball stretch of highway on the way to give his girl the ring.

Then it hit him, he had something very valuable and they could easily take it from him. He tried to remember where it was and realized that it was in his side jacket pocket. "Well, hell, I ain't got all day then, get that wallet out and let me have it." He continued the process of extracting the wallet from his back pocket. His heart was beating so fast that he hoped he didn't have a heart attack because of this fool pointing a gun at him right now. When he finally extended the wallet out the window, he was relieved to see that the policeman slid his gun back into the holster that flapped so freely on his right hip. "Now, step on out of the car." A.J. did as he was told and did it so slowly that he felt like he was being a smart ass by moving so slow, but he just couldn't bring himself to take any chances of getting shot.

By now, the other officer, who seemed quite a bit younger, made his way all the way around the car and ended up standing in front of A.J. while the old cop looked at A.J.'s license. A.J. noticed that he had simply dropped the wallet on the ground after he found his license. "One Alvin Jerome Mack we have here. Where you going with a busted taillight, Alvin Jerome Mack?" Alvin swallowed again, but this time it wasn't saliva, it was hate he swallowed. He hated being harassed like this and he knew they would certainly bust a taillight just for fun. "I been meaning to get that busted light fixed, SUH. I was on my way over to my cousins in Selma so he could help me fix it. SUH."

The young cop leaned over and picked up the wallet off the ground, and to A.J.'s surprise, handed it back to him. "Who you

## Chapter 11

work for, boy? Who owns this here cab and do they know you out gallivantin' around Alabama?" The young cop still hadn't said anything, but there was something in his eyes that A.J. couldn't figure out. It was dark, but the moon was pretty bright, bright enough for A.J. to see that the young cop seemed to not want to be here just now, almost as if he was annoyed by this.

A.J. started to answer that he owned the cab but thought better of it because that wouldn't be playing the game. "I believe a certain percent of it belongs to Mr. Orville Gibson in Montgomery, Alabama, SUH. I don't know how much percent cause I don't do my math suh good, but he owns it." A.J. was pretty proud of himself for laying down a poor, ignorant Southern accent so well, but prouder for thinking far enough ahead to not lie to these guys and still not tell them he owned the cab. "Come on, Jim, let's go. I'm hungry and I am missin' supper for this shit." Finally, the young cop said something and A.J. was proud of himself again for reading the right expression on the man's face. He was hungry and didn't want to be there. "You just hold your horses, your old lady ain't gonna eat the supper without her dumbass husband. Never know what she saw in you anyway." The insult was clear, and the young policeman didn't care much for it. "Well, I will tell you, if my old lady was as fat as yours, I'd be home before she ate all your food and the family pet, shit for brains. I bet the damn dog hides under your porch when your old lady's stomach growls."

A.J. almost laughed but decided better against it. He kept a straight face and for a minute he thought these two idiots would duke it out right there on the side of the highway. A.J. had his money on the young one, not only was he more physically fit, he apparently was more quick-witted than the old cop. "Boy, I ought to drop you like a bag a turds for calling my wife fat!" The young cop snatched the license that the old one was still holding from his hand and handed it back to A.J. As he handed the license back to him, he simply said, "Get that taillight fixed, boy." A.J. breathed a sigh as he thought it was over. "Hold on

*Choice of Honor*

there, I swear he reached for a switch blade knife when I walked up on him, search him and don't make no more comments about my wife or I will keep you out here all damn night."

A.J. figured the old cop outranked the young one, but it didn't stop the young one from putting the old one in his place a time or two, but he still did as instructed. "Turn around, spread your legs, and put your hands on the car, boy." The young cop instructed him in a very sarcastic voice, but A.J. did as instructed. The pat down didn't last long, but the young cop did find the box with the ring in it. A.J. felt his heart beating again. He couldn't let them take that ring. "Ok, turn around." The young cop had the box in his hand and was opening it when A.J. turned around. He heard the young cop whistle when he had the box open and shined a flashlight on the contents. The older cop came over to look at what he was whistling at. "Why, this son of a bitch done went and stole him a ring from somebody. Jim, I told you that he was no good. I bet you that ring belongs to some white lady and we are gonna have to get it back to her!" A.J. looked up at the stars and told himself that he would kill these two men right here on the highway before he would let them drive off with that ring.

The old cop tried to grab the ring from the young one, but he wasn't quick enough because the young cop drew it away before he could. "Hold on, Jim. Get your damn hands off it. I want to hear what Alvin Jerome Mack is doing with a big ass diamond ring like this." He looked at the young cop as he was obviously waiting for an answer. "It was my mother's. I was going to Selma to give it to the lady I am going to marry next month." Before A.J. could say another word, the old cop backhanded A.J. across the mouth. It wasn't much because A.J. barely moved his head. "Bullshit, boy! You're a lying son of a bitch! You just said you was goin' to your cousins to get that damn taillight fixed, now you expect me to believe you are going to propose to a woman! Damn liar is what you are! Calvin, hand-cuff him and put him in the car. Give me that ring, it's evidence now. We caught him lying!"

*Chapter 11*

A.J. was in a full-blown panic, but he kept his eyes focused on the young cop, who he now knew was named Calvin. "Jim, shut the hell up!" Young Calvin turned to Jim and it was clear to A.J. that regardless of rank or titles, Calvin intimidated Jim. Calvin turned to A.J., "What's her name?" A.J. was surprised by the question and was about to answer when Jim punched him again. This time, it was a clear balled up fist and it stung A.J. His knees buckled, and he had to use the car to catch himself so he wouldn't fall. He was determined not to fall this time. "Damn it, Jim, if you hit him again, I swear you will walk home." Calvin put his hand on A.J.'s shoulder and helped him get steady again. A.J. could feel his lip swelling up. He thought, "So much for kissing Kari tonight." He licked his lip and said, "Her name is Kari." Calvin looked down at the ring then back up to A.J. "I believe you. I don't give a shit, but I believe you. Where did you get this ring for real?" Alvin shook his head in frustration, "I ain't lyin', it was my mother's. She died before I came back from war. She died the same week my dad died. They left it to me, SUH." A.J. could see a small but noticeable smile come across Calvin's face. He could also see old Jim pacing behind them like a caged animal that wasn't caged.

A.J. was in a bad spot right now and he knew it. His real only hope was the fact that he thought that young Calvin just might be a decent man. "All right, I believe you. I was in that war, too. Here's the deal. Old Jim back here wants this ring really bad. I want to go home and eat supper and hopefully give my wife a good ride and make some babies, and you want to go propose to woman I ain't never seen. Now, that's what I call a difficult spot." He was about to say something when Jim interrupted again. "Listen here, you little shit, I ain't leaving here without that ring or I will report you to the station chief for covering up a crime. Now, give me that damn ring!"

Calvin turned to look at the raging idiot pacing the side of the road then he looked back at A.J. "See what I mean?" Calvin closed the lid on the ring box, looked up at the stars, then back to A.J., then down at the ring. The silence now was deafening, except for the pounding feet of old Jim, all was quiet on Highway 80 East of Benson. "I have the answer, may not be the best, but it's the best I can do." A.J. waited with anticipation and almost prayed that young officer Calvin would hand him the ring back and beat the hell out of old Jim, but he had a feeling that was not going to happen. Just as Jim was about to scream at everyone again, Calvin turned and threw the ring box out into the dark field on the other side of the road from where they were standing. A.J. nearly sprang off the car he was leaning on to go after the ring, but his heart sank when he heard the splash sound of the box hitting the pond.

A.J. wanted to scream at the cops, he wanted to beat the hell out of both of them. Scratch that, he wanted to kill both of them. His entire body stiffened, and he was no longer leaning on the car. Anger was not a strong enough word for what he was feeling. His hands were clinched in fists and his back was arched. "What the hell is you doing, Calvin! I wanted that ring, damn it!" Jim walked across the road and stood at the barbed wire fence that protected a pasture and the pond that now held A.J.'s ring. Calvin looked at his crazy partner and then looked back at A.J. He was speaking to Jim, but he was looking directly at A.J. when he said, "And you can have it, you just have to go get it, but I am leaving now. Either come get in the car with me or stay here and bob for apples with Alvin Jerome Mack, your call, it don't make a shit to me." He turned and started walking to his car.

A.J. fully expected him to turn around and say something, but he didn't. He just kept walking to the car. Jim obviously got the message because he came back across the road and walked right up to A.J. He stood there for a second, long enough for A.J. to see the pure rage and hate in his eyes. "Stay off my highway, boy, or I swear you won't be heard from again. You hear me!" He walked back towards the police car, stopped when he got to the back of A.J.'s car, and smashed the taillight out with his flashlight. "Get this damn taillight fixed, boy." A.J. didn't say

## Chapter 11

anything, he just stood there. He realized that even though it was a terrible and awful thing for Calvin to do, at least he knew where the ring was, and he was not leaving until he got it back.

He stood by his Packard until the police taillights could no longer be seen. He stood there, choking back the anger and the fear and all the other things those two morons brought out in him. One day he would get even with Officer Jim for hitting him in the face and he would get even with Officer Calvin for throwing his ring into a nasty cow shit filled pond. That would have to come later, though, at the moment, he needed to go diving for diamonds. Thank God for the Marines because before he went into the service, he had no idea how to swim.

He took his clothes off; walked across the road naked as the day he was born and waded into the pond. It was one of the most disgusting things he had ever done. It was too dark. The moon lit up the water some, but certainly not well enough to help any. He developed a circular search grid pattern and felt around with his hands and feet. When he thought he might have stepped on it, he dove down into the foul-smelling water to investigate, only to come up with a rock or some other worthless junk. After hours of searching, he found the ring box just before sun up.

He was nearly exhausted, and he was shivering from head to toe. He tried to dry off as best he could but had to put his clothes on while he was still wet. He was just too cold and a naked black man on the side of the highway was sure to bring more trouble. He knew he smelled awful from all the things that the cows left in that pond as they waded in it. While he was diving for the box, he could hear the cows walking around the pond, but thankfully they were afraid to wade into it because of its current occupant.

Regardless of the smell, there was no way he was going back to Montgomery. Kari was going to get that ring today; he simply couldn't risk another encounter with Officer Moron and Officer Asshole. He found an old mechanics blanket in the trunk and wrapped that around himself as he put the city of Benson behind him and made his way to Selma. The sun was rising, and he smiled, the irony of a new day after a terrible night hit him, *it is a beautiful thing to see a sunrise no matter what kind of mood you were in*, he thought, *you just had to slow down to appreciate it.* He had done as his uncle said...he played the game...hated every second of it, but he was starting a new day and he had his mother's ring in his pocket.

## Chapter 12

MR. CURTIS FREEHOLD HAD JUST sat down for breakfast with his missus, as he liked to call her, when he heard the car pull up in the front of his house. He really didn't care for the interruption because she had made his favorite that morning, biscuits with strawberry preserves made from his own strawberries, some pepper gravy, bacon strips, and three eggs over easy. "Who in the hell is rollin' in here at this early hour?" He said it out loud and wasn't really expecting an answer, but he got one from his missus anyway. "Curtis Freehold, you better not be cussin' at the table, you ain't even said grace over that plate yet." He smiled, reached over and patted her hand, "My forgiveness, Momma."

He slid his chair away from the table and grabbed the shotgun that was standing in the corner of the front room. It was a beauty of a gun too, it was a 16-gauge Remington that was always loaded with buckshot. It was not common to receive visits this early, so he never liked to go to the door without presenting the image that he meant business. More than once he had defended his home from both white folks and black folks.

Curtis made it to the front porch before A.J. could manage to get out of the Packard. When A.J. got out of the car and stood up, he could see Curtis Freehold standing there with a shotgun cradled in his arm like a newborn baby. "Boy, what are doing here at this early hour? You drunk, you lookin' for trouble?" A.J. decided that it was best if he didn't move any closer, he was getting really tired of feeling like if stepped wrong he would end up getting shot. "No, sir, I came to see Miss Kari, but I had to see you first." Curtis seemed confused, "Why so early, I thought you was supposed to be here yesterday?"

A.J. stuck his hands in his pants pockets, which were still damp from putting his clothes on when he was still wet. "I had a little trouble last night or I would have been here a lot sooner. Can I come in and talk to you?" Mr. Freehold let the shotgun drop from its cradled position and let it dangle with his right arm. It was a sign to A.J. that Mr. Freehold had relaxed. "Come on in, boy, you are just in time for breakfast." Curtis stood there on the porch waiting for A.J. to come up the steps. When A.J. was almost to the top of the steps, he turned to hold the door open for A.J. When A.J. was walking past him to enter, Curtis got a whiff of A.J. "Uh, hold up there, boy, you smell like shit! What the hell kinda trouble did you get into? Smells like you been romancing a stump broke cow! You ain't goin' in my house smellin' like that!"

A.J. stopped and lowered his head, he was nearly defeated, and no more fight left in him. He knew he stunk, but there was just something about having to explain the events of the night and he truly felt embarrassed to have to admit that he was powerless against those two policemen and they had made him fish around in a nasty cold pond in the middle of the night in order to find something that was already his. His embarrassment turned to anger, and he told Mr. Freehold the entire story, right there on the porch. He even included his reasons for stopping to visit with Mr. Freehold.

Mr. Freehold set the shotgun down on the porch, opened the door to the house, and hollered, "Momma - heat up some water for this boy. He needs a bath right quick." He turned to look at A.J. "Skin them clothes off, ain't no way those are coming inside. I will have the missus clean them for you. A.J. rolled his

## Chapter 12

eyes, more out of embarrassment, but despite the embarrassment, he started taking off his clothes. When he was down to his underwear, he stood there hoping that Mr. Freehold would show him a little mercy, but he didn't. "Them skivvies, too, boy, they practically sticking to your skin they're so wet." A.J. let out a deep sigh and slid his underwear off. Now he was standing on the porch of the main house of Mr. Curtis Freehold buck naked again and he was pretty tired of being naked when he didn't want to be. "Now go on through the house and out on the back porch, the missus will bring the water out to you, so you can wash that cow shit smell off of you. Hurry up, too, cause I want to eat."

A.J.'s eyes got big when Mr. Freehold told him to go through the house. "You want me to walk through your house naked?" Mr. Freehold let out a laugh, "Don't you worry, boy, my missus has seen bigger snakes than that, you ain't no threat to me." Mr. Freehold was having a good belly laugh this morning at A.J.'s expense, for sure. Just as promised, Mrs. Freehold brought him a huge bucket of warm water out to the porch with some soap and a towel to dry off with. Even though he knew it was coming, he was still embarrassed to be standing naked on the Freehold's back porch with Mrs. Freehold helping him clean up. "I'm sorry, ma'am," was all he could say. She just smiled and replied, "Don't you worry 'bout a thing now. Hurry up now and I will get you a plate." Mr. Freehold returned to the back porch holding a pair of overalls and what looked like a very worn flannel shirt. "These ought to do you until the missus can get your clothes cleaned up real good." A.J. took the clothes and put them on.

The clothes, along with the warm water for the bath, felt better than he could ever remember feeling. This wasn't the way he expected to be dressed when he officially asked Miss Kari to marry him but at this point, just feeling warm was all he could ask for. Mr. Freehold was already on plate number two when A.J. finally sat down at the table. "Now you smell good enough to have breakfast at my table!" Mrs. Freehold set a plate covered in food down in front of A.J. and poured him a cup of coffee. A.J. thought perhaps that was the best smelling food he had ever said grace over.

He didn't realize how hungry he was until he caught a whiff of Mrs. Freehold's biscuits. "I already said grace, so go on and dig in, you got some proper proposing to do." He patted A.J. on the arm, "Besides, I need you to hurry up and get on outta here. After the missus saw you on the porch in all your glory, she came back in here and thanked me for being the man I am and wants to give me a little before I start my busy day!" He laughed as loud as A.J. had ever heard anyone laugh. Mrs. Freehold was walking around the table when he said it and she managed to smack Mr. Freehold in the back of the head. When she did it, he laughed even harder. "Curtis Freehold, you behave yourself at my table and act like a Christian or you've had your last." He laughed some more, "Apologies, momma, just trying to get the boy in a better mood, he is plum pissy this morning." A.J. looked up at Mrs. Freehold, sort of embarrassed. She smiled at him as she left the room.

She was a beautiful woman. H flashed back to Kari Harper and pictured her being just as beautiful as Mrs. Freehold when she reached Mrs. Freehold's age. He couldn't wait to get started now. Mrs. Freehold came back into the room and she had the ring with her. She set it down on the table next to A.J. and put her hand on his shoulder. "I cleaned it for you, it's a beautiful ring and she is going to love it. I couldn't salvage that box, though. I promise you she won't care about that, all she is gonna see is that beautiful ring. Now go on and get to her little place and give her that ring." A.J. could feel the emotion building up inside him, especially when Mrs. Freehold put her hand on his shoulder. He needed a mother's touch just then and thank God she had been there to provide it.

It was as if when she touched him, she had managed to turn some invisible relief valve and all his stress came steaming out of him like a kettle on the stove. It was such a relief. "Yes, ma'am, and thank you for, uh, the, uh, ring and the, uh, breakfast." He

*Chapter 12*

stood up and nearly ran to the front door. When he got down the porch steps and opened the car door, he wished he had rolled a window down because now his car and his workspace smelled like the South end of a Northbound cow. He opened all four doors, rolled the window down on each, then closed the doors back and made the short drive to Kari's little house.

He pulled the car to the side of her little house. It was 12 x12, if that, just big enough for a bed and pipe stove to keep warm. It had a small front porch that jetted out enough so that she could sit under it shaded by the hot sun. Over the last eleven months, since the day after he blurted out his marriage proposal in his cousin's body shop, he had sat there with her on that very porch, holding her hand, talking about all he planned to do and how he wanted her to be a part of it. He was a gentleman every step of the way and had only kissed her on the cheek and hugged her as he left. Never in his wildest dreams would he think of trying anything more with her. He stepped on to the porch and gently knocked on the door. It was still pretty early so he wasn't sure if she would be awake. He tapped a second time and the door opened. Even though she had just woken up and barely had her eyes open, she was the most beautiful woman in the world.

His tongue immediately got thick and his mouth got dry. He couldn't contain himself anymore and before she could even say good morning, he dropped to one knee, pulled the ring from the overall front pocket, extended it out to her and said, "Miss Kari Rae Harper, I'd like you to my wife. I promise to protect you and love you like nobody ever loved another person the rest of your life." She hadn't quite gotten her eyes completely opened, but they were open pretty fast. She stood there just looking at the ring. It was her turn to have thick tongue and a dry mouth. She took the ring from his hand and slid it on her finger then she held her hand up close to her face so she could see the ring better. "Get up off your knees, Alvin Jerome Mack, you know I will marry you!" She smiled the biggest smile A.J. had ever seen and practically leaped into his arms.

He stood there holding her. His embrace was as strong as he dared to be. She felt so good in his arms, he could stay in this position all day if necessary. She held him tightly, too, and whispered in his ear as they embraced, "I love you, A.J., and I can't wait to be Mrs. Alvin Jerome Mack, but why are you here so early and why are you wearing those stupid looking overalls?" A.J. let go of her but kept his hands on her hips. They were nearly eye-to-eye as he stood there and collected his thoughts. He decided to tell her everything, all of the events of the evening and how he intended to present her the ring the night before. "Baby, I can't risk making that trip anymore. I need you to come back with me this morning. I need you to marry me today. I know I have another month on our deal, but I just can't risk it. You know I love you, so don't make me wait another month." She stepped forward and hugged him tightly again. "You fished around in that smelly pond all night to bring me this ring?" A.J. squeezed her gently again and said, "Baby, I'd fish around in the ocean all night if I had to. I'd do anything for you." He could feel her body heave against his and he realized she was crying. He could feel the warm tears smear against his neck.

He didn't know what to say, "I'm sorry, baby, I didn't mean to make you cry." She squeezed him even tighter. "I'm crying because I am happy, you silly man. Let's go get married today." A.J. didn't think he could, but he gripped her even tighter, tilted his back, and lifted her off her feet. She let out a little yelp, but she didn't let go. He felt his own tears welling up in his eyes and decided he needed to speak to keep it from spilling out into his voice. "Pack your stuff, Miss Kari Rae Harper, soon to be Miss Kari Rae Mack, I am taking you back to Montgomery this morning, we are getting married TODAY."

# Chapter 13

"DO YOU PROMISE TO LOVE her and cherish her in sickness and health for all the days of your life?" A.J. paused for a second, not because he didn't know what to say, but because he thought the line was supposed to be *for as long as you both shall live*. He panicked because he thought, *what if there are strict rules about the accuracy of the vows, what if I got through this then found out the Justice of the Peace was a quack and he screwed up and none of this was legal? My God, this can't be happening*. This has to be legal! His Uncle Marvin was standing behind him along with a lady that A.J. had never met. She had a giant hat on, and he thought she smelled a little funny. He couldn't put his finger directly on the smell, but he didn't care for it. His uncle told him that it was a lady he knew from his church. He didn't argue because he did know that there had to be at least two witnesses and since he only knew his uncle, he had to go with whomever his uncle could drag along.

The Justice of the Peace stood there looking at him, waiting for him to answer, but he still wanted clarification on the accuracy of the *you both shall live* as opposed to *all the days of your life*. He was sweating bullets; he could feel a sweat bead roll down from inside his armpit all the way down his arm muscle and on to his elbow where he assumed it got soaked up by his shirt. The tickle feeling of the sweat bead rolling down his arm gave him a little shiver. Kari caught the shiver and she took it as a sign he was shaking his head no.

She swallowed a huge glob of spit and was about to burst out in tears when A.J. realized what was going on and he said, "Isn't it supposed to be 'as long as we both shall live' instead of what you said? I want to make sure we get this right." Kari's eyes got big then they got narrow as she was about to get mad at A.J., but in a good way. She knew him well after sitting on her porch almost every night for the last eleven months. She knew he was meticulous about details and getting things right; he couldn't even leave the house unless his shirts and his pants had a perfect crease in them. He wouldn't let his food touch each other on his plate, he had to have everything separate or he simply wouldn't eat. He told her used to be a slob and then the Marines got a hold of him and made him the way he is. He was the most detailed man she had ever met, and she loved him even more for it.

The Justice of the Peace put down his book and held it by his side for just a second. He looked at Kari and sort of rolled his eyes, then he looked at A.J. and said, "Son, I've been doing this for nearly thirty years, but if you would like to trade places with me, I can marry your woman and you can stand here in my place wishing you were somewhere else at this very minute. I assure you the words are legal, and I am permitted to improvise on verbiage from time to time, but If you would like me to change them to your version, fine." A.J.'s mouth got dry, then he started thinking about a white Justice of the Peace marrying his beautiful black bride. Boy, wouldn't that be the talk of Montgomery! He was still day dreaming that scenario when he heard the JP say, "As long as you both shall live?" He momentarily came back to reality and was happy that the JP had corrected it to his version, and he said, "I cedar."

He was smiling because they were about through with the ceremony now and couldn't figure out why the JP had put his book back down at his side and was staring at A.J., as was Kari.

*Chapter 13*

"Son, that wasn't the answer I was looking for, not the answer she was looking for either. Kari hit him on the arm, and he turned to look at her, "You cedar?" A.J. squinted his eyes as he tried to figure out what she was saying. He thought maybe he was dizzy and was about to pass out because nothing made sense, why the hell was she talking about wood right in the middle of their wedding ceremony? "A.J.! you said, 'I cedar,' what does that mean?"

A.J. smiled and shook his head in agreement, "Yeah! She does smell like cedar! That's what it is!" He was so excited that someone else smelled the lady with the big hat. He turned to smile at his uncle who was not smiling back and then the reality hit him. "Uh, uh, your honor, I'm sorry. I am so nervous I don't know what I am saying right now. I've never been married before, this is my first time, see, and I am just trying to get it right is all. I'm sorry. Go on, please." The JP held his book at his side again, "First time you say? I wouldn't have guessed it. In that case, I now pronounce you man and wife. You may kiss the bride." A.J. heard that part then remembered he had never even kissed Kari, other than on the cheek, so he gave her a peck on the cheek. He was about to pull away when she put both of her hands on his face, pulled him close, and kissed him square on the lips. He froze in his tracks, her lips felt amazing on his. He wasn't sure what to do, but he wasn't going to move until she did.

As the kiss went, it was probably a short one by all measures, but it was enough to get the juices flowing and his heart started beating really fast. During the ceremony, and only after he figured out that the lady in the big hat smelled like cedar, he stopped sweating, but now - now he could feel the sweat rolling down the center of his back, and he knew for sure where that bead was headed and when that little kamikaze bead finally crashed into the old Grand Canyon, he was for sure going to feel that tickle again. Before he could feel the tickle, she let go of him in time for his uncle to step in between them and kiss his bride.

After he was finished giving the bride a kiss, he turned and gave his nephew a huge bear hug. A.J. could see through the bear hug that the big hat cedar lady was giving Kari a hug and smooch and all he could think of at the moment was that he hoped she didn't leave any of that cedar smell on Kari. In his ear, his uncle whispered to him, "I'm so proud of you, boy, I know they are watching us now, it was your daddy picking on you from heaven that made you act like an idiot. He's laughing his dang fool head off right now." A.J. laughed and returned the hug. "Thank you, Uncle Marvin. You mean the world to me." They both stood there looking at each other when his uncle turned to Kari and said, "He's the best man I know, you sure got a dandy!" She smiled and laughed she agreed, but then his uncle said, "Say, let me borrow him for just a few minutes before ya'll run off, we'll be right back." Uncle Marvin grabbed A.J. by the arm and before A.J. could even protest, he pulled him to the back of the courthouse and out the door. When the two men were outside the courtroom, Uncle Marvin looked sternly at A.J., but then his face relaxed a little. A.J. could tell he was struggling to say whatever it was he wanted to say. "Say, boy, your father probably talked to you about the rifle and all before you went off to war, huh?" A.J. was confused and didn't know what to say. Why in the world would Uncle Marvin want to talk about rifles now? Uncle Marvin could tell he wasn't getting it, so he tried again.

"You know, boy, your daddy talked about He'n and She'n right?" A.J. was still struggling with this conversation. "What are you talking about, Uncle Marvin, rifles and He'n and She'n? I don't understand." Uncle Marvin scratched at his chin and looked around the room as if he didn't want anyone to see them, then he leaned in really close and whispered, "You know, what a man and woman does on their wedding night. How to use the rifle and where the target is at and all?" A.J. understood now what he was trying to say and started to reply, but his uncle spoke again. "I imagine a Marine goin' off to war probably got

## Chapter 13

plenty of that kind of action, huh? You probably know what you are doin' already, huh?"

A.J. could feel the embarrassment rising up to his forehead. In fact, he had never talked about the subject, but he had heard plenty of stories. Truth be known, that subject scared him to death and so did women, for that matter. Until he saw Kari Rae Harper at the Freehold place, he had avoided even the thought of it. During his basic training for the Marines in North Carolina, a bunch of his buddies would go out on Saturday night and chase women, but he didn't care for it at all. He wanted a woman as badly as any man, but he wasn't about to go pay for it and he sure as hell wasn't going to have an accident with a woman he didn't want to spend the rest of his life with. His buddies talked him into going out one Saturday night and he had fun watching them, but when some young girl started pawing at him under the table, he panicked and ran all the way back to base.

When he saw Kari, he knew there would be nobody else, but he hadn't thought about tonight, the honeymoon night. He had been staying with his uncle and was sleeping on the couch, the thought hadn't even occurred to him what they were going to do. He didn't have any extra money to take her anywhere. "Uncle, I kinda know what to do and where the target is, but I ain't never done it. I'm sure we will figure it out, but I have a bigger problem. I don't have anywhere to go for, uh…target practice." Uncle Marvin stood there in silence for a few seconds and then he let out a big belly laugh, he actually doubled over, which A.J. didn't appreciate very much and started to say so, but his uncle stopped laughing long enough to say, "I figured so, boy. You go on back to the house, take my room. I ain't coming home tonight."

A.J. felt bad about him not staying at his own house, "You don't have to do that, Uncle Marvin, we will figure it out. I don't want to kick you out of your own house." His uncle started laughing again, "Boy, it's been a while since I had target practice myself. Ms. Big Hat, who you think smells like a cedar tree, has invited me over to her place for the evening. Something tells me she'd like to do a little He'n and She'n, too!" He laughed when he said it and seemed to be very excited at the prospect of his own evening. By this time, the two ladies came out of the courtroom and joined the men.

The big hat lady made a dash for A.J. because she hadn't properly congratulated him on his marriage. She hugged him and he couldn't help but smile. It was easier dealing with her smell after he had figured out what it was. Cedar wasn't so bad. She had probably dug that hat or that dress out of a cedar chest and wore it to the wedding. Besides, he didn't think his uncle brought her to the wedding for her aroma, he had other ideas.

# Chapter 14

HIS HANDS WERE SHAKING AS he pulled the car to a stop. Kari talked all the way from the courthouse to his uncle's house. He heard some of it, but when she was on a roll, all he had to do was nod his head. Sometimes when they were back on her porch he would get so caught up in her voice and smell and her skin and her beauty that he would lose track of what she was saying. He would often sit there on that porch and wonder what in the world she was doing with him. She was everything to him now. She was his wife and hopefully would be the mother of his children. He wanted to share everything with her. He knew that when he was with her, he was better. He was a better man, a better businessman, and especially a better person.

He turned the car off and she was still talking. She was saying something about getting the rest of her things from the Freehold place, but he wasn't sure. He put his hands on the steering wheel for no other reason than to keep them from shaking. He drew in a deep breath and decided to just lay it all out there for her. "Baby, I love you. You've made me the happiest man there ever could be. I don't know why you want me, but I promise you that I will protect you and provide for you and more than anything, love you as long as I have a breath in my lungs." She reached up and put her left hand on his cheek. She gave him a smile that he had never seen before. It was like an angel had touched his face.

He drew in another breath, "I'm scared cause I don't want to let you down, ever. You should know that I have never been with a woman before." She leaned over with her hand still on his cheek and kissed him. She kept her face nearly nose-to-nose with A.J. He could smell her perfume; he felt the stir in his stomach just looking at her. "Alvin Jerome Mack, I love you too, with all my heart. I have since the first second I saw you. I knew at that very moment in that dimly lit nasty old tent that there was nobody else that I wanted to be with. I've prayed for you to come along and God answered my prayers. I think love and nature will do its work for us in a few minutes because I've never been with another man. I say we go in and figure this out together."

She smiled that angel smile and kissed him softly again. He didn't want to, but he pulled away, opened the door to the car, practically ran around to her side, and opened the door for her. He stuck his hand out and she took it. She walked with her arm stuck under his all the way to the front door. When they got to the front door, A.J. turned and said, "I'm sorry this is not our home. I think I am supposed to carry you through the door of our home, and I promise to do that when we get one, which, uh, I promise will be soon. You deserve it baby." He turned and grabbed her, swooped her up in his arms. He was surprised by how light she was. She felt good in his arms as he crossed over the threshold of his uncle's home. He kicked the door shut and headed straight for the bedroom. He thought, *no point in delaying this any longer.*

The room was totally dark, but he could see the outline of her body. He had his arm draped over her as he held her tightly. He could feel the rise and fall of her body as she breathed so peacefully. Before the day started, he didn't think he could love her any more than he did, but now, laying here next to her, watching her sleep, he was certain he had just learned to love her even more. He thought about all the things he had been through to

## Chapter 14

get to this point. He wished his parents were still alive so that they could know her and love her as their new daughter they never had. He laid his head down as close as he could to the back of hers so he could smell her hair. He closed his eyes and slept as peacefully as he could ever remember sleeping in his whole life. "I feel you looking at me, Alvin Jerome."

He had no idea how she knew, but she was right. He didn't sleep much, but the sleep that he did get was the best ever. Now, he raised up on one elbow, resting his head in his hand watching her breathe again. "I can't help it, Kari, I never in a million years thought I would be right here next to you." She spun over from having her back turned to him to being face-to-face with him. "What are you thinking about?" She moved her hand up to his cheek again, he had learned to like that very much very quickly. She had the softest touch and he also learned that when she put her hand on his cheek, a kiss was soon to follow.

She kissed him as expected, but she moved her hand down his shoulder along his arm until she clasped his hand. "Want to just stay here all day?" The way she said it made him actually think about it, but he knew he couldn't. He was at the very end of his one-year deal with Mr. Gibson and he needed to finish it. "Baby, after last night, I can think of nothing better than that, but I have to finish my contract with Mr. Gibson." She smiled and moved in even closer. He held her as tightly as he dared and to his surprise, dozed off again.

When he woke, she was not next to him. The first thought that came to his mind was that he had been dreaming, that maybe he had not just slept with the most beautiful woman in the world, but then it hit him, if he were dreaming, then why was he in his uncle's bed? He turned on his back and he caught the smell of bacon. He got up and started for the kitchen and realized that he was naked. He turned to find some pants, but somehow in the haste of what he badly wanted to do the night before, he couldn't find his pants, but he found his underwear. He put those on and started down the hallway where he luckily ran into his pants crumpled on the floor. He grabbed those and put them on; they made him feel better, less exposed. He knew she was his wife now, but he wasn't going to scare her by walking into the kitchen naked. She was a lady and he intended to treat her as such the rest of their days. *Damn JP screwed it up*, he thought.

He walked into the kitchen and saw her there. He was speechless; she was in a baby blue robe, bare feet, and looking as lovely as an angel. She saw him come into the kitchen and immediately made her way towards him. When they met in the middle of the kitchen, he grabbed her and lifted her off her feet. She embraced him with all her strength and the two just stayed locked that way in the middle of the kitchen. "The bacon is going to burn, baby, let me down so we can have breakfast, our first breakfast as Mr. and Mrs. Alvin Jerome Mack." She couldn't see the smile on his face, so he put her back down on the floor so she could see it. "It smells fantastic, Mrs. Kari Rae Mack. I can't wait to eat breakfast with you."

They sat there at the little table his uncle had and talked as they ate. She wanted to know what his plans were and when he would be home. She told him that she had surveyed the kitchen, the ice box and all its contents, and making a meal tonight would be hopeless if he didn't bring something home. He wrote down the things that she wanted and told her that he would pick them all up at the Piggly Wiggly on his way home. She put her coffee down and asked the question that he knew she would ask but he dreaded having to answer it.

"What does Mr. Gibson have you do when you drive for him? Where does he want to go and how come he can't drive himself?" He thought about the best way to answer the question and decided that the truth would be his best bet. "Baby, I promise I will never lie to you, so don't judge me when I tell you this. I swear I had no idea he would want me to take him to some of these places when I agreed. I thought he was just a rich old man, but he is more than that." He started to explain

## Chapter 14

some more but she smiled and said, "You don't have to tell me if you don't want to, A.J. I just like to talk and sometimes I ask to many questions."

He then put his coffee down in almost a panic, he certainly didn't want to turn this into an argument. He wanted to tell her everything, he just didn't know how she would handle it. After all, Mr. Gibson wasn't breaking the law, but he was breaking some biblical laws, and considering the current opinions in this part of the country about people of color, he was taking some pretty big chances. It only took A.J. a few weeks to figure out why he specifically wanted A.J. to drive him around on the weekends. He cleared his throat, took a deep breath, and began, "Mr. Gibson has a girlfriend." He paused to see what her reaction would be, and she had a blank face. She gave him nothing in body language, so he got a little jittery. "Baby, I am sorry, but he doesn't have just a girlfriend, he has Olivia Compton." He looked at her like she would know, but he temporarily forgot that she was not from Montgomery; she was from Selma.

She finally smiled at him, which made him feel much better. "A.J., am I supposed to know who that woman is?" A.J. picked up his coffee and grumbled just a little as he took a sip. "Well, no, but most folks in our circle do. She is the daughter of L.C. Compton, one of the most religious men in the state of Alabama. He is one of those Bible-thumping, fire and brimstone kind of guys. You see, L.C. has an upholstery business on the South side, and he preaches every chance he can get. He makes a pretty good living from what I can see, but his daughter is a housekeeper for the Gibson family. As far as I can see, she is doing pretty well, too, actually, very well for a housekeeper."

He could see that Kari was confused and unsure of where he was going with this, so he decided it was best to just plow ahead. "Baby, Olivia Compton is as black as you and me and folks in these parts don't take much to white fellas and black women gettin' together and they think even less of a white woman and black man gettin' together." Her eyes got really big and then she laughed out loud. "What's so funny, baby?" She leaned over and kissed him on the cheek. "You are silly, Mr. Mack! You think I would judge you for the actions of a dumb white man with a thing for a black woman?" She leaned back and waited for him to answer, but she made sure to smile as she waited.

"I don't know, baby. I just feel bad when I sit and wait on them to finish their business. Sometimes it lasts all day Saturday and sometimes they are done in an hour. I know he bought her that little house that he meets her at, and I know he selected it for its seclusion. That poor girl thinks he loves her, and he sure might, but she's not gonna ever be nothin' more than a place for him to park his thing on the weekends." She laughed again, "Why did he pick you to drive him?" It was his turn to laugh, which he did hardily. "Because he knows I can't play the secret against him. Nobody would ever take my word over his, so he figures his secret is safe with me."

He went on to explain the details of one Miss Olivia Compton to Kari. She was half Mr. Gibson's age and could have probably been his daughter under different circumstances, but A.J. had an idea that she was just a little slow witted. She was certainly attractive, not nearly as attractive as his Kari, but she would be a catch for someone, but because of the choices she made, nobody would touch her because they all knew what the situation was with Mr. Gibson. The only person that didn't know was her daddy, L.C. He would probably beat her to death if he found out. He was a little crazy and he might have killed Mr. Gibson if he knew about what he was doing to his daughter, but he didn't, so she kept Mr. Gibson happy on the weekends and he kept her in a nice little home and in groceries on the weekdays.

Kari sat there, sipping her own coffee listening to his stories; she loved hearing him talk. She asked what he did while he waited on Mr. Gibson to finish and he told her that he liked to read, he would read anything he could get his hands on. Mr. Gibson once gave him a very thick book that was filled with lots of poetry and stories and he read it from front to back. He told

## Chapter 14

her about some of the stories in the book. She let him know that she liked to read, too, and wanted to read the book he was talking about. "We don't just always go to Miss Olivia's house, though. Mr. Gibson has a buddy that he likes to bet on things with."

She took another sip of her coffee, "Bet on what?" A.J. frowned a little, "They bet on dogs fighting, chickens fighting, and men fighting. Pretty much anything they feel like throwin' money at. I hate to admit it, but it sure is hard watching those dogs fight. I can handle the chickens and even the men, although I think it is a stupid waste of money, but those two fellas sure like to bet. I don't care much for Mr. Gibson's betting buddy, he is mean and crazy and worse, he hates black folks like there is no tomorrow. I know for a fact he's pretty high up in the white sheets." Kari looked a little confused.

"The Klan, baby. He is in the Klan, may be the leader for all I know." She sat up in her chair and now had a very scared look on her face. "Baby, you have to get away from those people. You can't be anywhere near them!" He reached out and touched her hand that was now tightly wrapped around her coffee cup. He cleared his throat and then gave her that reassuring smile that she now had come to count on. "Honey, a deal is a deal. I have one more month with Mr. Gibson according to our deal and then I can concentrate more on the company and on you. Don't you worry, I will be just fine, I know how to keep my distance."

She leaned over and kissed him on the lips and held it for a bit longer than he expected. "I can't lose you to nobody, especially some of those damn fools running around in sheets in the middle of the night. You stay clear of that other man, Mr. uh, what's his name?" He had his nose about a half an inch from her nose and replied, "Ansil Anderson, everybody calls him Ance, but I don't. I've never even talked to the man and don't want to."

## Chapter 15

HE ROLLED UP TO MR. Gibson's house and parked his cab where he always parked it. He was instructed to never park his cab in view of anyone, so he was given a spot in the back of the house behind a huge oak tree. He walked towards the side shed where the 1946 Cadillac Series 75 Fleetwood limousine sat and waited for him each Saturday. A.J. was told, and it was only a rumor, that Mr. Gibson ordered the limousine before the war was even over, but he couldn't be sure of that. A.J. thought it was a silly waste of money and he thought it was pretty dumb to drive a car like this around town and then not want to be seen at Miss Compton's place.

A.J. didn't figure anyone would ever see him at Miss Compton's because the house he bought her was right smack dab in the middle of 30 acres on the Southeast side of town. Nobody would ever see the car at her house, but they would sure see it pull off the road and onto her property. Just to be safe, A.J. would drive past her entrance and check both ways to make sure there were no other cars around, and then he would circle back and head towards her house. A.J. tried not to concern himself with the details, he simply wanted to complete his contract and move on, although he did like driving the car. It was as smooth as anything he had ever ridden in and, my God, it smelled good.

## Chapter 15

All that leather everywhere mixed with the pipe tobacco that Mr. Gibson kept stashed in the glove compartment because he didn't want Mrs. Gibson to know he still smoked a pipe. She said the pipe smoke gave him gas and she didn't appreciate him breaking wind in his sleep. She was certain it was the pipe smoke that was causing it.

"Good morning, A.J. I am in a hurry this morning, so let's get rolling." A.J. turned from where he was standing next to the car to see Mr. Gibson entering the shed carrying a briefcase. "Good morning, Mr. Gibson. I am ready when you are." He reached for the back door of the limousine to open it for Mr. Gibson. "Don't forget your hat, A.J." A.J. nodded in agreement and closed the door behind Mr. Gibson. He rolled his eyes as he turned to open the driver's door. "Where are we headed this morning, sir?" He adjusted his rearview mirror so he could see Mr. Gibson in the back seat. "Same as usual first, but we won't be there long. Hand me that Kaywoodie out of the glove box."

A.J. reached into the glove box and handed the pouch of pipe tobacco back to Mr. Gibson. While Mr. Gibson fidgeted with the pipe tobacco, he eased the limo out of the shed and was on the highway headed towards Miss Compton's place before Mr. Gibson even had the pipe lit. He caught a waft of the smoke as they cruised down the highway. "Keep it under the speed limit, A.J., we wouldn't want to attract any unnecessary attention." A.J. smiled and nodded. "Yes, sir." He heard Mr. Gibson break wind and he knew that Mrs. Gibson would be unhappy with him for smoking the pipe, but she'd probably be more unhappy if she knew he was having an affair with another woman, a black woman no less.

"You don't smoke, A.J.? I figured a tough Marine like you would have some kind of vices to deal with, no?" Before A.J. could answer him, Mr. Gibson came back with a whole slew of questions, which was the way it always was. Mr. Gibson asked a thousand questions when he was in the mood, and obviously he was in the mood today, but this was a little different than

*Choice of Honor*

normal. This was a rapid-fire question session born out of nervousness, which A.J. couldn't figure out why he was nervous. He had been going to Miss Compton's virtually every Saturday for nearly a year. "What do colored men think about today's environment? What do they think of women in general? Do men like you carry two women, generally?"

A.J. felt his blood pressure rising and wanted to slam on the brakes, jump in the back seat and beat this man within an inch of his life, but he heard his uncle's voice in the back of his head, *play the game*. "No, sir, I am a one-woman man. I just got married and don't want no one else." He started to explain the wonderful qualities of his beloved Kari, but he was cut off again. "Then you have a problem with me and Olivia's arrangement?" He started to answer, but once again, he was cut off. "Wait until you've been married for a few years, young man. The nagging will get to you and then the sex is gone, then the beauty, and pretty soon you forget why you even married her. Trust me, it will happen to you."

A.J. figured out after a short while that this was really not a conversation, this was Mr. Gibson venting, or he was trying to make himself feel better about his fornicating with another woman. "I bet you think that the minute I close the door to her house that we just hop into bed and go to work? Well, I don't. She is a good woman with a good heart. I mean, we eventually get to it, but I like to hear what she has on her mind and I like to tell her about what I am doing. She listens, see, she doesn't nag at me to fix this and fix that and go to this stupid party and show up to this dumb charity. You see, Olivia just wants to be with me for me, and no other reason."

A.J. was trying not to laugh, was this man serious? Olivia wasn't with him for him, she was with him for his money and no other reason. Mr. Gibson continued to ramble on, "Montgomery is a mess, Alabama is a mess, hell, this whole damn country is a mess. I will tell you this, we all need to get over this black white nonsense. A man ought to be able to see whoever he wants to see

## Chapter 15

regardless of what color they are." They rolled into Miss Olivia Compton's driveway and Mr. Gibson was still talking to himself.

A.J. finally figured out through Mr. Gibson's rantings in the back seat that he and Mrs. Gibson had gotten into a pretty big argument, and at some point during the argument, Mrs. Gibson had hinted that she knew of his Saturday destinations, but didn't come right out and say it. A.J. sat in the car for most of the day. He got out every now and then to stretch his legs and wander around the place. He didn't like to wander off too far because Mr. Gibson would get upset with him if he wasn't there ready to open the car door for him when he was finished with Miss Olivia.

The two men were quickly back on the road after Mr. Gibson was done doing whatever he did inside with Miss Olivia. Mr. Gibson wasn't nearly as talkative on the way back to the Gibson place. About three miles away from the Gibson home, Mr. Gibson finally broke the silence. A.J. was thankful that he did because it was so quiet that even A.J. thought about speaking, but he didn't know what to say. What was he going to say, how was it? That just didn't seem like a good question. "I told her I couldn't see her anymore. I won't need your services any longer. Consider your contract upheld after today. Keep that three percent coming, though." A.J. could hardly wait to park the car and be done with this part of his contract with Mr. Gibson. "I appreciate that, sir. I will keep the three percent coming for sure. I appreciate your help when you gave it to me." He parked in the shed, jumped out of the driver's seat, opened the door for Mr. Gibson, and just like that, he was finished with Mr. Gibson.

# Chapter 16

IT WAS 4:00 A.M. A.J. was on his back staring at the ceiling like he did most every morning. He had so many things on his mind and he found that this was his best position for thinking. Kari had her head on his shoulder with her arm draped across his chest. He had no idea how they ended up in this exact position every single morning, but he was happy they had found the routine. After he thought about it for a little while, he wasn't sure if it was this position that he did his best thinking because the truth be known, he did his best thinking when Kari was next to him. Even when his arm would go numb from her body pressing against it, he never moved. He couldn't think of attempting to move.

His uncle had graciously moved out of the only bedroom the house had and let his nephew stay in the room with Kari. When he told him to take the bedroom, A.J. and Kari both argued with him that they would sleep on the couch, but he wouldn't hear of it. This morning, he stared at the ceiling thinking of his business and how he could make it better, thinking of his marriage, how good he felt with Kari but how they would eventually need to move out of this house with his uncle. He slowly eased his out from underneath Kari's head, doing his best not to wake her. She stirred just a little, but then went back to sleep. He grabbed

## Chapter 16

a robe from the chair and made his way into the little kitchen where he saw that his uncle was already up, had the coffee made, and was sitting at the little table sipping coffee reading the Bible.

His uncle loved to read the Bible. He wasn't an overly-religious man and didn't go to church on Sundays, but he had a passion for understanding everything that was in the Bible. He could quote scriptures like no one else that A.J. knew and he could recite some great stories from the Bible that were often applicable to whatever situation A.J. was trying to think through. He was relieved to see his uncle was already up. He liked talking to Uncle Marvin very much. He seemed to have a way of explaining things so that it helped him make better decisions. "Good morning, Uncle Marvin." He walked past him but touched him on the shoulder as he walked by. "What's in the good book this morning?"

He kept walking as he spoke and took out his favorite coffee mug from the cupboard. It was a simple mug, but it was oversized. He had no idea where Kari found it, but she bought it for him as a Christmas gift, along with a pair of socks that he badly needed. He smiled every time he reached for the mug because when he opened it, she laughed and told him that maybe he wouldn't wear out his socks going back and forth to the coffee pot anymore. He filled the coffee mug to the top and then smiled knowing that he would still make a few more trips back to the pot. He loved the coffee almost as much as his uncle did. "Oh, just about anything you want to know. You should try reading it, son." A.J. pulled the chair out from the table and sat across from him. He smiled and looked at the pages that were open. "I thought you stayed away from the Book of Revelations?" A.J. chuckled a little as he said it. "Oh, I have to dive into it every now and then. There is some awful scary shit in that book. If I get all those seals, riders, and horses stuck in my head, I get a little edgy and it helps to confront it head on." He laughed a little when he said it and leaned back in his chair.

A.J. took a sip of his coffee and smiled. "Is there something that caused you to think about the seals and riders and stuff?" Uncle Marvin shook his head, "No, actually I had just flopped it open when you came in the room. From the look on your face, looks to me like you got something on your mind." No matter how hard A.J. tried, he could not hide his feelings from his uncle. He marveled at Uncle Marvin's ability to read through his body language, A.J. could have a huge smile on his face and his uncle would figure out that he was faking it and plow ahead. He wished he could read people that way and often tried, but he wasn't very good at it yet. "How did you know, Uncle Marvin?" A.J. shook his head in amazement as he said it. "Boy, you are as easy to read as any book ever written. Tell me what's weighing on you so heavy this morning."

A.J. looked around the room and then looked back at Uncle Marvin, "A few things been weighing on me pretty heavy, to tell you the truth. Me and Kari sure been trying to have a baby, but we been trying for nearly three years now and nothing. I am starting to worry that maybe I ain't got the right juice in me for it." Uncle Marvin had a slow but very noticeable grumble in his voice. "What's your hurry, boy, trying to make a young'n is the best part!" He laughed when he said it, but he didn't laugh too loud because he knew Kari was still asleep and didn't want to wake her. "You said there were a couple things weighing heavy on you, what's the other? That first one is a helluva problem to have." He chuckled again. "Well, my business is going pretty good now, I got myself the third cab this week and I keep them all running. I keep pouring all my money back into the business and, uh, well uh, I can't keep ridin' on your dime. You been sleeping on this old couch for almost four years now and I think it's time me and Kari let you have your house back. It can't be easy for your back sleeping out here."

Uncle Marvin closed the Bible in front of him and got up to get another cup of coffee. At first, A.J. took it as a sign that he had upset his uncle by suggesting that he and Kari move out and

## Chapter 16

leave him alone, so he tried to repair it as quickly as he could. "Uh, we were thinking about getting a house that has a few more rooms and you could come live with us, too." Uncle Marvin poured his coffee and returned to the table. He sat down with a heavy thud. "Boy, you worry 'bout too much stuff. My back is just fine, I've slept in a whole lot worse places than my own living room, but I've been wondering when this day would come. I reckon it's here."

A.J. reached across the table and put his hand on his uncle's hand, "I could not have gotten started if it hadn't been for you. When I came back from the war, I didn't really know you like I know you now. I won't leave you alone, ever." Uncle Marvin looked down at his hand that was now covered by A.J.'s, looked up and smiled. "Your daddy would be so proud of the man you've become. I don't need you worrying about me. The man upstairs takes care of all of us. Proverbs 16:9 says, *"In their hearts human beings plan their course, but the Lord establishes their steps."* A.J. smiled as he was once again amazed but his uncle's ability to quote scripture. "What does that mean?" Uncle Marvin gave him a long stare and big smile, "It means that you think you are in control of what you are doing, but the Lord already knows and is already guiding you whether you want Him to or not. It's when you resist His help that things get so damn messy. So far, you ain't resisted nothin' that I can see, so I think you need to just keep taking your steps and I will keep takin' mine. The Lord did a mighty fine job of settin' me up here and I don't see much need to move nowhere else."

A.J. knew there would be no arguing with him. His uncle was a very proud and very stubborn man, convincing him to live with him and Kari wouldn't happen this morning, but he certainly wouldn't give up on it. Uncle Marvin had gotten a little old for working on cars, so now he was just doing odd jobs around the garage, which mainly consisted of sweeping and cleaning. He never minded, he always said that he was just happy working. He may not have been able to yank an engine block out of a car any longer, but the other guys in the shop always brought him over to consult for they all knew that Marvin Moore had probably forgotten more about automotive repair than any one of them would ever know. It didn't stop A.J. from worrying about him being in the home alone.

A.J. decided to change the subject so as not to upset the apple cart anymore. "Say, Uncle, you think there will ever be a time when black folks don't have to be second-class citizens?" He knew that if he brought up civil rights his uncle would get going again. His uncle was very active in the black church and community and he knew the heartbeat of Montgomery better than any man A.J. knew. "Oh, son, that day is close, but let me tell you, don't you ever for a minute think you are a second-class citizen. You got the same rights as all these numb nut white folks around here, they just ain't figured out how to get un-stupid yet!" A.J. smiled but not too much. He knew his uncle had forgotten now about the offer to move out with him and Kari when the time came, so he just sat back and listened for a while. "I hear that there is a young preacher over in Atlanta that can snatch the pitch fork from the devil and preach the hate right out of him. Yes, sir, folks say he will be coming to Montgomery soon and I will be there to listen and help him if he needs it. Things is getting ready to change and there ain't gonna be no sittin' in the back of no bus, I can tell you that for sure."

A.J. smiled at the way his uncle became so passionate about the things that were going on all over the country and especially the things that affected the black community. He got up from the table, grabbed an iron skillet from the bottom cabinet, opened the icebox, and extracted enough eggs for him, Kari, and Uncle Marvin. She would be waking up soon and he liked to make her breakfast. "You want bacon or ham this morning, Uncle Marvin?" Uncle Marvin rose from the table, stretched his arms out and said, "Oh, Lord, so many choices. I swear I have gained a hundred pounds since you kids moved in and started shoving food down my throat." A.J. still had the iron skillet in

## Chapter 16

his hand as he pretended to raise it as if he was going to smack his uncle on the head with it. "Ain't neither one of us shoved any food down your throat, dear Uncle. You are doing just fine without any help!"

They both were laughing when Kari came into the room. Both men stopped the banter when she came in and both acted as if they were two boys caught horsing around in the kitchen. A.J. put the skillet on the stove really quickly. "Good morning, baby." He walked towards her and gave her a hug and a quick kiss on the lips. "You look like an angel." Uncle Marvin finished pouring another cup of coffee and sat back down in his chair. "Yes, sir, you sure look like an angel, what in the world you doin' with that old numbskull I will never know." Uncle Marvin laughed when he said it. Kari walked over, bent down, and gave Uncle Marvin a hug, and as she was kissing him on the top of his head, she said, "Because I have a soft spot for numbskulls, I guess." A.J. laughed as did Uncle Marvin. "Boy, you sure hit the jackpot when you found this woman. Good Lord, she is perfect!"

Kari went over to the coffee pot and poured herself a cup of coffee. She turned to see if A.J. wanted some help making breakfast, but she suddenly got a little dizzy and ended up stepping out the back door as fast as she could so she could throw up. A.J. didn't see her spin around and go out the back door, but he heard the screen door then he heard her throw up. Uncle Marvin just sat there, but as soon as A.J. heard her wretch up whatever she had in her stomach, A.J. bolted out the back door almost knocking her off the stoop with the screen door. "Baby! Are you ok?" He stood behind her and then he put one arm around her waist to help steady her. She was still slightly bent over and was chucking up a little of whatever didn't come out the first time.

A.J. had seen a lot of bad things during the war, things that most people would never even believe; he had stuck his finger in a man's chest to keep him alive for crying out loud, but one thing he still struggled with was puke. Anytime he saw someone puke, he would have to fight off the urge to puke, too. He tried

*Choice of Honor*

not to look at the mess Kari had just created on the grass just off the back-door stoop, but when he saw it, he let go of her hip but kept his hand on her back and tossed the contents of his stomach on the ground beside hers. With his hand on the small of her back, he was hunched over right beside her. He could feel her body shake a little and thought she was about to heave again, which now, just the thought of her heaving again caused him to finish whatever he hadn't expelled on the first chuck.

What he learned was that she wasn't about to heave, she was laughing. She now had her arm around his waist and was trying to help him get steady again. She patted him on the back. "Baby, it was just a little throw up, I didn't mean to make you sick. Come on, it's over now. Let's go back inside and I will finish making breakfast." He tried to stand up straight from his current hunched over position, but he was dizzy. She sensed that and helped him stay steady. She slowly walked him back into the kitchen through the back door and ushered him to the table and sat him down. "Sit right there, baby, and I will get you some coffee."

She brought him a cup of coffee and then went back to the bathroom and brushed the bad taste out of her mouth. When she came back to the kitchen, both men were looking at her. "I don't know what happened, I just felt sick. I feel fine now. I will get breakfast started." She moved toward the skillet when A.J. said, "Well, we are going to the doctor, skip the breakfast. I can't have you sick. No way!" A.J. had sincere panic in his voice and he was about to rise from the table when Uncle Marvin laughed out loud. "Boy, sit your weak stomach back down. You may be sharp as a tack when it comes to runnin' a business, but you are dumb as a gunnysack full of bent hammers when it comes to women."

A.J. was rubbing his stomach and forehead. The motion of attempting to get up from the table had made him dizzy and nauseous again, but he looked up at his uncle for clarity. "It's called morning sickness. I reckon your pea shooter might have some peas in it after all!" He clapped his hands together and stomped

*Chapter 16*

his feet on the floor. For a second, Kari thought that he might actually fall out of the chair, then it hit her, too. "Oh, my goodness! You think so, Uncle Marvin? Could it really be true?' Uncle Marvin was still laughing and A.J. was still rubbing his forehead and he still hadn't caught on yet.

A huge smile came across her face, "I reckon you will take me to see the doctor after all." A.J. looked back and forth from Uncle Marvin to Kari. Kari slowly walked over to him, put her arms around his neck as he sat there at the table, kissed him on the cheek and said, "Your uncle thinks I might be pregnant, baby." A.J. stopped rubbing his forehead, looked up at Uncle Marvin and then to Kari. Uncle Marvin started laughing again. "Well, look who just figured out what morning sickness looks like!" A.J. bolted up from the table and out the back door he went. Both Kari and Uncle Marvin laughed as they heard him squeezing the rest of his stomach out on the back stoop. "Honey, I wouldn't throw up in front of him no more, might just kill him next time."

Uncle Marvin stood up from the table and gave his niece a big long hug. "I hope I am right. That boy wants a baby with you more than anything in the world. He'd trade all his cabs if it meant you'd plunk a baby in his lap. You look just like my missus did when she was getting ready to bake one." Kari held on to him and started a soft cry. "I want him to have whatever he dreams. I want you to be a part of it, too. I love you, Uncle Marvin." He drew in a deep breath and thought about how much better his life had become when these two kids entered it. He was lonely before they showed up and now all of the sudden his house was hopping every day and he felt useful again. "I love you, too, baby. Now go give that numbskull some crackers to settle his stomach so he can celebrate, too."

## Chapter 17

A.J. WAS SURPRISED TO SEE Mr. Gibson walk into his little cab company office since it was quite a way out of town. He purchased a third cab, another Packard, except this time he didn't have to put much work into it other than the paint job. It had plenty of miles on it, but his uncle looked it over and told him it was in pretty good shape. Since he had what he considered to be a fleet of cars, he decided he needed a place to park them and open up a location where folks could call and ask for service instead of him and his two drivers just waiting on fares around town. He found an old filling station that had long since closed. The previous owner used the lot as a salvage yard, but based off what A.J. could tell, it was a place where he just dumped everything he didn't know what to do with. It was a little over an acre lot, which A.J. really didn't need, what he wanted was the building that had a closed-in service bay and small building attached to it that he turned into an office. He did most of the oil changes and brake work right in the bay, so he saved himself a lot of money. It took a lot to clean the property of all the junk, but little by little, A.J. got rid of everything he wanted to get rid of and kept what he wanted. It took him over two years to get things just the way he wanted.

Things were going so well that he hired his uncle to oversee the maintenance of the vehicles. The fact that his uncle left his

*Chapter 17*

job in the Montgomery Garage owned by Mr. Gibson and went to work for A.J. was a huge decision. When Marvin Moore walked into the office of his former employer to tell them that he would be leaving them and wanted to know what a good time frame was to give them time to find a replacement, they got mad and fired him on the spot. It really hurt his uncle that he had been employed with that same garage for so many years. He couldn't even remember a time he called in sick or missed a day for any reason and they had fired him that day, even told him he was selfish and disloyal and a bunch of other stuff that couldn't be said in public.

He found the old filling station one day when he was out for a drive with Kari. It was out on Old Route 9 just East of Highway 331. The previous owner heard they were building a big fancy highway they called an Interstate Highway to the West of 331 and he decided to get in front of it and bought land for a new filling station to the West. A.J. drove by the service garage and said he knew right when he saw it that it would be perfect. He had been told by many that if he wanted an office building for his company, it would be best to have one far outside the city limits. Everyone warned him against showing his success too close to Montgomery. As best as A.J. could tell, nobody in Montgomery even knew a black man owned the cab company. He never talked about it and when he was asked, he always referred to the ownership that Mr. Orville Gibson had in the business. He just never offered up that Mr. Orville Gibson only had three percent of the sales and, in fact, had no real ownership of the business. It was deceptive, of course, but it was not a lie. A.J. hated to tell lies because he was sure that he would not remember one lie from the other and eventually one would trip him up, so he stuck with the three percent. It did frustrate him from time to time when he had to drop off the three percent at Mr. Gibson's office every month. He just couldn't figure how a man could sit on his butt, do nothing, and collect money from the people that were doing all the work. None of it made sense, but he was still doing way better than he expected.

A.J. jumped up from his desk when he saw Mr. Gibson walk in the door. He walked around to where he was and as he was approaching Mr. Gibson, he stuck out his hand as he always did. "Mr. Gibson! I didn't expect you to ever come out here. It is nice to see you, SUH." It slipped out again even though A.J. had slowly began to convince himself that he didn't need to play the game as hard as he used to, but without even thinking, the SUH just popped right out there. He was frustrated even more by the fact that Mr. Gibson, instead of extended his hand, reached for his handkerchief and blew his nose in it like he always did. A.J. put his hand back down to his side.

"What brings you all the way out here? Can I get you a cold drink? A soda pop or something?" Mr. Gibson looked around the room and followed the walls with his eyes. He saw a picture that A.J. had hung of his parents over the wall behind his desk and walked towards it. A.J. racked his brain trying to think of a reason that Mr. Gibson had come all the way out to his office. He had paid everything on time, he hadn't said anything about Mr. Gibson's Saturday destinations of years past, he had no idea why he was here. "Who are these people?" Mr. Gibson stood directly in front of the picture. "SUH, that's my momma and that's my daddy." A.J. was full on deferring to the game. When he referred to his parents with his friends and family, he referred to them as his mother and father, but standing here in front of Mr. Gibson, he had just referred to them as his momma and daddy.

He was thinking he would be just as well-off if he did a little dance and played a fiddle for this man. His stomach was churning and if he didn't figure a way to settle himself, he would chuck it all up just like he had done with Kari the day he found out his baby maker actually did work. "They alive?" Mr. Gibson once again pulled his handkerchief from his back pocket and blew his nose in it. A.J. thought that if he stayed long enough that handkerchief would be so full of snot that the man would have

## Chapter 17

blown what he had left in his coat pocket. The thought made him smile and it settled his stomach, mission accomplished. "Uh, no, SUH, they passed while I was off in the war." Mr. Gibson finally turned to look at A.J. then reached for the back of A.J.'s desk chair, pulled it back, and sat down at A.J.'s desk.

A.J.'s stomach started churning again, mission was not over at all. "This is a nice set up you have here, A.J., you're doing quite well for yourself. I see you added another car to the operation." A.J. was trying to figure out where all this was going, but for the life of him, could not put his finger on it. "I like those deposits you bring by at the end of each month, but I am just not seeing the increase in the amount. How can you be adding all these cars and have this big nice fancy office and my three percent doesn't seem to change much?" A.J. knew that wasn't true because he was excellent at math and always paid the man fair and square with three percent of revenue, even though it killed him to do so. He knew that he had invested quite a bit in the shop, property, and drivers, and even though he was doing better, he still struggled with the profits. "Uh, I do the math myself, SUH. I can show you the books if you don't believe what I am sending you is accurate." Mr. Gibson leaned back in A.J.'s chair and put his feet up on A.J.'s desk. "Oh, and I see you got a phone line established here, too. You really are doing well, son." A.J. drew in a deep breath, but he did it so that Mr. Gibson couldn't see it. He was afraid that he might give away his anger.

He didn't say anything but was about to when Mr. Gibson continued, "I got a call from Southwestern Telephone Service the other day and you know what they said?" A.J. knew exactly now where this was going. "They congratulated me on my new business venture way out here on Old Route 9. Now, you might imagine my surprise when I got a call like that when I had no idea I was in a new business venture out here. I absolutely didn't know what to say and I gotta tell you, I am never at a loss for words. Words is my business and I am good at it, so you know what I said to the boss out there at Southwestern Telephone

Service?" A.J. clinched his teeth and tried to swallow back the words that he really wanted to explode with and instead let out a breath and said, "No, SUH, I don't know what you said to them."

Mr. Gibson now put his hands behind his head and looked up at the ceiling and said, "I said *thank you*." He then looked straight at A.J., took his feet off the desk, then leaned forward and placed his elbows on the desk. There was a coffee cup on the desk that was half full that Mr. Gibson managed to knock over, spilling the contents on some of the papers that were on A.J.'s desk. Mr. Gibson never reacted to it. He simply ignored the coffee that was now pooling on some papers. "Been hearing all over town how well my cab company is doing, you see." A.J. felt a little awkward, his stomach stopped churning and now he was just mad H he pulled a chair against the office wall and slid it up towards the front of his desk and sat down in it. He hated sitting in front of his own desk, but he heard his uncle's voice, *play the game.* Even his uncle's voice in his head wasn't working as well as it used to, this was nearly 1952 and a black man should not have to hide behind a white man for any reason. "I reckon you are here to renegotiate our deal?" Mr. Gibson leaned back in the chair again but pretended to just now notice the coffee that was spilled on the desk. He looked around as if he was looking for something to clean it up with and when he couldn't find anything, he slowly picked up the papers that the coffee was pooling on and dumped them in the trash can beside A.J.'s desk.

"I sure am sorry about that. Hope they weren't important." He clapped his hands and rubbed them like he was trying to rub two sticks together and start a fire. "No, sir, I am a man of my word, the three percent works just fine. It helps keep my missus in pearls, she loves pearls, that woman. I swear, every time she goes to Atlanta, she buys another string. Oh, and furs too! You should see the last one I bought her, full-length mink. I was told by the store manager that the damn thing come all

## Chapter 17

the way from Russia. Can you imagine that? We are now tradin' with those red commie bastards. Oh, well, I guess that's progress."

A.J. felt a little relief that his percentage wasn't about to go up, but he knew he was being toyed with at the moment and there was certainly something else that this man wanted, and he wished he would just get to it. He couldn't give a hoot about his wife's pearls and mink coats. "No, sir, a deal is a deal." Mr. Gibson stood up from the desk and walked around the office, pulled his snot-filled handkerchief from his back pocket and instead of blowing, he jammed his finger in his nose, probing like there was no tomorrow. A.J. felt a little queasy again, he was not above mining for a booger himself every now and then, but never in a million years would he ever do it in front of anyone, even if he did use a hanky instead of the old bare digit. When Mr. Gibson was finished with one nostril, he made a hard charge into the other one but continued to talk, so his voice was a little raspy and muffled.

"I just need me a weekend driver again is what I need. You see, I been borrowin' one from old Ance Anderson and that dirty son of a bitch is charging me a fortune. He's robbin' me blind is what it is. I just won't pay his market price no more because you just can't trust old Ance when it comes to secrets and whatnot. Not that I have any secrets, mind you, I just don't like doin' business with close friends, you see. You or one of your boys wouldn't be available on the weekends, now would you?" He continued with the nostril and apparently had missed an intruder the first go around and went back to the nostril he started with. "I am sure we can arrange something for you, Mr. Gibson. I am sure one of my drivers could use the extra money."

Mr. Gibson finished his booger pickin' and stuck the handkerchief back in his pocket. All A.J. could think about now was how awful it would be to shove a snot and booger-filled rag back in your pocket. That man needed to carry at least a dozen hankies. "Well, good. Then it's settled. We start this Saturday, be sure and pay them well, too, because I don't need any loafers

*Choice of Honor*

in my outfit." A.J. sat there in the chair across from his own desk trying to absorb what he had just heard. Pay them well? He started to speak but Mr. Gibson must have read his mind, "Phone lines are a luxury, boy, I'm told the colored aren't quite high on Southwestern Telephone Services and Telegraph's lists of priority customers right now. They might get all in a tizzy if they find out they ran a line all the way out here for a colored man." He started to walk out the door, and with his back now to A.J. and leaving his office, he said, "You are doing real good for yourself, I'm impressed, I'm thoroughly impressed." A.J. sat there, he didn't move, he just sat there in silence. How long would that fool hold this stuff over his head? Why couldn't he just tell old fancy ass Mr. Gibson to go jump in a lake? He turned to look and see what Mr. Gibson was driving and he could see through the window that he was in a new black Cadillac, longest Caddy he had ever seen, but the length of the Caddy wasn't what caught his attention.

What got his attention was the person holding the door open for Mr. Orville Gibson, none other than Curtis Freehold. Not the senior, but the young Freehold that A.J. had met on a dark path leading to the alcohol tent way back in Selma when he first got to town, the same Curtis Freehold, Jr. that he had broken his wrist in front of everyone on a crowded dance floor.

A.J. sat there in his office in the visitor's chair for an hour after he was interrupted by Mr. Gibson, thinking about what life would be like without Mr. Orville Gibson and how good it would be and what he could do with the three percent he was giving to that man every month for nothing more than the use of his garage over four years ago. *What a complete mess*, he thought.

# Chapter 18

∽

HE WAITED OUTSIDE THE ROOM where the doctor was examining Kari. Even though it was becoming clear that she was going to have a baby, A.J. insisted that she see a doctor. She wasn't allowed to use the hospital doctors, but there was a doctor that his uncle knew of that wasn't a real doctor, but he understood medicine and had been very trustworthy, according to his uncle. His uncle said that because of the doctor's light skin, he passed off as an Indian man and got into medical school at Princeton but ran out of money and had to leave. He did get a full-fledged degree from Selma University before being accepted into Cornell Medical School. Uncle Marvin said that Cornell would have never let him go to school if they knew he was black. Uncle Marvin didn't know how long Dr. Tom had actually spent in medical school before he ran out of money or quit, but he told A.J. and Kari that folks around here trust him, and he is a straight shooter. "Mrs. Mack, is this your first child?" Kari sat there in a chair provided for her; she was extremely nervous, she had never been to a doctor before and didn't know what to expect. "Yes, sir, it is."

Dr. Tom was flipping through some papers and looked up. He paused and could instantly see that Kari was nervous. He put down his papers and took off his tiny little reading glasses. He reminded Kari of Mr. Curtis Freehold Senior. He had a full beard and it was well trimmed, but it wasn't gray like Mr. Freehold's was. His beard was jet black, but he still had gray hair just over the top parts of his ears. His eyes were worn and heavy like he was tired, but he didn't seem tired. He smiled when he talked, and he had a very soft voice. "Mrs. Mack, you do understand the process, would that be accurate?" She could feel her cheeks heating up, "You mean like how the baby gets born?" He smiled and leaned forward closer to her.

"No, sweetheart, the brain surgery portion of this. See, we have to take a look inside every woman's head before she gives birth to see if we can find any sustainable theory as to why a woman would put herself through this for any man." At first, she thought he was serious, and she was trying to decide to get up and run, but then she saw him smile very big and when he smiled, he reached and touched her forearm. She smiled and giggled, she was a little embarrassed to have been taken in by the joke. "Yes, sir, I understand, I think we do it for love and through instinct."

Dr. Tom let out a huge laugh. "See, Mrs. Mack, you already understand that I am not a necessary part of this process at all. I am told that women have been having babies for thousands of years and I even heard that women long ago would be working in the fields and would go off behind a tree, have a baby, bite the umbilical cord off, and go back to work. God knows how to make it simple for us. You don't need me, you will already know what to do. It is your husband that will worry himself sick and that is why we suggest brain surgery." She laughed out loud.

"Just tell me how you feel, how many times you relieve yourself in a day, how much work you do, and have you noticed any swelling in your feet or ankles?" She thought about all of it for a minute then answered all the questions, but she could not come up with how many times she went to pee in a day because she had never counted. "Well, that's fine, it is normal to go quite a bit as you get closer to term. Have you been sick?"

## Chapter 18

She smiled and remembered the incident with A.J. the first time she got sick. "Oh, yes, sir, pretty much every morning for the last four weeks." He smiled again and picked up the papers he was reading when they first started the exam.

"That's good, quite normal. I like to think that is your body kicking out any bad stuff so that your baby can have all the good stuff." She had never thought of it that way and it really did make her feel better about upchucking in the morning, although she still had to do it way out of view of A.J. or he would throw up more than her. "I think my husband gets sick more than me, Dr. Tom." He laughed and scribbled something down on the papers he was reading. "I just made a note to have your husband checked for child birth." She laughed so loud it came out as a high-pitched squeal, she covered her mouth with both hands to keep her voice from squealing again.

"In all seriousness, Mrs. Mack, you are a very healthy woman, you have nothing to worry about. I am going to give you the address of a lady that we like to call Mimmi. I am not actually sure if that's her name, but folks have been calling her that for nearly thirty years. In our profession, she is called a mid-wife." Kari watched him scribble on a paper, but she was confused. She had no idea what a mid-wife was, and when the doctor looked up, he could tell she was confused. "She will help you deliver the baby when the time comes." Kari took the paper from him, "I thought you said we've been doing this for thousands of years and nature would do the work?" He patted her on the arm again, "You are correct, my dear, nature will do most of the work, but sometimes nature needs a little help or a steady hand. Mrs. Mimmi is the best in the world at it. She is also the best in the world at keeping panicking husbands from driving their beautiful wives insane."

He stood up from his sitting position and stuck out his hand. She took this as a sign that the exam was over and was relieved that she didn't have to take off her clothes or anything else. Although she had convinced herself before she ever even walked into his office that he would probe her every which way and she would leave feeling worse than when she came in, it was the exact opposite. This doctor had made her feel good just by talking to her. He was nothing like what she expected. She reached for his hand to shake it, which was odd because most men never bothered to shake a woman's hand, black or white, but not only did he shake her hand ever so gently, he raised her hand slightly then bent over and kissed her hand like she was a queen or something. Now, that was something she had never expected or experienced, but she liked it very much.

She told herself that when she was done, she was going to make sure that A.J. and Uncle Marvin began addressing her in the same fashion. "You are a true lady of monumental proportions, God has blessed you with beauty and brains and now he has blessed you with a child. See to it that you forever nurture that delightful creation you now carry and prepare him or her to be good servants of the Almighty and forever humble in all of their endeavors." She was shocked and nearly speechless listening to him as he continued to hold her hand. She had never in all her existence heard so many beautiful words all strung together like that. "Thank you, Dr. Tom. I will do just that." He let go of her hand and then ushered her to the door where he held it open for her to walk out. Once they were in the little room outside his office where A.J. had been standing and trying to listen through the key hole without much luck, the doctor stood squarely in front of A.J. His demeanor became a little more rigid as he looked A.J. in the eyes and began giving A.J. what he called father instructions.

He explained the mid-wife and that the closer they got to the date, Mrs. Mimmi would come stay with them full-time. "Mr. Mack, I hope you are listening to all of this. Your wife is slender in nature and will have a hard time adjusting to the changes in her body. She will certainly be able to handle all of it, but it will be much easier if you assist her in all of her chores and treat her as the immeasurably beautiful queen that she is." Dr. Tom was a pretty tall man, so he was looking down at A.J. as he was giving

## Chapter 18

him the what for. A.J. was not arguing one bit and seemed to be a little scared of the doctor, but Kari knew that he wasn't, for she had seen A.J. mix it up with folks and he was quite a fighter when he had to be.

It made Kari giggle a little watching this all happening in front of her. "Yes, SUH, doctor." What was he thinking, he didn't need to play the game with this man, he was a black man just like A.J., but yet A.J. felt like he needed to revert back to that? His head was spinning. "Good, I am glad you understand." The doctor stuck his hand out to shake A.J.'s and Kari wondered if he would kiss the back of A.J.'s hand like he did hers, but he didn't. She giggled to herself wondering what A.J. would do if he had. "Oh, and one more thing, Mr. Mack, one month before the due date you cannot touch this woman in a biblical way. You may resume your dealings one month after she has had your child. Do you understand?" A.J.'s eyes got very big, but so did Kari's. Holy cow, this doctor just told them they couldn't he and she for two months! Kari didn't think she would pay any attention to that instruction at all. She never could get enough of Alvin Jerome Mack. "Uh, uh, yes, SUH. No touching, got it good, Doc." With that said, the doctor released A.J.'s hand, went back into his office and shut the door, leaving A.J. and Kari standing in total silence. Kari decided she would break the silence and she took a step closer to A.J. and put her arms around his neck and kissed him on the lips. When she pulled back, she said, "I guess we better get home and get busy before the time runs out on us." She smiled and kissed him again. A.J. drove them home and when they got there, they both walked right by Uncle Marvin without saying a word and went straight to the bedroom and closed the door.

# Chapter 19

HE PULLED INTO THE GIBSON driveway and parked in the back like he remembered and turned the car off. He was still driving his cabs everywhere; he never felt the need for his own car. He had convinced himself that the reason why his cabs were doing so well was because he and his drivers all worked hard, but mainly because folks liked the colors. He went to the shed where Mr. Gibson kept the car parked, but the car wasn't there, the shed was empty. "That new Caddy won't fit in there. I had to build another shed on the other side. Damn thing was just too long."

A.J. turned around to see Mr. Gibson carrying a shotgun and was dressed way differently than he had ever seen. He looked like he was going hunting. "Good morning, Mr. Gibson. I thought maybe you was starting without me." Mr. Gibson walked him to the other side of house to the new shed. As they passed the back door, A.J. could see Mrs. Gibson standing in the doorway and she didn't wave at him like she normally did. In fact, A.J. thought she looked like she had been crying. She had her arms folded across her chest and just stared at them as they crossed the back yard. A.J. had to admit that she was never a very cordial woman, but most of the times when she saw him, she would offer up a wave.

## Chapter 19

The few times when he came to knock on the back door and Mr. Gibson didn't answer, she would acknowledge him but not come to the door. She would stand back away from it like she was scared of something and would shout at him from a distance. A.J. offered a wave but she didn't return it, so he just put his head down and kept walking. When they reached the shed, A.J. opened the shed doors and saw the big long black Caddy he had seen at his work just a few days ago. It was certainly a thing of beauty. "Just got this one a few months ago. Gave the old one to my son over in Mobile. It doesn't get as good of gas mileage as the last one but this one sure rides better. You'll see, let's get rolling." A.J. did as he was instructed, except he almost forgot to open the door for Mr. Gibson. It had been so long that he wasn't used to opening doors for anyone now but Kari.

When they were both settled, A.J. adjusted the seat and mirrors to suit him and as he was adjusting the rearview mirror, he asked, "Where to, Mr. Gibson?" Mr. Gibson was still holding the shotgun across his lap, which made A.J. a little nervous. He was certain he would tell him to head out to Anderson's farm, but instead he said, "Same place as always." It caught A.J. off-guard because the usual was Miss Olivia Compton's place, and on the last drive away from Miss Compton's place, Mr. Gibson had said that he had told her he couldn't see her no more.

Mr. Gibson read the body language, or lack of. A.J. had stopped adjusting the mirror and, in fact, he froze. "Just go, A.J. Life has its ups and downs and twists and turns." A.J. did as he was told and drove straight to Miss Compton's place. He suspected he knew now why Mrs. Gibson was standing at the door with those puffy looking eyes and her arms crossed. He knew she wasn't a stupid woman; she had to know where her husband was going every Saturday. When he pulled in front of Miss Compton's place, she came out onto the porch to meet them like she always did. Wearing a white calico dress, but barefooted. She looked as good as she ever did, but it shocked A.J. to see a toddler following her out the door, a toddler that looked to be about two or three years old. All he could think was, *holy shit, that there is Mr. Gibson's baby boy.*

A.J. was speechless. Miss Compton was light skinned and, of course, Mr. Gibson was Lilly white, and if A.J. didn't know better, this boy could pass for any white kid in town, the only give away was the hair. A.J. knew he'd never seen hair like that on a white person. He'd heard that it was possible, but he sure hadn't come across it yet. Mr. Gibson broke the silence and said, "Come on up to the porch, A.J. You can wait for me there." A.J. got out of the car then opened the back door for Mr. Gibson. "Yes, sir." He said it clearly, he was hell-bent on not playing the game with this man anymore. He may have to drive for him until he could figure out a way to get out of it but was going to leave the SUH behind from now on.

When the two men reached the top stairs of the porch, Miss Compton gave Mr. Gibson a hug and tried to give him a kiss, but Mr. Gibson wouldn't allow it. Nevertheless, the exchange between Mr. Gibson and Miss Compton made A.J. feel uncomfortable, but it surprised him when she let go of Mr. Gibson and came to A.J. and hugged him. That made A.J. feel even more uncomfortable. "Nice to see you again, Mr. Mack." She kept her left hand on his right arm as she spoke. I want you to meet O.G. She made a sweeping motion with her hand and stepped aside to reveal the little boy that followed her out the door when they drove up. A.J. didn't know what to say, so he just nodded his head and said, "Nice to meet you, uh, uh…" He couldn't bring himself to say it, but she thought he had forgotten. "O.G. It's O.G." He nodded again and just said, "It's nice to meet you." Mr. Gibson stood for a second but grabbed Miss Olivia by the forearm and nearly dragged her inside the door. As they were crossing the threshold, Mr. Gibson said, "A.J., stay out here on the porch and get to know O.G." And with that, the screen door slammed shut and then the inside door slammed shut.

A.J. swallowed hard and looked around for some help, but then he looked down at that little barefooted boy who was

## Chapter 19

staring at the door that had just shut behind him. He knew he wouldn't get an answer, but he said, "Boy, looks like we are stuck out here on the porch and I don't know doodly squat about no babies. Good Lord, what the hell am I supposed to do with you? I'm a driver, not a damn baby-sitter." He realized he was speaking loudly, but then he realized he had just cursed in front of the boy and quickly apologized. "Sorry 'bout that, little man. I'm as confused as you are now." As if the words upset the little boy, he began to cry; this wasn't just a whimper either, this was full lung capacity wailing.

At first, A.J. thought he needed to keep him quiet to give them their peace, but then he realized from the sound of the bed springs he heard though the walls that this boy's crying wasn't interrupting Mr. Gibson one bit at all. A.J. reached down and picked the little boy up and started down the steps. When he was down the steps, he took a path away from the house that led to the outhouse, but he kept going. The boy had stopped crying and actually had his little arms wrapped tightly around A.J.'s neck. A.J. couldn't help but think that this was no way for this boy to grow up, watching some old white man roll up in a big car, leave him out on the porch, and having his mother worked over inside while he waited. He got really frustrated with the whole situation. He could feel his grip tightening on the boy and decided he needed to relax a little or he might squeeze the life out of this poor little boy.

He kept walking along the trail when he heard the boy burp and then he heard the gush. Immediately, his neck, chest, and back felt wet and, my God, that smell. This kid had just upchucked on him and now he was going to upchuck himself. He panicked, "Good grief, kid, you just made me..." He couldn't finish. When he bent over with his arm behind the boy's head so he wouldn't drop the kid on his head, he unleashed a fury of vomit all over the ground and, unfortunately, all over his arm that was holding the kid. He wanted to set the kid on the ground, but he was afraid a bug or something might bite him, so he held on tightly.

He looked down at his arm and saw his stomach contents on his arm and he wretched again. "My Lord, help me get back to the car so I can sit down." He said it pretty loudly and that must have scared little O.G. because he started wailing again.

This was a bad situation and A.J. did not have an answer; he had no idea how to puke and keep a kid from puking and crying all at the same time. He stood there bent over holding the little boy tightly and decided to sing the only song he could think of, *"What a fellowship what a joy divine, leaning on the everlasting arms..."* He didn't know all of the words, so he sang what he could and when he came to parts he didn't know, he just hummed the tune. It was one he could remember his mom sang to him when he was a boy. He figured he knew more songs than that, but he just couldn't think of any, it was all just too much pressure at the moment.

It must have worked because the boy laid his head back down on his shoulder and squeezed his neck. A.J. had to do something about this puke smell though, so he gathered himself, turned, and headed back towards the house. As he was making the last turn past the outhouse, he saw the pump handle and decided that was as good as it was going to get. Despite having his arms full with a baby, he managed to wash the puke off his arms and neck, all without causing the boy to start crying again. He climbed the steps to the porch and sat down in the swing that had been hung since the last time he was here. He slowly rocked back and forth, and to his surprise, the boy fell asleep.

It was quiet inside, so he was expecting Mr. Gibson to come out soon enough, but he didn't. Just as A.J. was enjoying the peace and quiet with the only sound being the springs and chain of the swing, he heard the bedsprings start up again. He looked down and could see the boy was asleep, so he wasn't worried about the boy hearing stuff he shouldn't hear, not that he would know what that noise was, but he had been thrust into the role of this boy's protector for the moment and he intended to do a good job of it.

*Chapter 19*

"Helluva a baby-sitter you turned out to be." A.J. somehow had managed to fall asleep on the porch swing.

He wasn't sure if it was the silence and peacefulness of the porch with this little boy breathing and sleeping on his chest or if he had worn himself out throwing up earlier. Usually when he upchucked, he wanted to just crawl into bed and stay there for a while, but today's events didn't allow that. He looked up and saw Mr. Gibson standing over him. "He threw up on me," was all A.J. could manage to say. The screen door squeaked as Olivia Compton came out of the house barefooted wearing a silk robe that wasn't tightly tied in the front. One of her boobs popped out as she bent over to take little O.G. from him. She didn't seem to mind, but it embarrassed A.J. enough that he looked away and pretended not see it. "Hope you had a good nap, I am ready to do some bird hunting. Let's go." Once Olivia was no longer standing in his way of getting up, A.J. rose from the swing. Olivia laughed when she saw the baby puke on the front and back of his shirt. Mr. Gibson caught a whiff of him, "No way you are getting in my car smelling like that!" He turned to Olivia, "Go get one of my shirts for him to wear. Take that one and wash it for him. He can pick up next Saturday."

Olivia immediately turned and went inside the house. A few minutes later, she was holding a bright red and black flannel shirt and handed it to A.J. "Let me have the one you have on." A.J. looked around the porch and felt a little uncomfortable taking his shirt off. Mr. Gibson must have sensed his embarrassment, "Honey go inside and clean that boy up. Don't forget, we will be here next Saturday morning bright and early to pick you up." With that said, Olivia took a step towards Mr. Gibson and started to kiss him, but he pushed her away, "Never in front of anyone, now go on so this boy can get out of that foul-smelling shirt."

She stopped and turned towards the door. As she turned and looked at A.J., he caught a slight smile, but he also caught embarrassment of her own. "Nice to see you again, Mr. Mack." The screen door squeaked as it opened, and she stepped through it.

*Choice of Honor*

Little O.G. was still sound asleep. "Well, get that shirt off and let's go. A.J. quickly put the shirt on, which fit him a little too tight, but it was better than the puke-covered shirt he just had on. He started towards the car when Mr. Gibson said, "Grab that shotgun out of the back seat."

A.J. stopped moving, he actually froze because he had his back to Mr. Gibson at the moment. His mind went through a series of panicked thoughts. *What in the world was he going to do with that shotgun? Go back inside and shoot them? Maybe he was going to shoot little O.G. and settle up any claims to and inheritance now? Maybe he was going to shoot them both? Maybe he was going to shoot them both and then shoot A.J. and just leave them all out here to rot?* Hell, as far as A.J. knew, nobody but Mr. Gibson came out here.

A.J. unlocked his legs and continued towards the car, opened the back door, and reached in and grabbed the shotgun. It was an over and under silver plated Mossberg 12 gauge. It had more fancy designs and etchings than A.J. had ever seen. As he was about the close the door, Mr. Gibson hollered, "Grab that box of shells from the trunk, too, A.J." A.J. held the gun, fumbled in his pocket for the keys to the trunk, and dropped them on the ground. When he reached down to pick them up, he saw Mr. Gibson's boot come into his view and he raised up before he grabbed the keys.

"What's the matter with you?" Give me that shotgun before you drop it in the dirt." A.J. handed the shotgun to him then bent down and picked up the keys. He handed the box of shells to Mr. Gibson, but he wouldn't take them. "You carry them, ever been bird hunting?" A.J. had never been bird hunting, he didn't care much for shooting because the noise still made him jumpy. "Uh, no, sir, I have never been bird huntin'. Hadn't done much huntin' of any kind." Mr. Gibson scanned the entire property then looked at A.J. "Well, good, you can learn something new."

A.J. was confused, less nervous, but the jitters were still with him. "This land has been in my family for a long time. My father

## Chapter 19

would come out here every Saturday, as did his father and his father before that." He clicked the lever on the Mossberg and the two barrels released and came free from the stock, making an L. "Hand me a couple shells." A.J. opened the box and did as he was told. "This land has some of the best quail hunting in the state. Dove, too, but they are not as easy to shoot as the quail." Mr. Gibson popped the two shells in the barrel and clicked the barrels back to the stock. He started walking towards the same path that A.J. had taken the little boy, but A.J. didn't follow. Mr. Gibson stopped and turned to A.J. "Well, come on, I need someone to help me make noise and scare up the quail. We can talk as we walk."

# Chapter 20

UNCLE MARVIN WAS SITTING ON the couch that doubled as his bed, reading the Bible as he always did. If he wasn't reading it at the kitchen table, he was sitting on the couch reading it. Kari came in from the back yard. She had been out spreading some scratch for the chickens. She collected an apron full of eggs, put them in a bowl, and slid them in the icebox.

She came into the living room holding two cups of coffee. "I know you can handle a cup of my coffee." Uncle Marvin closed the Bible and sat it on the couch beside him. "Oh, baby! You are so good to me. I sure can! How in the world do you read my mind? I was just about to get up and get one myself!" He laughed and took the cup from her hand. "What are you reading about now?" He took a sip from the coffee and let a huge smile come across his face. "Doggone you make the best coffee!" She took a seat on the couch next to him. "Well, it seems that even though David was just a little fella, he became real popular when he conked that big Philistine on the head with a stone when nobody else would fight him."

He took a sip of coffee, "You'd think he would have had it made. Hell, they even made him king, but he went and took up with a woman he shouldn't have and had her husband sent off to battle and killed so he could have her full-time for himself." Kari

## Chapter 20

took a sip of her coffee and giggled a little then she replied, "You men and your swords, you just need to learn to keep them in the sheath." Uncle Marvin laughed and spilled a little coffee on his wrist. He sat the cup down and wiped his wrist on his pant leg. "My A.J. better not ever find him someone else."

She smiled but she had a concerned look on her face as she did. Uncle Marvin sensed that she had something on her mind. "What's you pondering this morning? Seems like every time I go out and throw down some scratch and watch how them chickens behave, it gets all the gears in my head turning. Does it do the same to you?" He waited on a response, but she didn't give one. "If you are worried about A.J. finding someone else, you better quit on it. That boy is as crazy about you as any man could be. I swear I think he'd stop breathing if you didn't return his love. I know that for a fact."

She laughed, "Oh, I know that, I was just wondering where that Mr. Gibson is making him go to now. I thought we was done doing that old fool's business and now all of a sudden, he gets A.J. wrangled into hauling him around all over a stupid phone line. I don't like having that man messin' around with us. He ain't nothing but trouble." Uncle Marvin shook his head so that she could see he was listening. "Well, you are right for sure, that man thinks the world evolves around him and when it don't spin right for him, he tries to change it and no matter how hard he tries, he can't." She was silent again. "That baby you got bakin' in there doin' good? You still feeling poorly in the morning?" She smiled and shook her head no. "Thank goodness I don't throw up anymore. I don't know which I was more tired of; me throwing up or A.J. throwing up because I was throwing up! I swear I have never seen anyone with a weaker stomach." They both started laughing.

"We have to give you some space, Uncle Marvin. You can't sleep on this couch much longer and you sure can't sleep listening to a baby cry all the time. We don't want to leave you alone, so why don't we just all find something bigger for us to all live in?" Uncle Marvin was shaking his head no before she could even finish. They had had this conversation it seemed like a thousand times and it always ended the same way, Uncle Marvin would laugh and say he had been in this house for nearly forty years now. He would recite all the things that happened in the house, the children that were born, the children that died, his wife's passing on in her sleep and the loneliness that his wife's passing caused him and the joy and happiness that he found when she and A.J. came crashing into his life.

He always told them that they could have ten babies and it wouldn't bother him the least little bit. He never really talked about it, but he had four children of his own, but all of them had passed on. He would often mumble when he read a story in the Bible or saw something in a newspaper about a child death. *"Parents ain't supposed to bury their kids."* She could always tell that Uncle Marvin carried a certain amount of pain with him everywhere he went.

The door opened and A.J., stepped through wearing a shirt neither Uncle Marvin nor Kari had ever seen. After both Kari and Uncle Marvin looked at each other then back to A.J., Uncle Marvin was the first to speak, "What the hell you got on, boy?" A.J. let out a sigh and immediately began unbuttoning the shirt that was formerly Mr. Gibson's. When A.J. had the shirt off and he was standing there in his tee shirt, he crumpled the shirt up and threw it in the corner on the floor. He let out a sigh and rolled his eyes to let them know that he was frustrated, "Let me get a cup of coffee and I will tell you both all about it."

A.J. came back with a cup of coffee and different shirt that fit. He told them about the bird hunting, the walking and talking, and Mr. Gibson shooting birds as they walked. He said that he didn't do much talking, Mr. Gibson did all the talking, and as far as A.J. could tell, he really didn't have a point to anything he was talking about except when he got to the part about his wife confronting him about his mistress that morning. He said that Mr. Gibson suspected she had known about it for as long as it had

## Chapter 20

gone on, but she never brought it up. He laughed when he said that every Gibson man in the family for as far back as he could recite kept some form of service on the side.

He even bragged about how well the service women of choice were treated; how they were given places to stay, fed and clothed, and the only exchange required for such "lavish treatment" as Mr. Gibson described it, although A.J. found nothing lavish about the house that Miss Compton stayed in. A.J. noticed that you could actually see through some of the cracks in the side boards and the porch floor was rotted in a few spots. A.J. had never actually been inside the house and never wanted to, it was to provide the Gibson men with a little comfort and escape from the pressures of being such powerful men in the state.

As they walked through the dense brush of the property around the "lavish" trying to scare up birds, it seemed to A.J. that Mr. Gibson was actually trying to make the situation right with A.J., but he wasn't sure. It's when he got to the part about the little toddler that things got confusing. Mr. Gibson claimed that when he broke it off with Miss Compton a few years back that Miss Compton shifted her focus to other men, and he wasn't sure who the father was, but that he truly loved Miss Compton and felt the need to support her and the boy.

"That boy looks just like Mr. Gibson except for the hair." A.J. took a sip from his coffee and let out a deep breath, "He never did say, but I think Mrs. Gibson confronted him about not only Miss Compton but the boy as well." A.J. paused as if he was trying to come to a logical conclusion as to why that morning Mrs. Gibson stood at the door with puffy tear-filled eyes. Uncle Marvin shifted in his seat a little, "Boy, you got to get away from that mess somehow. That man is gonna cause everybody trouble, including you." A.J. nodded his head in agreement. Kari put her hand on his thigh, "What are you thinking, baby? Can you get away from him?"

A.J. looked around the room as if he was searching for answers in the wall of his uncle's home, "If I come clean with the phone company and let them know that they really ran a phone line for me instead of Mr. Gibson, then they might cut it off, and I need that line to grow the business. Uncle Marvin slid forward in his seat and put his elbows on his knees and said, "And they might not." The comment surprised A.J. as it was his uncle that was always telling him to *play the game*, and by fibbing just a little to get the phone line hooked up, he felt like he was playing the game, now his uncle was telling him not to? "Uncle Marvin, I did it that way because I thought that you would have done it that way." Uncle Marvin sat back in his chair, "You are right, I would have a few years back, but times are changing now. I sure need to think this through before you do anything, but I know some folks down in Atlanta that sure might be willing to help us if they tried to cut your phone off just because you was black."

They all sat in silence for a little while before Kari spoke, "I don't want you to do anything right now. We have a baby that will be here soon. Just drive for him on Saturdays and let him go out there to that old whore and dip his wick and maybe in a few years things will change enough to where you ain't got to hide your business behind that philandering old white man." A.J. leaned over and kissed her on the cheek and put his hand on the now very visible belly. "You are right, baby. I will keep up the charade until things change, but don't be too hard on that girl, she is doing what she can to survive."

Uncle Marvin made a grunt as to agree with him, which didn't go over well with Kari. "A woman spreadin' her legs to survive is not the answer, Alvin Jerome Mack, and don't you ever think it is! What if this here baby turns out to be a girl, you want your baby girl he'n and she'n with some old fool just for a place to live? I bet that girl's daddy don't know what she is doin' or he would put a stop to it!" Both A.J. and Uncle Marvin retreated from their argument quickly just to keep the peace. They both could tell that Kari Rae Mack was having no sympathy conversation for Miss Olivia Compton.

# Chapter 21

A.J. HANDED THE MAN THE cash and the man handed him the deed to the house, the house right next to his uncle's house. Uncle Marvin lived about two miles South of Montgomery city limits. The area that he lived in was lined with houses on one side of the dirt road and the other side of the road was a cow pasture. There was talk that somebody was going to build some more houses on that side of the road, but it never did happen. All of the houses were so close together that Uncle Marvin used to joke that he could turn the page of his neighbor's newspaper for them if they both happened to be sitting in the front porch at the same time.

The houses originally were painted all white, but many of them had let the paint wear off to where they just kind of looked gray now with a few white flecks, except Uncle Marvin's house. His was always immaculate white. He painted it every year and if he could trade and swap for enough paint, he would also paint the neighbor lady's for her. All the houses looked the same except for the paint and each of them were built with huge front porches. Uncle Marvin called them shotgun houses.

Because Uncle Marvin had that big oak tree in his front yard and one just to the side of his house, his wasn't as close to the other house as all the rest, but he still liked to joke about flipping the newspaper pages for his neighbor. A.J. considered it luck and good fortune when the old woman who had been Uncle Marvin's neighbor for nearly forty years passed away. He didn't consider it luck that she passed away and was actually corrected by Kari one day when he was describing his luck to a friend, so whenever he would talk about the passing of his uncle's neighbor, he would always say something like *When the Lord called her home* or just simply *She traveled up to heaven*, but no matter how he told the story, he always sounded excited and it just didn't come out right.

It didn't take him long to buy the house from the old lady's brother. The brother lived in Monroe, Louisiana and had come to town to make the arrangements for his sister. When A.J. met him, he mentioned in the conversation that he intended to sell the house as he had no desire to move to Montgomery, so right there on the spot, he and A.J. came to a reasonable price and they shook hands. The brother did stipulate to A.J. that he didn't want to officially sell it at that moment and that he would rather wait until his sister was in the ground before he sold off her things. He said it just didn't seem like the Christian thing to do, so they agreed to settle the day after the funeral, which they did.

It was Uncle Marvin who found her sitting slumped over on her kitchen table, face down in the plate of noodles she was eating. Uncle Marvin seemed more shaken up about his neighbor's passing than A.J. thought he should be, after all, he never really spent much time with the woman that A.J. knew of, but he would check on her every so often. "Everybody I know is gettin' planted in the ground, boy." That was Uncle Marvin's response when A.J. asked him why he seemed so upset. "When you get to be my age, all you do is watch your friends and family die off." A.J. patted his uncle on the shoulder in a show of emotional support, but it was what he said next that caught A.J. off-guard, "Me and that old lady helped each other through some rough times. Her old man died right about the time my wife died. She was a good woman."

## Chapter 21

A.J. listened as his uncle continued, "A man, no matter how old he gets, has needs, and for that matter, so does a woman. Now she done went and died." A.J. was becoming more curious now and had to ask a few questions, "You never said much about her since I have been here, how often did you check on her?" He had a slightly sneaky smile on his face as he said it. His uncle looked up at him and saw the smile and cracked a smile of his own. "I checked on her enough to keep us both happy. She was a good woman." A.J. couldn't help it because he wasn't much for skirting an issue, he liked to address things head-on. "So, you been gettin' busy with that woman all these years? How come I didn't know that?"

Uncle Marvin smiled, "You don't know everything you think you know, Mr. Smarty Pants. I know how to get things done, too." A.J. and Uncle Marvin both laughed as he said it. A.J. then sat and listened to his uncle talk about the secret love affair his uncle had with the lady next door for many years now and nobody even knew it. He was amused to hear that he would sneak over there after dark, go through the back door so nobody would see them and tarnish her reputation, which was apparently very good because she was well-known in the church and community for being practically a saint.

Uncle Marvin said it started about a year after her husband passed and his wife passed. She asked him if he could help her fix the sink in her kitchen because it was leaking and apparently the payment turned out to be pretty good. He could easily sense that his uncle thought more of her than just a bedmate because as he recanted the story of all the secret rendezvous the two had, he would choke up in certain parts. He admitted that it wasn't necessary to sneak around and that the two could have married, but neither wanted the commitment and the arrangement was pretty convenient. "She was a saint in my book, just because she let me have it whenever I felt like I needed it, and I tell you this much, there was plenty of times she snuck in my back door, too!" A.J. shook his head, he was learning more about his uncle every day.

This was not only unexpected, it was highly amusing. "I am sure she was a saint, Uncle Marvin. I ain't questioning that, but what gets me the most is how good you keep secrets!"

After the funeral for the neighbor lady, A.J. and the brother took the time to go through the house with Uncle Marvin, taking inventory of the things that needed to stay with her brother, the things that maybe they could sell off, and the things that just needed to be tossed. Uncle Marvin got choked up a few times, but he always managed to recover. Once the house was cleared of all of Uncle Marvin's secret girlfriend's stuff, Kari and A.J. set up their first home ever and they didn't have to leave Uncle Marvin in his house by himself, which was one of their other concerns.

Uncle Marvin didn't seem to be able to think clearly anymore. He often brought up the same subject he had brought up just minutes before, as if he was talking about it for the first time. Kari and A.J. would correct him at first and remind him that they had just talked about that very subject, but after a while they could see that it would frustrate him, so they would both pretend that they were hearing it for the first time.

# Chapter 22

A.J. NEARLY JUMPED FROM HIS porch to Uncle Marvin's porch, he almost made it but was just a little short. His foot hit the side rail of the porch and he did a summersault, which landed him right in front of Uncle Marvin's door. He stood up quickly and ran into the house, "Ms. Mimmi! Kari is hurtin' real bad! She is hollerin' for you!" He was yelling as he ran through the living room, through the kitchen, and then on back to the bedroom. Ms. Mimmi had moved in with them just like the doctor ordered, which turned out to be a blessing because she was also helping with Uncle Marvin. He would forget things like pants and would walk out onto the porch with his coffee naked from the waist down. It had never occurred to him to put any pants on. They hadn't really needed her for Kari because Kari continued to do everything she had always done right up until this very moment.

It was a Sunday, Kari was hulling out some purple hull peas in the kitchen, which were A.J.'s favorite, but he hated shelling them. He hated the fact that it took weeks for that purple color to wear off his thumb after he had shelled a bunch of them. He heard her let out a little scream, so he ran into the kitchen where he found her standing beside the counter looking down at the floor. He looked down at the floor to see what she was looking at and he could see a little puddle of water.

He thought she had spilled something, but when she looked up at him, she smiled and said, "You better go find Ms. Mimmi." It took him a minute, at first, he thought it was silly to go get Ms. Mimmi simply to clean up an accident and it wasn't her fault anyway, so he thought he would be a big help and grab a dish rag off the stove and wipe up the mess. As he bent down to clean it, Kari playfully smacked him on the back of the head, "Silly man, get Ms. Mimmi, that puddle you are trying to clean up came from me!"

He shrugged his shoulders in half-way agreement, "Of course it came from you, you are the only one in the kitchen. We don't need Ms. Mimmi for this, baby, I can clean it up in a jiffy. You just sit down and relax, and everything will be all right. Don't you worry your pretty little head none." She smacked on the head again, only this time it was a little more forceful. "Baby, I am tryin' to help you, whackin' me in the head ain't helping one bit at all." This time she pinched the top of his ear and began to pull him up to her. "Ouch, baby, that hurts, you know I have sensitive ears, a pinch like that could stay with me for days."

When she finally had him looking at her, she smiled again and said, "Baby, that puddle of water is called amniotic fluid, it means that the baby is coming. Now, go get Ms. Mimmi, please." It took A.J. just a minute to put the pieces of this puzzle together but when he did, his eyes got as big as silver dollars and he nearly fainted. "Oh, Lord! Is the baby drowning? What's happening?!" He looked around the kitchen, but he had no idea what he was looking for, he just felt like he needed to be looking for something. Kari caught him by the arm, "Calm down, baby, everything is just fine, just go get Ms. Mimmi." With that, he bolted through the kitchen door, through the living room, and out onto the porch, and that is where he tried to make the leap from his porch to Uncle Marvin's.

Once he was inside and had checked the living room, kitchen,

## Chapter 22

and was now entering the bedroom, he sure didn't expect to see what he saw. Today was just full of surprises. Uncle Marvin was standing beside the bed with no pants on and his gentleman was just as straight as an arrow. Ms. Mimmi was scrambling around the room looking for something and he wasn't sure what she was looking for, but he thought it really wasn't unusual for Uncle Marvin to walk around without his pants on and it wasn't all that unusual for his tally-whacker to illustrate to everyone that it could still stand up straight. "Uh, Ms. Mimmi, you need to come quick, Kari is leaking water all over the kitchen floor and she said it was time for me to come get you!"

Ms. Mimmi found what she was looking for, crumpled it up in her hand, and stuck it in her front apron pocket. "Well, honey, let's go then, I can't get through that door with you standing in it." She pushed passed him and made her way out the front door. As A.J. was leaving, he turned to see Uncle Marvin still standing there without anything on below the waist, smiling back at A.J. with his gentleman still standing up straight. "Put some pants on, Uncle Marvin, I already told you that you can't run around here without any pants on!" A.J. turned to catch up to Ms. Mimmi but she was already out the front door. A.J. was surprised at how fast she moved for an older woman.

When he got to the kitchen, Ms. Mimmi had Kari up from the chair and was holding her by the arm. "A.J., you get me some clean water, some of that rubbing alcohol from under the sink, and a few towels and put them in the bedroom. Me and Kari are about to experience one of God's true miracles together and you and that crazy old fool over there are going to stay out of my way until I tell you."

A.J. stood there for second trying to process all that was happening. He wanted to go pick Kari up and take her to the bedroom, but he was afraid Ms. Mimmi would yell at him some more, so he did as he was told but had a hard time focusing, especially when he turned to see that Uncle Marvin had followed them over to their house without any pants, of course, but at least now he wasn't so perky. "Damn it, Uncle Marvin, you go back and find your damn pants!" Uncle Marvin was still smiling as he turned and left the kitchen.

He stayed on the front porch trying to relax but he couldn't. He would sit in one of the two wood rockers they had on the front porch for a few seconds then he would pace around the porch and then back to the chair. Uncle Marvin finally came back over wearing pants in time to hear Kari scream and when she did, A.J. started to run in the house, but Uncle Marvin grabbed him by the arm. "That's natural, boy, hurts a lot for a woman to push a baby out of her system. That's why they let the women have the babies, we men couldn't handle that kind of pain, so we'd just quit he'n and she'n all together." He laughed as he said but his attempt at humor fell on deaf ears.

A.J. was as intense as he had ever been. "Ms. Mimmi will holler for you if she needs anything. I expect she has probably delivered at least a thousand babies around these parts. Yes, sir, she knows what she is doing." Uncle Marvin sat down in the other rocker and began rocking back and forth. "Yes, sir, she knows what she is doing." A.J. looked at his uncle who was smiling again and was staring out at the cow pasture across the road. A.J. made another circle around the porch and went back to the chair. Just as he was about to sit down, Kari let out another loud scream and it caused him to flinch and he missed part of the chair, knocked the chair over, and he landed hard on his backside.

Uncle Marvin stood up to set the chair right again, "Boy, I swear you got to just relax! You gonna kill yourself out here on this porch as jumpy as you are. That girl in there is tryin' to give you a baby and you out here acting a fool!" Uncle Marvin got the chair back upright and reached down to help A.J. up. That's when they both heard a baby cry. "See there! I told you everything gonna be all right. You got a baby in there with a fine set of lungs sounds like to me." Uncle Marvin laughed and finished helping A.J. up.

A.J. could feel the excitement rising from his feet to his head. He wanted to rush in there and see his wife and new baby, but

## Chapter 22

he was following orders. He was sure that if Ms. Mimmi didn't holler for him soon, he was going to say the hell with her and bust through that door and he didn't care what Ms. Mimmi said. The two men heard Kari let out another scream and this time, Uncle Marvin didn't say anything. It was as quiet as church on the porch. A.J. expected him to say something to try and help him calm down, but he didn't. When A.J. looked at Uncle Marvin, he could see the concern on his face and when Uncle Marvin saw that A.J. was looking at him, he changed his expression from one of concern to another smile on his face. "Just give it a minute, boy."

They could both hear Ms. Mimmi mumbling though the walls, but they couldn't make out what she was mumbling. The wait was killing A.J. He expected Ms. Mimmi to either come out and hand him a baby or he expected her to call him into the bedroom so that he could see both his wife and the baby were healthy, but she hadn't. All he could hear was mumbling and it was driving him crazy. Kari screamed again and this time Uncle Marvin started for the front door. He had the screen open and A.J. was about to follow in behind him when they both heard the baby cry again.

They froze in their positions of being half inside the house and half out. "Ya'll come in here and see this new momma!" Ms. Mimmi hollered as loud as she could, but neither men moved. Both were frozen in their positions. Just a minute ago, both men were ready to rush in the room, but neither had an idea of what they would do once they got there. Now, standing in the doorway, half in and half out of the house, both men were scared. Finally, A.J. gave Uncle Marvin a shove in the back to get him moving again and both men headed straight for the bedroom.

A.J. walked into the bedroom behind Uncle Marvin and nearly had to push him out of the way to see his wife and new baby. When he saw Kari lying there in bed looking as beautiful as he had ever seen her, smiling at him holding two babies, he nearly fainted. Uncle Marvin saw his nephew get wobbly and immediately grabbed him to help steady him. A.J. looked at

Uncle Marvin with a stunned look on his face, he had no idea what to say. Uncle Marvin was about to break the silence when Ms. Mimmi broke the silence for everyone. "Alvin Jerome Mack, meet your two boys." She smiled as she said it. A.J. looked at her and then he looked at Kari, she was smiling from ear-to-ear.

The couple had never even thought about the prospect of having twins. "Well, aren't you gonna come say high to your boys?" Kari whispered because it looked like to A.J. that one of the boys was already asleep and the other was staring up at his beautiful mother. A.J. looked around the room as if he needed permission from someone else, but he didn't. Uncle Marvin gave him a little nudge, "Well, go on, boy, them two babies want to meet their daddy. Go on and say hello." A.J. smiled and practically leaped the few steps that separated him from his wife and now two children.

He reached the bed and sat down beside Kari on the side where the baby was awake. He put his hand on her thigh then leaned over and kissed her. He felt explosions in his stomach, but they weren't the kind that made him throw up, they were the kind that his uncle called "butterflies." He got them when he was nervous, but he hadn't felt the butterflies like this since the day he saw Kari for the first time. As he kissed her, all those thoughts came exploding back into his head. He thought she looked as beautiful right now in that bed holding those two little boys as she did the first time he saw her. "I've never loved anyone more than I love you right now, baby. You are the most beautiful woman in the whole world and right now, you holdin' these precious boys of ours, you somehow got even more beautiful."

A tear rolled down his cheek and he tried to wipe it away before it rolled all the way down to his jaw, but it was futile; another tear followed right behind that one. Kari smiled, "And you were worried that your workings were messed up and look here what you did, you went and stuck two babies inside me without telling me what you were doing." She was still whispering, but even Uncle Marvin heard her with his bad hearing, and they all got a laugh out of the humor.

## Chapter 22

Kari looked over at Uncle Marvin and said, "Well, I'm glad you wore pants for the birth of our boys." They all laughed again, but A.J. corrected her, "Well, not at first he didn't, I had to tell him there was a dress code for child birthin' around here." Uncle Marvin stammered around a little because he really couldn't remember when and why he did not wear pants. It seemed odd to everyone that he could remember some of the finest details of things like cars and engines and even family members that had long since passed on, but some days he couldn't remember to brush his teeth or even put on pants.

Ms. Mimmi stepped towards Kari and put her hand on her forehead to check for a fever. "You feel a little warm, baby, you feel all right?" Kari smiled, looked at both her boys then stared straight at A.J. and said, "I'm the luckiest woman in the world, I feel wonderful." Ms. Mimmi kept her hand on her forehead and moved it to her cheeks just to make sure she got a good feel for Kari's temperature. "Well, you gonna need to rest, givin' birth to one baby is hard and here you went and did it twice in the same hour." A.J. continued to look at her as if he was seeing her for the first time again. He would have been happy just sitting there on the side of that bed staring at his wife and babies, but Kari broke the silence, "Well, this one here is Alvin Jerome Mack because he came first."

She moved her head in the direction of the baby that was sleeping and continued, "But we never talked about another name, other than for a girl, and I don't think he would care much for being called Jane like we discussed if it was a girl." She looked up at him and smiled. He smiled back and without hesitation he said, "Little man with the big watchful eyes that's been staring at you the whole time we been here is James Robert Mack for sure. There just can't be any other name." Kari nodded as if she agreed but asked, "Is that someone in the family? Why that name?" A.J. got nervous for a second because he thought maybe she had another name in mind, "We can name him another name if you don't like that one, baby."

Kari chuckled a little, which caused Alvin Jerome Mack III to open his eyes for a second, but he closed them just as quickly as he opened them. "No, baby, I love the name. I just want to know when people ask if he is named after anyone in the family." A.J. leaned over and kissed her forehead and softly said, "My Marine family, baby, he is named after someone in my Marine family."

A.J. never really talked to Kari about his days in the war and some of the awful things he had seen and some of the awful things he had done in order to survive. It bothered him that he was nearly seven years removed from that mess and he still had nightmares about it. He was afraid if her told anyone about it, including Kari, some of those nightmares might pass on to them, so he just kept it all inside. "All right now, we got to feed these boys and clean up some more. Things happened so fast that I am not organized like I like to be. A.J., you got to fetch me some clean sheets and I will change and wash these."

The minute Ms. Mimmi started barking orders, Uncle Marvin was out the door. He was not about to stay long enough to get roped into doing any chores he didn't care to do. A.J. kissed her on the forehead and started to get up, but Ms. Mimmi wasn't finished. "Now, look here, young man, this woman is gonna be sore for quite a while. She done went and pushed two watermelons through a radiator hose and she don't need no monkey business. You hear me?"

A.J. was trying to figure out why everyone thought he was such a sex-starved animal that he would start humping his wife while she was holding the newborns in each arm. It frustrated him, but he knew they all meant well, so he just nodded and agreed. There was no point in arguing about his sex drive. Ms. Mimmi continued, "Honey, it's tough enough suckling one child, but you got two at the same time. I'd say by the looks and feel that both them boys is probably a good seven pounds apiece, so they are sure to be big eaters." Kari smiled and A.J. could tell she was a little shy about having this awkward conversation in front of him. She started to say something, but Ms. Mimmi continued,

## Chapter 22

"Them boys are gonna wear your goodies out. They gonna make you so sore that so much as a silk shirt brushin' up against them milk jugs is gonna make you wanna cry."

Kari flushed in the face a little, "I think I understand, Ms. Mimmi, I do appreciate the rather blunt instructions." Ms. Mimmi was undeterred in her instructions, "Now, I have a special salve that I want you to rub on those things every day. It will help with the soreness but mind you…" Ms. Mimmi stuck out her finger and then pointed it directly at Kari, "You wash it right off after letting it set for a few minutes. If them boys suckle and any of that salve is still on your nipple, you'll have two drunk little boys with a bad case of the drizzles for a few days. There is a special ingredient I put in my slave that babies don't need in their system."

A.J. was getting a little embarrassed by Ms. Mimmi's bluntness and decided it was a good time to go get the sheets. He kissed Kari on the lips, then gave each of his boys a kiss and left them room. Ms. Mimmi was still giving him instructions, but he paid her no more attention. He was going to get the sheets then go sit on the porch with his uncle, have a shot of Maple Nut whiskey he bought his uncle for Christmas last year, and smoke a cigar that he had bought just for this occasion.

# Chapter 23

"COULD YOU ROLL OUT FOUR yards of this for me, please." A.J. brought Kari into town to buy some things for the babies. One thing in particular on the list was buying enough cotton blend fabric to make more diapers out of. A.J. was amazed at how the boys could mess up so many diapers throughout the day. It seemed to him that the minute you got one of them in clean diapers, the other would make a mess in his. A.J. had a weak stomach and this diaper changing business was pushing him to his limits.

Ms. Mimmi had agreed to stay with them for a month beyond the birth to help Mrs. Kari with the twin boys. She wasn't going to at first, but A.J. offered a little more money for the extended stay and then he referred to the day Kari went into labor. The day was a blur to him at first, but after a little time, he would laugh to himself when he thought about actually trying to jump from his porch to Uncle Marvin's. Even in his younger days, he knew he couldn't make that leap, but on that day, he damn near made it. What flashed through his mind was finding Uncle Marvin and Ms. Mimmi back in the bedroom. It wasn't uncommon for Ms. Mimmi to help wherever she was needed and at it certainly wasn't uncommon to find Uncle Marvin without any pants on, but it was uncommon to see Ms. Mimmi searching the

## Chapter 23

bedroom for something, which A.J. could now see more clearly as he had time to recount the day's events.

He realized one night while in bed that Ms. Mimmi was searching for her underwear! When he figured it out, he sat straight up in bed and made so much noise that he woke up the babies. Kari gave him hell for waking up the boys since getting them both to sleep at the same time was quite a chore, but she laughed when he told her what he had remembered about the day. She reminded A.J. that both Uncle Marvin and Ms. Mimmi were adults and could do whatever they wanted. He knew she was right and never brought up the subject again until the day he asked her to stay longer than agreed.

When she was kicking up a fuss about the extra stay, she made mention that she had to get back home to her family and that her husband needed her to look after him. A.J., being the smart business man he had now become, seized the moment and let her know that he was sad to see her go and wished she could stay, but he totally understood and simply asked her that if he found any of her skivvies laying around Uncle Marvin's place after she was gone, did she want him to bring them to her. He hated holding that over her head, but he knew no other way to keep her.

He would never let Kari go into town by herself, it was just too tense around Montgomery at the moment. The tension between black folks and white folks was as high as A.J. had ever seen it. The couple needed things from the store and there was no way he was going to haul Kari and the babies into town during this tense time. He had no idea that Ms. Mimmi, who was now Mrs. Mimmi, was married. It was good information to use, he didn't feel guilty about holding it over head too long.

"That's a lot of fabric, I am not sure I have four yards left on this bolt." The clerk at Woolworths rolled the bolt out on the counter, measuring off each yard as it unfolded on the counter. She got to three yards and the cardboard insert fell out on the floor. A.J. bent down to pick it up and put it back on the counter.

*Choice of Honor*

"I'm sorry, hun, I only got three yards. I will have the manager order some more today and it should be here..." She turned to look at a calendar on the wall behind her, "Well, if he phones in the order, it can be here in about two weeks, but if he mails it in, it might take a little longer than that." The clerk folded the three yards of cotton blend and pinned a ticket for the amount to it. "Our manager just hates to phone any orders in, he says that long distance calls cost too much money." She walked towards the register as she was talking. A.J. and Kari followed her from their side of the counter when the bell on the front door clanged as another customer walked in.

"Well, Mr. Anderson, sure didn't expect to see you back so soon. I will be with you in just a second." The clerk hurried through the sale as she punched the keys and pulled the lever. It made a loud noise and the drawer popped open. A.J. handed her the money and she slid it in the drawer and closed it. As she was handing the bag to Kari, Mr. Ansil Anderson came over to where A.J. and Kari were standing next to the counter. "You're that driver for old Orville, ain't that right?" A.J. turned to look at Ansil Anderson, as did Kari. A.J. felt a tinge of nervousness come up over him as he had no idea where this was going, but he knew he wanted to quickly pay for the diaper material and leave Mr. Anderson to his business. A.J. had never officially met Mr. Anderson, but he knew of his reputation. He had heard that not much good ever came from knowing Ansil Anderson.

He tipped his hat to Kari, which sort of caught A.J. buy surprise because white men of power, especially this one, did not show any respect to black men or women. "Ma'am, if you wouldn't mind, I'd like to have a word with your husband, and I am afraid you'd be sour on the conversation in no time." Kari looked at A.J. to see if he really wanted her to walk away so they could talk. A.J. could see the worry in her eyes and he did not like it. He hated for his Kari to have to worry about anything. "Baby, why don't you look around some more, it sure seems like we are missing some things. I will go outside and visit with Mr. Anderson while you shop."

*Chapter 23*

    A.J. smiled at her to reassure her and then looked at Mr. Anderson for some kind of confirmation that his impromptu meeting plan was ok. It turned out to be because Ansil Anderson had already turned and headed back out the door. Kari stepped towards A.J. and grabbed him by the arm. She whispered to him so that Mr. Anderson could not hear her, "What do you want me to do?" He smiled and kissed her on the cheek and then whispered in her ear, "Stay beautiful and love me forever, that's all I want you to do." He smiled as he said it. "I will be fine. Just shop some more, buy something nice for you and the boys."

    She let go of his arm and returned his smile. A.J. always knew how to calm her and make her feel like she was a queen. She didn't stop worrying about Mr. Ansil Anderson, though. She knew of his reputation even when she was living in Selma, but then he was a mythical figure, now she was standing in Woolworths in Montgomery, Alabama staring at this beast that she had heard of and he had actually tipped his hat to her; she didn't expect that at all. A.J. turned and walked out of the store with Ansil Anderson walking right in front of him. Kari choked down the lump that was in her throat and continued to browse the store. She knew she wasn't going to buy anything else, she just needed to kill some time while her husband and Ansil Anderson were on the sidewalk. She could not help but wonder what in the world that man wanted with her husband.

## Chapter 24

ANSIL ANDERSON WASN'T AN OVERLY big man, he was roughly the same height as A.J., but there was something about him. A.J.'s father would have described Ansil Anderson as wirey, the kind of man that has just something a little extra in his system that kept him fighting long after others had quit. His skin and hands were rough; he had certainly done his fair share of work while he was bootlegging.

Ansil was quite a bit older than most of the people he hung out with. A.J. guessed he was in his sixties, maybe even seventies, he couldn't tell. He knew that Ansil made all his money bootlegging before the war. He controlled all the alcohol coming in and out of Alabama during prohibition. If you operated a still, you had to get it approved through one Mr. Ansil Anderson and, of course, pay his excise tax, but if you tried to operate behind his back, you generally weren't ever heard from again. Everyone said he was a man who had absolutely no compassion and because of his lack of compassion, he had no remorse. If you got cross with Ansil Anderson, you paid the price.

There was a story that circulated around town quite frequently about a man that traded with Ansil back before the war. The story changed many times, but it was always the same result,

## Chapter 24

the man didn't fare to well. The story says that Ansil and the man had done a deal that involved a mule, a horse, and a couple acres of land. The man traded the mule and horse to Ansil for a really small piece of property. The next day after the trade, the mule went and bit Ansil's little girl on the arm when she was trying to pet him, and that pissed Ansil off something fierce.

He took the horse and mule into town where the man was said to be in the feed store doing some business. Everyone said he was buying some seed for planting, but who knows. Anyway, Ance finds him at the feed store, goes into the store, and starts beating the man with an axe handle and drags him outside the feed store. Once he was outside the feed store, he pulled a gun from his belt and shot the horse and the mule right in front of the man.

Both animals dropped right where they stood. The man was beaten and bloody and to this point, had no idea why this was happening to him and as far as the story goes, he never did. All Mr. Ansil Anderson said as a huge crowd of people was now gathered to see that this was about was, "No deal. Here's your damn animals back." That was the kind of man Ansil Anderson was. Even up in his years now, nobody tangled with Ansil Anderson. It was said that the poor man left town, confused, and with the only horse he had left now and was never heard from again. It was safe to say that A.J. had heard all the stories and would just as soon keep his distance from the man with that kind of reputation.

He felt nervous just standing on the sidewalk with him, but he wasn't about to let this man know it. Ansil Anderson stood on the sidewalk looking out over the street waiting for A.J. to close the door to Woolworths behind him. When he heard the clang of the bells attached to the door, he turned to look at A.J. The expression on Ansil's face was not one that A.J. expected, in fact, he really didn't know what to expect, but he certainly didn't expect a soft warm smile, which is what he got from Ansil.

"Folks will question why I am standing on the sidewalk talking to one of you, but you know what I say to those folks?"

A.J. didn't answer, not because he didn't sort of already know what a man like Ansil Anderson thought, but because he figured that Ansil wasn't really looking for a response from A.J. just yet. "I say, 'Fuck 'em.'" Ansil Anderson removed his warm smile and A.J. didn't know how he did it, but he changed the intensity of the conversation, that was still just one-way, with nothing but his brow.

With a simple change of facial expressions, the man literally went from being the grandfather you wished you always had to being the schoolyard bully you always avoided. "People need to stay in their own lanes and quit tryin' to make the world fit into their cute little picture window." He looked around the street, but he held his palms and touched the tips of thumbs together to form a frame he could look through. "Yes, sir, we got us a pressure cooker brewin' down here." He put away his make shift picture frame and crossed his arms across his chest. "You people want to eat at the same counters, piss in the same toilet, and I hear that you folks up North are snatchin' up white women like they are candy."

A.J. took a deep breath; he still had no idea where it was going, so he decided the best thing to do was remain quiet until he knew for sure where the conversation was going. "Yes, sir-ree, Bob, we got some real stuff brewin' here in Montgomery and you know what I say?" A.J. knew what was coming, so he felt like it was time to speak up, "Fuck 'em?" Ansil Anderson burst out laughing. "Well, I'll be damned! Ole man Gibson said you was one smart son of a gun and I'll be damned if wasn't right!" He started laughing again.

A.J. looked around to see if anyone had noticed the two men having a conversation on the sidewalk, especially since Ansil Anderson was laughing as loud as he was. Ansil Anderson caught A.J. looking around with a little apprehension on his face. "I reckon it makes you a bit skittish to be standing on the sidewalk with a white man, huh?" A.J. recognized this as a direct question and knew it was his turn to respond and hopefully try and figure

## Chapter 24

out what Ansil Anderson wanted from him. "I've seen men get beat for a lot less in these parts, Mr. Anderson. I am not afraid of any beating myself, but I happen to be shopping with my wife and I don't want no trouble for her."

Ansil Anderson shook his head to acknowledge that he understood. "I see your point." Mr. Anderson took a step closer to A.J., which made A.J. take a step back and nearly back into the door of Woolworths. "No need to get jittery with me, boy. From what I hear, you could thump me and a few other men like ripe watermelons if the mood struck you." A.J. was completely confused by that comment as he had never been in a scrape anywhere in Montgomery, and truth be known, he would never go looking for one. He hated to fight. "Just settle down and relax a minute. I am only here to meet the man who knows how to get things done."

A.J. was confused even more as he searched for the words. He felt like he was on dangerous ground dealing with Ansil Anderson, but he also felt like Ansil Anderson was telling him the truth. He had no intention of trusting this man standing in front of him, but he would at least play along for a little while to see where this was going. "Suh, I wish I could place my mind exactly where yours is right now, but I sho cain't." A.J. reverted back to his Southern voice, the one he used to play the game. Just like always, he hated doing it, but he could hear his uncle's voice in his head when he ran into white man like Ansil Anderson. He never pronounced "can't" as he just did, and it made him sick to his stomach to do it.

Mr. Anderson apparently hated it, too. "Cut the damn backwoods swamp-running crap with me." A.J. was a caught off-guard by that comment, so he did exactly what Mr. Anderson said. "Mr. Anderson, I have no earthly idea what you want to talk to me about and why you have to drag me out the store and scare my wife to do it, but I can assure that I don't care for it and neither does my wife." He took a step towards Mr. Anderson, an action that surprised both he and Mr. Anderson, but neither men flinched. A.J. could tell that this man was not afraid of anything and he certainly wouldn't be backing down from A.J., so he didn't advance any further.

A.J. could feel himself tense up and realized that his fists were clinched, but more importantly, he realized that nothing good could come of this meeting if he didn't try to relax. Ansil Anderson stood perfectly still, but he smiled. "Ole Gibson has his flaws, but lyin' ain't one of them, at least to me. He lies to his wife all the time, but she knows he has some 'hide one on the side,' you might say; she don't care for his infidelity or his choice of colors, but she puts up with it. He thinks he is getting' away with it, but she knows. What he does know, and I know is that his wife is crazy as a shit house rat, but that ain't none of my business." Ansil Anderson chuckled as he said it, but as he was providing his opinion of Mrs. Gibson's mental state, he patted A.J. on the shoulder with his right hand and then with the same hand, lightly patted A.J. on the side of head as if he was petting a stray dog. A.J. didn't move. He didn't care for the gesture, but in some weird way, he could tell that Ansil was trying to be sincere.

"He said you were smart, tough, and a helluva business man." After Mr. Anderson was finished petting A.J. on the head, he took out a newspaper clipping and handed it to A.J. "You are gonna want to read that. I hate to see a young man tryin' to make his mark on the world get derailed simply because other folks make bad choices and I can tell you right now, this world is full of idiots making bad choices." The clipping was folded over a few times, so A.J. took his time unfolding it. He couldn't help it, but he could see that his hands were shaking as he tried to unfold the newspaper clipping. He got internally angry at himself for not being able to control the shaking hands better than what he was currently doing.

He took a slow deep breath with the hopes that he could steady his hands, but it didn't work, his hands were still shaking. "Those stories you hear about me aren't exactly true, so try and relax." A.J. took a break from unfolding the paper, lifted his head, and looked Ansil Anderson in the eyes. "I go get what's mine and I take care of what's mine and I don't let any son of a bitch stand in my way or cross me. You might say it's a personal code, but it seems to have worked for a long time and I don't intend to change." The more that Ansil Anderson spoke, the more confused A.J. became.

A.J. finally got the newspaper clipping open. It was an article clipped from a New York paper. A.J. tried to read it as fast as he could. The article was about the need for segregation changes across the United States and especially in South. The article specifically mentioned Montgomery and the good works that were being done by the members of the local chapter of the NAACP. The article wrote about the need to abolish Jim Crow laws and that *Separate but Equal* was not a solution, but rather a slap in the face to a nation that was built on the premise that all men were created equal. A.J. finished the article but was more confused now than he was before he read it. He could not figure out why this man would drag him out of a store and show him this.

He folded the article back to the way it was given to him and handed it back to Mr. Anderson. "I appreciate you sharing this with me, but I am confused as to why that concerns me." Mr. Anderson took the article, crumpled it into a ball, and threw it at the trash can that was placed on the sidewalk. He missed, and it rolled towards the front door of the store. "I figured you would be. Businessmen like you and me ain't got time for nonsense like this. What people do is their business until it starts to affect me and then it becomes my business." A.J. was still confused, but didn't know what to say, so he simply shrugged his shoulders in a gesture that conveyed he neither agreed or disagreed.

"Mr. Anderson, I still don't understand what this has to do with me." Mr. Anderson put his hands in his pants pockets, took a look around the streets as if he was searching for something. "Times are changin', don't know if it's for the better or the worse. but I know this: It is a natural reaction for people to resist change and when they do, things sometimes get ugly. It's up to men like us to make sure that things don't get ugly." A.J. continued to stare into the face of one of the most respected and, unfortunately, one of the most feared men in the state of Alabama but was still confused. "Say *hello* to your Uncle Marvin for me and give my apologies to your lovely wife for interrupting her shopping."

Mr. Anderson once again patted A.J. on the arm and then patted his head, but this time he wasn't smiling as he was before. When he was finished with his petting, he turned and walked away from A.J., leaving A.J. standing there on the sidewalk wondering what this conversation was about.

He heard the clang of the bell that rang every time someone went into the store and came out of the store. The noise of the bell brought him back into the moment and he turned to see that Kari was coming towards him in a hurried fashion. She had obviously been watching the two men through the window of the store. When she got to A.J., she dropped the two bags she was carrying and wrapped her arms around his neck and hugged him as tightly as she could. A.J. was surprised by the gesture, but he liked it. It made him almost forget everything that had just happened. He figured he could stand here on this sidewalk holding this beautiful woman in his arms for all of eternity and he would be as happy as he could ever be. Kari had a way of squeezing all the stress right out of him. She loosened her grip on him enough to allow her to look him in the eyes.

When she looked up at him, he was smiling. "You smiling because of him or me?" She was half joking when she said it, but she really wanted to know what this was all about. "Baby, ain't nobody in the world can make me smile like you can." He lowered his head and gently kissed her on the lips. It was a quick peck because he was still uncomfortable with public affection, but he figured she needed it at that moment, and to be honest, so did he. She pulled away from him and picked up the bags. "That man is scary, what did he want with you, baby?" A.J. let out a

## Chapter 24

breath that could have been heard across the street, shook his head, and said, "I really wish I knew, baby. He made me read some dumb ole newspaper article that didn't make a lick of sense to me."

She looked at A.J. and could tell he really was perplexed. "What newspaper article, baby?" A.J. looked around for a second until he saw the crumpled-up article lying by the door to the store. "That one." He pointed at the door. It took her a minute to realize that he was pointing at what looked like a piece of trash on the street. She put the bags back down and went over to pick up the paper. She spent a few seconds getting it un-crumpled so she could read it. She stood there for a few minutes and her hand began to shake as she held the paper.

A.J. could tell that the article meant more to her than it had to him and he could also tell that it upset her. When she was finished reading the article, she quickly folded it up and shoved it between the top buttons of her blouse. A.J. had seen her do that with money, but never with what he considered a piece of trash. "What is it, baby? Why are you sticking that in your shirt like it was money?" She looked at A.J. as seriously as she could and said, "We need to get home, we need to talk to Uncle Marvin."

She picked up the bags again and started walking toward the car. She offered no more explanation and A.J. had known her long enough now to know that all he needed to do was to follow her, keep a safe distance, and hope that he wasn't the reason for her current behavior. She might be the most beautiful woman in the world to A.J., but he knew she had a volatile side and when she decided to erupt, Lord help the person or persons that caused the eruption. She was a true force to be reckoned with.

## Chapter 25

SHE WAS QUIET ON THE ride home. When A.J. pulled under the tree in their front yard, he jumped out of the car as quickly as he could so he could open the door for her. He knew when she was in this type of mood that she would not stand to wait for any length of time, and he wouldn't dare let her open the door on her own. Because of the stuff he had seen in the war, the way his own father and mother had raised him, and for no other reason than chivalry made him feel good. He took pride in the way he dutifully waited on his Kari, she meant everything to him.

He opened the door for her, and it was just in the nick of time. She was fumbling for the handle when he managed to get her door opened. "Thank you, baby" came from her mouth, but it was muffled and hurried. She was about four steps away from him when she turned and said something about the bags, but he didn't need complete clarity, he knew she was telling him to grab the bags and bring them inside. He did as he was told, but all the while wondered why in the world her mood had changed so rapidly after she read that article.

Ms. Mimmi met him at the door with her arms crossed under her ample bosoms. This was also a pose that he was familiar with. This pose meant that he had done something wrong and

## Chapter 25

she needed an explanation, only this time, he had done nothing wrong, at least not to his best recollection, but he was willing to stand there and take whatever he had coming. "What in the world did you do to that poor child? I am 'bout tired of you men causing all kinds of trouble around here and then acting like some ole stray dog that ain't got no idea they just peed on the porch." She tried to keep her voice down because the boys were asleep, but she wasn't very good at it.

He started to answer, but he was interrupted by Kari, who had now returned from the back bedroom where she had checked on the boys and was now ready to tackle the problem that had been manufactured by her reading the article. "Ms. Mimmi, please stay with the boys, Mr. Mack and I are going over to visit with Uncle Marvin for a few hours." Having a very strong-willed women in the house was a challenge for A.J., but he managed it pretty well. Sometimes Kari and Ms. Mimmi would cross swords, but it always ended peacefully. Ms. Mimmi turned to look at Kari and said, "Young lady, I am here as a midwife, not a baby-sitter, you need to make other…"

Kari cut her off before she could finish. "Ms. Mimmi, we would not be able to manage without you, we are forever in your debt, as is Uncle Marvin. Should you ever feel the need discontinue your service to us, I will be sure and have Uncle Marvin send a currier to return your underwear, laundered free of charge, of course." A.J. felt a smile coming up from his throat and he forced it down as quickly as he could. Kari had just shut Ms. Mimmi down and it was amusing to see these two women match wits, and even more amusing to see that he had married a serious fighter. Not only was she beautiful, but she cut to the bone quickly and left a path of destruction when she wanted to.

Ms. Mimmi did not return fire because Kari had just let her know that she knew that her and Uncle Marvin were taking care of business whenever they could and for all he knew, while they were at the store shopping for fabric and the boys were asleep. Ms. Mimmi and Uncle Marvin had already shared some afternoon delight. A.J. found the thought of the two of them he'n and she'n a little repulsive, but he didn't mind, he knew that his Uncle Marvin would stick his thing in a knot hole in a fence if he thought it would give him any satisfaction. Uncle Marvin was not choosy at all, he just enjoyed the thrill of having a woman next to him and A.J. couldn't blame him. A.J. figured when he got to be Uncle Marvin's age, he would want a woman next to him, too, but he damn sure hoped it would be Kari.

The two entered Uncle Marvin's house without knocking. Kari led the way, of course. A.J. was still confused as to what their mission was, but he was not about to ask any questions now, his Kari was on a mission. "Uncle Marvin, come out here now, please." She was not yelling, but she had certainly raised her voice a few octaves. Even when she was mad, she knew better than to go back to Uncle Marvin's room. His habit of not wearing pants was getting worse by the day, but they discovered that if you gave him enough warning, he would snap out of whatever fog he was in and realize that he didn't have any pants on and would correct the situation before he took another step. They stood there in silence for just a little while, but because the house was so small, they could actually hear him zip up his pants. It was a relief to both of them to hear that.

Uncle Marvin came from the back bedroom without a shirt on, but that was okay to everyone. "What in the world are you kids waking me up from my nap for? Don't you know that a man my age has got to get at least twenty-two hours of sleep and two hours of He'n and She'n a day?" He laughed when he said it, but he could tell that Kari was not in the mood for jokes. He realized as he said it that he didn't have a shirt on and said, "Hold on, let me get my shirt." It was just a minute before he came back buttoning up an Oxford collar shirt that looked like it hadn't been ironed or washed in the last four weeks.

Kari removed the newspaper article from her shirt and took a few steps necessary to close the distance between them so she could hand the article to him. "You told me that you were not

## Chapter 25

involved in this!" Uncle Marvin looked at the article and tried to read some of it, but he crumpled it up and threw it in the trash can that was next to the coffee table that A.J. and Kari bought for him a few months back because he had very little practical furniture. "Baby girl, you worry too much, and how did you know I had anything to do with this?" Kari threw her arms up in the air after hearing that. "I didn't! You just verified it, you old fool!"

She spun around to look at A.J. "And you didn't know your uncle was the Vice President of the local chapter of the NAACP." It came out as a statement and not as a question, so A.J. didn't say anything. He was still confused about what to say or do. "No, I didn't, but why would I care? I am actually not surprised, and I am very proud of my uncle, Kari." He scratched at his backside for a second before he realized all eyes were on him. Kari had her arms crossed over her chest and Uncle Marvin had struck the same pose as Kari, and for a second A.J., thought they both looked like Christmas nutcrackers, both backs straight and faces fixed very hard on their targets, and the target was him. "Baby, change is inevitable and sitting on the sidelines waiting on someone else to do all the heavy lifting is not a good plan. Unfortunately, that is exactly what I have been doing." He scratched his backside again but decided it would be best if he crossed his arms over his chest and that way, they could all match.

"Why are you so mad at him, baby? I just don't understand." Kari uncrossed her arms and marched over to stand right in front of Uncle Marvin. She stood in front of him for a few seconds. A.J. couldn't see her face from where he stood, but Uncle Marvin could as he was looking directly at her and she was looking directly at him. Her eyes began to fill up with tears. She wiped one away, but couldn't stop the flow, so she stuck her arms out and put them around Uncle Marvin's neck. She started to cry more than A.J. had ever seen her cry. All this caught Uncle Marvin off-guard a little and he was unsure what to do, so he simply put his arms around her and patted her on the back.

Though the sound was muffled, she began to speak through her sobs. "White folks around here are all stirred up, they aren't taking kindly to the changes, and they are lashing out at folks just like you. They are mean and they mean business and I can't see why either of you fools don't understand that right now with the way things are,"

She let go of Uncle Marvin, took a step back, and turned toward A.J. "The very best thing to do is stand on the sidelines and let other folks carry the water!" She was visibly shaken, and she had raised her voice to make sure that both men understood exactly what she was talking about. "Our time will come and when it does, we will be ready, but dammit, I can't lose any of the men in my life! I just couldn't bear it!" She nearly sprinted across the living room floor of Uncle Marvin's house and leaped into A.J.'s arms and began to cry again. A.J. was still confused and couldn't help but try and clear up the confusion. "Baby, I don't understand how you knew Uncle Marvin had anything to do with the article?"

He could feel Kari loosen her grip on his neck. "For such smart men, I am amazed at how stupid both of you can be." She wiped her face on her sleeve because she couldn't find anything else. She gathered herself a little more and continued. "That visit today from that crazy man who shoots donkeys in the street and then beats a man to death with a baseball bat was not a visit for him to get to know you, A.J.!" Her voice filled the room as it reverberated off the bare walls. Uncle Marvin hated anything hanging up on the walls, so to Kari, she thought that Uncle Marvin had very poor taste in decorating. "You said that he gave his regards to your Uncle Marvin, right." She didn't ask it as a question and didn't wait for either of the men to respond before she plowed through what she wanted them to hear. "It was a message! He is warning you that your uncle is doing things to agitate people! You men are so dense!"

Both A.J. and Uncle Marvin stood still long enough to make A.J. uncomfortable, but he wasn't sure he was ready to speak. He

## Chapter 25

liked to give Kari all the space she needed when she decided to vent, and she definitely was venting on the two of them. "Baby, why would that man worry about me or Uncle Marvin?" He said it somewhat sheepishly and uncrossed his arms. He put his hands in his pockets as he tried to rationalize what she was saying. He was about to follow-up with another question, but Uncle Marvin interrupted him before he could get started. "What I do is nobody's business and I don't care what that old mule-killing idiot says or does. My ass is tired of drinking out of a different water fountain or riding on the back of the bus and being intimidated so's I won't show up and vote when it's my damn legal right to do so!" Uncle Marvin had also uncrossed his arms and became very animated. His arms were flailing around as he spoke. A.J. had never seen his uncle be this excited about anything, including the long list of women he apparently kept intimate company with. Even Kari was taken by surprise.

Uncle Marvin wasn't finished, though. "Things got to change, and I cannot sit back and wait on them to change. I've earned my way in this world and I don't know how long the good Lord wants me to stay on this Earth, so I am going to make the best of my time so that you and those two little boys next door won't have to put up with the shit we put up with today. That mean old bootlegger might be sending a message for sure, but maybe you're reading into it wrong." He stopped to draw in a deep breath and continued, "I've known of that man pretty much all my life, and one thing I know, he sold bootleg whiskey to everybody he didn't care what color you was. The only thing I knew for sure is that not one single person can give me a story about that man dirty dealing the black folks in anyway."

A.J.'s head was spinning now. His wife was dressing both of them down for something that he didn't understand and now his uncle, the same man who was timid and laid back and had told A.J. about *playing the game*, was sounding like a man on a mission that was intent on single-handedly changing the way things were in Montgomery. He was confused, but he was actually proud of both his wife and Uncle Marvin. He started to speak again, but Kari cut him off. "That's fine and dandy, but what do me and those two little boys do when those men in those sheets show up one night and decide your time is up!" She started crying again. This time, A.J. didn't wait to react, he stepped forward and grabbed her in an embrace that she didn't fight. She almost went limp in his arms. It was as if her emotions were drained and she couldn't support her own weight. He held her tightly and rubbed her back with both of his hands.

He looked up at Uncle Marvin, who had crossed his arms again, but his face said that he was through stumping for the night. He apparently didn't like to see Kari upset any more than A.J. did. "Baby girl, I didn't mean to upset you, in no way would I ever do that, but sometimes a man can't sit on the sidelines no more." Uncle Marvin took a few steps toward the spot where A.J. had Kari in a tight embrace and rubbed the back of her hair. He leaned forward and kissed her on the back of the head and then patted A.J. on the shoulder. "You kids mean the world to me. My life has been so much better since you all came into it. I mean that, I truly mean that." He let his words hang in the air just a little while longer.

He made eye contact with A.J. and somehow, he could tell that both men understood the moment and the emotion attached to it. "I can't back off because someone threatens me, or anyone else. I would rather die than see harm come to you two kids or them baby boys over there and it scares me to do what I am doing with the local chapter, but there are some things that cause you to just choke down that fear and keep moving. This is one of them." Uncle Marvin turned, opened the front door, and stepped out onto the porch. A.J. could hear the flick of a match as he knew that when Uncle Marvin felt uneasy, he had to light a cigarette. He didn't smoke often, he actually tried to hide the fact that he did smoke, but this was a time for sure that he needed a smoke.

Chapter 25

A.J. could feel Kari relax in his arms and he could feel the strength come back into her legs as she was no longer limp. She pulled away from A.J. and looked him in the eyes. "Did you know he was in the local chapter?" A.J. kissed her on the forehead and shook his head no. "I had a suspicion, but what he does is his business, baby. I can't disagree with him in what he is doing, either." He pulled her close again and said, "Folks are getting hurt, even killed, because of this stuff. Uncle Marvin is a grown man and he's made up his mind."

He could feel her shaking her head against his chest, but this time, she was shaking her head up and down as a sign that she agreed. She may not have liked it and it scared her, but for some reason, she could not explain at that moment, she understood.

# Chapter 26

A.J. SAT AT HIS DESK dreading the idea of heading out to Mr. Gibson's home. It was Saturday and he had gotten to the point that he hated leaving his boys and wife just so this man could go out and bump uglies with his mistress. It had been almost a year since Kari had her melt down when she found out that Uncle Marvin was Vice President of the local chapter of the NAACP, and everyone had pretty much calmed down.

Despite every effort he made with the phone company, they still wouldn't switch the name of his company over to him so that he could no longer be strong-armed by Mr. Gibson, so he continued his Saturday drives out to the Gibson place and continued to be greeted coldly by Mrs. Gibson, when she greeted him at all. He couldn't help it, but he felt like she treated him as if he was the one responsible for Mr. Gibson's infidelity. It was a fact that he dreaded Saturdays more than any day of the week. The only good that had come from his weekends with Mr. Gibson was that he managed to buy Mr. Gibson's 1946 Cadillac Series 75 Fleetwood limousine and had begun the process of offering limousine service along with his cab company.

Mr. Gibson had bought another Cadillac to replace it, but it wasn't a limousine. This Caddy was a four door 62 Series. A.J.

## Chapter 26

thought it rode a little rough and didn't handle nearly as well as the limo, but he didn't really care. He just simply endured the day and tried to get home as fast as he could. Some days it was a quick trip and some days it lasted all day and well into the night. He figured the amount of time that Mr. Gibson spent with Miss Olivia Compton was in direct proportion with how much stress Mr. Gibson was feeling at work or the little attention Mrs. Gibson gave him at home.

He pulled into the driveway and parked behind the shed, as usual. He pulled the brake on the Packard he had chosen for this trip and, in hindsight, he wished he would have taken the limo instead. The cab was becoming quite popular with its marine scarlet red and gold colors. It was hard to miss.

He went to the back door as he had always done and knocked on the door. There was no answer at first, but then he thought he heard a faint cry. It was either a cat or a baby and he was pretty sure that Mr. Gibson had neither, at least not here with Mrs. Gibson. He stood at the door for a minute and decided to knock again. "Hello? Mr. Gibson? Mrs. Gibson? Anyone there?" He started to get an uneasy feeling and the hair stood up on the back of his neck. It was rare that he had that feeling, but it was for certain happening now. He remembered that feeling in the war when he had his finger stuck in a man's chest and people were all around them, hunting them like animals.

He took a step back off the stoop with the idea that he was going to just get in his car and drive off. Whatever was going on, he wanted no part of. Before he could get to the bottom of the back stoop, he heard a sound he hoped he would never hear again, a gunshot. He flinched and ducked out of nothing more than pure instinct, but he didn't know where the gunshot came from. He looked in all directions and saw no one. He looked back up at the door and he saw a hole in the screen at just about the spot where he had been standing. His heart raced as he now knew the gunshot was meant for him, or was it? He tried to tell himself that it was an accident, and everything would be fine, but it didn't work. He was still close to panicking, but he didn't. He rolled out of his ducking position that he had assumed from hearing the sound of the first gunshot, and it was a good thing he did. He heard another gunshot and the thud of what he was sure was a bullet hitting the ground right beside him.

Had he not had rolled out of his ducked position, it would surely have hit him. He was one hundred percent certain now that he was the target of whoever was doing the shooting. He surveyed the area and decided it was best to make a dash for his car that was parked behind the shed. He heard another gunshot and needed no more decision-making time. He ran as fast as he could to the car. He heard a few more gunshots, but he had no idea where they were coming from. He just knew that he needed to get away from this place as fast as he could.

He made it to the car parked behind the shed when he heard another gunshot, only this time it couldn't possibly hit him; he was behind the shed and if the shots were coming from inside the house like he thought, no way they could hit him from this position. Despite being safely tucked behind the shed, he still approached the car door with caution. He stayed in a crouching position and reached for the door handle when he felt a hand on is back. He nearly jumped out of his skin when he felt a hand on him and spun around to see Mr. Gibson standing behind him. "Crazy woman inside that house, let's go."

A.J. could hardly believe that the man was standing behind him just as cool as he could be and worse, he wanted to continue the normal routine, despite the fact that his wife was shooting at A.J. "Mr. Gibson! Don't you think you should call the police or a doctor or something. She could have killed me!" Mr. Gibson stood there and shrugged his shoulders as if there was nothing he could do. "Why is she shooting at me? I didn't do nothin'!" Mr. Gibson opened the back door to A.J.'s Packard and sat down in the back seat, but left the door open as if to imply that A.J. should close it and begin his new fare. At first, A.J. just stood there, but he

## Chapter 26

heard another gunshot and decided it was best to go with his original plan and get the hell out this place, even if he had to take Mr. Gibson along with him.

"In a minute, she is going to come out of the house, and I must tell you that she is a very good shot when given time to take proper aim. She actually won a few skeet competitions at the club and she is currently learning the art of shooting long-range rifles. It was something I encouraged her to do to fill some time in her day, but in retrospect, I fear that I erred in judgment." Mr. Gibson made a sweeping motion with his hand that was clearly meant as a beckoning motion. A.J. slammed the door on his fare and jumped into the driver's seat. He started the Packard and pulled on the break release. "If you spin around to the South of the barn, she won't have a clear shot and we will be fine."

A.J. hit the accelerator and did as he was told, he swung South of the barn and did it quickly. Once he was back up on the main road and safely out of shooting distance from Mrs. Gibson, Mr. Gibson started laughing. "Good God, you should have seen the look on your face! You were scared out of your shorts!" He laughed again as if it was the funniest thing he'd ever heard or seen. A.J. did not see the humor in the situation. He slammed on the brakes and pulled over to the side of the road. He got out of the car and began pacing back and forth in front of the car.

He heard the door open but didn't bother to look until he heard Mr. Gibson speak. "She is drinking a lot. She has always known about my extracurricular actives and for the most part has been ok with it, but today she got a call from the doctor and he says she has a tumor. Pissed her off something fierce, maybe I should have stayed with her, but I am not in the mood for this today. I am in the mood for other stuff. She will calm down after she has had enough gin, and everything will be just fine."

A.J. could hardly believe what he was hearing. This man's wife had just been told over the phone, on a Saturday, that she had a tumor and her husband was going off to be with another woman. He wanted badly to beat this man with his bare fists and haul him back to his wife where he should be, but he didn't. "Then she should be shooting at you! Not me!" Mr. Gibson laughed again and started back towards the car. With his back to A.J., he said, "She shot at me before you got there. She hates where I am going and what I do, but with you, she just hates your kind. She thinks all you boys want to rape her. That's why she was shooting at you." He laughed again and got into the car and left the door open again. A.J. hated this man and wished she had hit her mark before he got there.

    He stayed quiet for the entire drive to Miss Compton's place. When they pulled in front of her house, she came out of the door and stood on the porch with her hands on her hips. She was barefooted and wearing her trademark calico print dress; the front buttons of the dress that were designed to keep her cleavage at bay were unbuttoned about half way down, leaving very little for any imagination. He heard Mr. Gibson grunt from the back seat, which A.J. took to mean that Mr. Gibson saw the same thing. Mr. Gibson didn't bother waiting for A.J. to get out and open the door and before A.J. could even set the brake, he was out of the car and had taken two big steps up the porch and had embraced Miss Compton. Before A.J. could turn the engine off, both Mr. Gibson and Miss Compton disappeared inside the house.

    A.J. decided to sit in the cab with the windows rolled up. He knew that if he got out, he would hear the bed springs or maybe worse, he might have to baby-sit little O.G. again. A.J. was not in the mood for either. Well, the truth was he was in the mood to hear his own bedsprings making their noises as he showed Kari Rae how much he loved her, but because of the boys, that was something that they had not been able to do much of. They could sneak in some fun stuff when the boys were babies in the crib, but now that they were both up and walking and getting into everything, they always seemed to end up in the bed with he and Kari. He smiled at the thought and nearly forgot what he was doing.

    It had gotten quiet in the house; he rolled down the window

## Chapter 26

every now and then to see if he could hear anything. Just when he thought they must be taking a nap or something, he would hear the bedsprings start up again and he would roll the window back up. He wondered if that little O.G. was inside watching all this and would feel bad for the boy, but this wasn't his concern. It must have been the adrenaline rush that got to him because his eyes started feeling heavy and he felt himself nodding off. He didn't like to sleep when he was around this man because he never knew what would happen next, but he couldn't help it. He fell asleep.

He heard the tap on the window as Mr. Gibson walked by the driver's side door then opened the back door of the car and slid in. He left the door open, so A.J. got out and shut the back door then climbed into the driver's seat. He was still a little slow because he had managed to get some really good sleeping in. He had no idea what time of the day it was, but he now knew it was time to go back to Mr. Gibson's house, and that thought alone woke him up. "You're getting lazy, A.J., never known you to sleep on the job." A.J. didn't say anything, he started the car and released the brake. As they were getting closer to Mr. Gibson's house, he slowed down and looked in the rear-view mirror. "What if she is still mad and wants to shoot at me some more?"

Mr. Gibson checked his shirt and to A.J., it looked like he was tucking his shirt in. "Then you better be quick, boy." Mr. Gibson let out a belly laugh as if he didn't have a care in the world. "She won't, she has had plenty of gin by now, she's probably lying in bed. She gets real 'anxious' when she drinks, if you know what I mean." He laughed again. "She will want me to give her a little pickle tickle and I swear on everything holy I don't know if I got the strength right now." He laughed again. "Just pull up to the back door and I will get out and you can just go on home." A.J. did exactly as he was told, but he sort of scrunched down in the seat so that Mrs. Gibson would have less off a target if Mr. Gibson was wrong about the gin.

# Chapter 27

"HONEY, WAKE UP." SHE NUDGED him gently, but over their time together, he became a sound sleeper. When they first got married, she remembered him tossing and turning all night, he would moan in his sleep and grit his teeth. He made the most awful noise when he would grit his teeth. She learned to simply drape an arm around him and pull herself up very close to him and she could almost feel his body relax. It wasn't easy, but now he slept hard, and all night. He told her that he had bad dreams about the war, and he figured he would have to wrestle with those demons for as long as he lived, but Kari had an effect on him like no other. She knew she calmed him, and truth be known, he calmed her too.

She nudged him a little harder and he stirred just a little. She thought she heard him mumble, but she wasn't sure. One more nudge and he came to life, a little. "What is it, baby? You ok? The boys ok? What's wrong?" He rolled over so he was facing her. The room was dark, but he could see the light flicker in the window that was across the room from them. She whispered, "Something is going on outside."

He sat up in bed, still groggy, but she was right, it was usually pitch black in the window that faced Uncle Marvin's house, but

## Chapter 27

tonight, there was a light flickering. At first, it didn't register, but then it hit him. "Shit!" He said it in a cross between a whisper and a throaty cough. "Get in the room with the boys and stay there." He threw the covers back and grabbed his pants. He slid his pants on almost in one fluid motion. He went to the dresser where he kept his WWII souvenir, a Type 14 Nambu pistol. It was a pretty common weapon carried by Japanese officers. At the end of Iwo Jima, he stumbled across one that he found tangled up in an old cargo net that was piled up in one of the caves that he and some others cleared. It was somewhat simple in nature, but you still had to know how to chamber a round, which was slightly different than American side arms.

He jammed the clip in the gun and pulled the tube, chambering a round. He went to the window and gently pulled back the curtain just enough to see, and there it was. He turned to look and see if Kari was still in the room with him, but she had already made her way to the boys. He stood there peeking out the curtain for a minute, trying to think. He needed a clear head. He stepped away from the window and made his way down the hall to the boys' room. He saw Kari sitting in the rocking chair next to where the boys were sleeping. He was amazed at how calm she was at times when he felt like any other woman would be pitching a fit.

"Stay here, I will be right back." He moved out of the room and went into the kitchen; he reached behind the cabinet and found what he was looking for. He grabbed it and went back to the room with Kari and the boys. It was a room that had no windows, one way in and one way out. He handed her the 20-gauge pump shotgun, but before he handed it to her, he pumped a shell into the chamber for her. She looked at him with her beautiful eyes and smiled. "Baby, you know I don't know how to shoot a gun." Her voice was so calm that he couldn't help but smile. His mind raced, but it slowed long enough to take in a very long stare, thinking to himself that he was probably the luckiest man in the world. She was as beautiful today as she was the first time he saw her at Freehold's barn dance serving drinks. She truly took his breath away then and she took his breath away now, right here, sitting in that rocking chair smiling at him as if she didn't have a care in the world.

He leaned down and kissed her as softly on the lips as he could. "All you have to do is point the barrel end and pull the trigger. The gun will do all the work." He smiled and looked at the bed where the two boys were sound asleep. He moved away from Kari, went to their bed, leaned over, and kissed each boy on the forehead. Yep, he was the luckiest man in the world, for sure. "I will be back, I gotta go check on Uncle Marvin and I promise I will be back." It was then that he saw her expression change from love to fear. Even in the dark room, he could see the tears well up in her eyes. "Baby, I promise you I will be back." He kissed her on the forehead, and, in a flash, he was out the door.

He slowly opened the back door and stepped out on the stoop. The cold winter air hit him harder than he expected, but the stepped out on the same stoop he had held Kari around the waist as she dealt with morning sickness. He took a crouching position and made his way to the side of the house that was parallel with Uncle Marvin's. There was a field behind both houses that was full of thistle brush, so he knew no one would come at him from behind. He checked behind and in front while staying crouched. He was at a point where he could peek around the side of the house and see some of the front yard that he and Uncle Marvin shared.

He could see the light flickering from this angle, he could hear the crackle and he knew what it was, but he couldn't see for sure. He had the Nambu at the ready and made a dash across to the back of Uncle Marvin's house. He leaped on the stoop and eased the back door open. He knew that Uncle Marvin's screen squeaked something terrible, so he did his best to be slow and not make any noise. He also knew that if Uncle Marvin was awake, He might get shot coming in the back door, so he kept very low. The screen squeaked as expected, but there was little he could do

## Chapter 27

about that. He stayed low as he eased into Uncle Marvin's kitchen. He slowly pulled the screen and then the door shut.

"Sure took you long enough to get here. I swear you gonna sleep through the rapture if you ain't careful. God's gonna call us home and you gonna be snorin' like a hibernatin' grizzly." Uncle Marvin was sitting in his usual kitchen chair reading the Bible by candlelight. "You old fart, you know I don't believe none of that Revelations stuff." He lowered the gun and slowly made his way past Uncle Marvin, through the hall, and then to the front living room. He stayed close to the walls until he got to the front window. He pulled the curtain back slowly so he could see. "Damn." He let the curtain fall back into place and pushed his back firmly against the wall, took a deep breath, and stayed in that position for what seemed like an hour.

He gathered himself and went back to the kitchen and sat down next to Uncle Marvin at the table. "You sittin' here, readin' the good book while some fools burn a cross on your lawn?" Uncle Marvin put his finger on a page and tapped on it for effect. "Look here, A.J., right here!" He continued to tap the section of the Bible he happened to be reading. A.J. tried to look, but his mind was on the problem at hand and shook his head. "Uncle Marvin! Wake up, man, I ain't got time for this and neither do you!"

A.J. started to get up, but Uncle Marvin grabbed his forearm with more strength than A.J. estimated his uncle actually had. "This is Psalms, boy, you may not want to look or believe it, but I do." He closed the Bible, let go of A.J.'s arm, and leaned back in the chair. He crossed his arms and took in the surroundings. "I will tell you it is from Psalms 9:9-10 and it says, *The Lord is a refuge for the oppressed, a stronghold in times of trouble.*" Uncle Marvin shook his head and sighed. "That's some potent shit for a time like this." Uncle Marvin smiled and this time leaned forward. "I saw what was going on outside. I came back here to fetch my shotgun and I saw that Bible laying there on the table and flipped it open without even thinking about what I was opening it for and that's the verse I read." Uncle Marvin was shaking his head as if he was either confused or amazed. "You can't tell me that God didn't make me do that. What just happened right here in this kitchen is a bonafide Christmas miracle. That's what it was, for sure!" Uncle Marvin said it loud enough that A.J. was certain that Kari heard it next door and if anyone was outside the house, they heard it too. A.J. shook his head.

He got up, went to the front window again, and peeked through the curtain. He came back to the table and said, "Well, the miracle ain't workin'. Words in that book ain't gonna change the hearts that set fire to that cross in your yard." A.J. was growing visibly upset that his uncle didn't seem to be worried at all. "They hate you, me, and anyone that threatens their way of life. I suggest you go with your original thought and grab that damn shotgun instead of that Bible." Uncle Marvin pushed his chair back, stood up from the table, and stretched like he didn't have a care in the world. "It's just a scare tactic, A.J. They don't want no trouble tonight or they would have just rushed in here while I was sleeping, yanked me out of bed, and that would be the last you'd see of me."

A.J. crossed his arms now but didn't stay that way for long. He was agitated and couldn't help but show it. "Well, their scare tactics are working on me and they are damn sure working on Kari. She is over their scared out of her mind." Which wasn't really true, Kari was calmer than he was. The image of her face, sitting there in that rocking chair smiling up at him, became so vivid that, for a second, he thought he was dreaming. Uncle Marvin came around the table, put his arms around A.J. and pulled him in one of the biggest hugs that A.J. had ever received. "Go back to your woman, A.J., she needs you more than I do. Everything is gonna be just fine." There was something about that hug that A.J. loved and hated at the same time.

He had hugged his uncle before but not like this. He hated it because the hug felt sort of final, like Uncle Marvin was giving him a hug that he would never give again, and he loved it because he loved Uncle Marvin as much as he could love anyone. He would do anything for his uncle and

## Chapter 27

at that moment, he felt like he needed to do something, but he had no idea what to do. "Listen to me, old man, you better not be planning on doing something stupid." Uncle Marvin squeezed him just a little tighter, something that just a minute before, A.J. thought was impossible. "Boy, you worry too much. I am gonna be just fine."

Uncle Marvin let go of his nephew and turned back towards the table, picked up the Bible, then turned back to A.J. "What's your plan if, God forbid, somethin' happens to you?" A.J. seemed a bit confused by the question thrown at him at this very moment. "What do you mean? There ain't nothin' gonna happen to me." Uncle Marvin sat back down at the table. He was sitting in such a way that A.J. could see the flicker of light from flames coming from the front yard in his uncle's pupils. It was almost peaceful. "I know that, boy, but for a man that always has a plan, you seem to take an awful lot for granted." Uncle Marvin rubbed his chin a little as if he was pondering the subject more. "Ok, I will play along." The two men had countless conversations over the years and A.J. knew when his uncle was trying to get him to arrive at a conclusion that his uncle had already come to. Sometimes it worked and sometimes it didn't, but A.J. was grateful for it because when it did work, it kept A.J. out of a whole lot of trouble.

"If anything happens to me, Kari and the boys will sell that house and the company and move in with you. That should be enough money to get them boys a good education and hopefully go off to college." Uncle Marvin nodded his head as if he was agreeing with him then added, "And what if I ain't here? Then what?" Up until that very moment, it surprised A.J. that he had never really thought about life without his uncle. He tried to seem unconcerned, but that question really had taken him by surprise and his uncle was right, for a man that seemed to plan for everything, he hadn't considered this one. "You plannin' on goin' somewhere?"

Uncle Marvin flipped the Bible once again then looked up at A.J. "Boy, I'm pretty near eighty years old now. I am strong as a bull, but God don't let us live forever." A.J. started to reply, but he thought that whatever was about to come out of his mouth at this moment was going to sound stupid or worse, his uncle would know for sure that his nephew hadn't bothered to consider the most obvious of dilemmas. Instead, he went back to the front window and peeked through the drapes. He still couldn't see anyone, and the flame was dying down. "I ain't havin' that thing burning in your yard any longer." A.J. opened the front door and stepped out onto the porch. He was a little upset with himself because he knew it was a stupid thing to do right now, but he figured he would rather face whatever was outside than to have to admit to his uncle that he didn't have a plan for his wife and kids. He heard his uncle say something, but he couldn't quite make it out. When he was on the porch, the air hit him a little harder than expected and he remembered he was still clad in just his underwear. He stepped off the porch and made his way to the cross his uncle had merely called a scare tactic earlier. He didn't see anyone and couldn't hear anyone and frankly, at this moment, standing there in his uncle's front yard, in his underwear, he didn't care if he did see someone, the rage he felt building up inside him meant that he would have killed anyone that dared to try anything.

    He looked around the yard and saw the metal lawn chairs sitting underneath the big oak tree that his uncle would sit under almost every evening. He grabbed one of the chairs, held it up to his chest, and rammed it into the side of the cross. It wasn't a very big cross and A.J. thought it was pretty flimsy. It fell over from the force of the chair and the minute it hit the ground, it extinguished itself. The yard became dark and peaceful again. His uncle was right, the idiots left their calling card in hopes of scaring them and had left.

# Chapter 28

HE CAME BACK INTO THE house and brushed his bare feet off on the rug that Kari put by the back door for him to wipe his feet when he came home from work. She was adamant about a clean house and would politely give him the what for if he failed to wipe his feet. He made it back to the room he had left Kari and the boys, and they were not there. His heart skipped a beat as his first thought was that he had left them unprotected and should not have. He went to their bedroom where just a few minutes earlier they were both happily sleeping. He found Kari and the boys all in the same bed. They were all asleep.

Kari was not about to let anything bother her and the boys. She was truly one strong woman. He stood over the bed for a few minutes just staring at her. He was about to go into the living room and lay down on the couch so that he wouldn't wake them when he heard her sweet voice whisper, "There is enough room for you. I hope you wiped your feet, though." She couldn't possibly see the expression on his face in the dark room, but he was smiling. This woman changed his mood in minutes.

He slid into the bed next to Kari, the boys were behind them both. He slid his backside next to her so he could feel her against him. As soon as his butt touched her, she flinched because he was cold and the bed was warm, but she slid her arm around his waist and proceeded to gently rub his chest anyway. A.J. thought for a minute that if there was a heaven, it had to be like this. He couldn't believe that just a few minutes ago he was dealing with hatred first-hand and now he was dealing with love, love at its finest. He fell asleep in a matter of minutes.

He was still groggy, but he caught a whiff of something that smelled really good coming from the kitchen. He could actually hear the bacon frying from his position in the bed. He rolled over to see the twins were still with him but had turned in separate directions. He was always amazed at how much the boys squirmed in bed. They would twist and turn in ways he never thought possible, but they were always in unison with their movements. When one turned, so did the other. He quietly slid out of bed, being very careful not to wake the boys.

He walked barefooted into the kitchen where he saw Kari standing by the stove. He walked up behind her and put his arms around her. "I love you." He kissed her on the back of the neck. He could hear her giggle just a little. "Stop it, silly. I don't want to burn myself with this bacon grease. It's popping hard this morning. Too much fat in the strips." He kissed her again and squeezed her as tightly as he dared. "You quit that now and go see if Uncle Marvin has had anything to eat yet this morning."

He let go of her, but he was smiling. "Yeah, I gotta go get rid of the shit in his yard before I go to work." She took the long fork and started pulling strips of bacon out of the pan and putting them on a plate. As she was stacking the strips up nice and neat, she said, "Do you want to talk about last night or do you want to pretend it didn't happen?" He put his head down because he really didn't want to talk about it. He hated what happened as much as a man possibly could, but he had learned from war that it simply did no good to dwell on bad events too long. The best he could do would be to put it behind him and move on. Kari, on the other hand, liked to discuss things until she had her mind wrapped around the subject. It would drive A.J. crazy because he

*Chapter 28*

was more decisive. He knew Kari was decisive, too, but it took her longer to get to the decision. "I really don't want to talk about it, but I do want to talk about one thing." He paused for a second because he hadn't expected to discuss it, but Uncle Marvin had hit home with some of his comments the night before. "If anything happened to me, ever, I want you to contact Buddy Patton. You know his real name is James Robert, same as our son."

He felt a lump rise up in his throat and he couldn't put his finger on why. Just thinking about the possibility of having to ask someone to help him with all he ever really cared about made him anxious, but he continued. "Uncle Marvin asked me to think about what you and the boys would do if something happened to me." She interrupted him by sticking her finger on his chin, which was something that she did when she was both mad at him and when she was happy with him. She would place her index finger right in the middle of his chin because he had a huge dimple that he was not find of, but Kari was.

He wasn't sure which mood she was in now. "Nothing is going to happen to you, baby, and I'm sorry I brought it up." She turned towards the stove again but turned back quickly. "Why are you so set on trusting a man that you haven't talked to in years? You don't even know if he would help us if the time came. It just sounds like some kind of war buddy mumbo jumbo that only lasts as long as the war, and that war is over." A.J. tried to come up with a proper response, but he knew that anything he said wouldn't make sense to her. As much as he loved her, he knew she would never understand the bond of a Marine, and especially the bond of Marines in combat.

A.J. looked at her with a look of frustration. It was probably the first time that he visibly showed his frustration and it surprised him more than Kari, although she could see that she had pressed an emotion in him that she was not completely familiar with. He gathered himself and immediately tried to change his expression, "Baby, the bond of men in combat lasts til death. He saved my life and I saved his. There isn't much more I can say about it because it is difficult to explain." His comments must have worked because she smiled her beautiful smile, closed the distance between the two of them, and hugged him as tightly as she could. "Baby, I trust you, and if you trust that old Marine, then I do to." She kissed him on the neck, which he always loved, it made him very frisky and took his mind off anything else that was troubling him.

He took the opportunity to cup her backside with both hands, another little treat that he enjoyed because every time he did that, it led to other stuff, which he really liked. This time, though, she pushed him away a little, but giggled in the process. "There is no time for that, the boys will be awake, and you need to go get Uncle Marvin and bring him over here to eat." He tried to hang on to her, but she broke free. "All right, baby, are we ok?' He looked at her as seriously as he could because he could not stand it one minute if he thought she was mad at him. "Baby, I love you, ain't much more ways to say it." She smiled when she said it and he returned the smile. "I can think of a few more ways to say it, but you got to come back over here and let me grab that backside of yours again." She shook her head and turned back to the stove and that extinguished any hope of a little extracurricular activity he was hoping for.

He turned away from her and made his way out the back door. The screen made its usual noise. Instead of going directly to Uncle Marvin's house, he went to the front yard to survey the results of last night's activity. As soon as he turned the corner and was standing in the front yard, he was surprised to see that there was no trace of anything. He stood there and scratched his chin, looked around to see if maybe in the dark, he had misjudged where the bonfire was located. He even looked for the old metal lawn chair that he used to knock the thing over, but it was back under the shade tree right where Uncle Marvin always sat every evening. He could see some scorched grass in the front yard, but even that was pretty faint. He figured maybe Uncle Marvin must have come out early and cleaned it all up, but he was relieved that he didn't have to clean up the mess.

## Chapter 28

He looked up in the tree as he was heading to the front door of Uncle Marvin's house, not for any particular reason other than he loved that tree. It was big and beautiful, and he guessed it was well over a hundred years old. He liked to imagine what trees could tell him if they could talk. All the history they could share, all the things they had seen in their times, but they never gave up their secrets. They simply withstood the winds and the rains and came out stronger because of both.

He opened the front door and let himself in. The door was never locked, and Uncle Marvin wouldn't think of locking it. Uncle Marvin used to tell him that if had to lock a door in any place he lived, he didn't need to live there. "Uncle Marvin!" He yelled like he always did. "Kari said to bring your old ass over for breakfast!" He smiled because he knew that Kari would never say such a thing and Uncle Marvin knew it, too. He didn't get a response, so he figured he may be in the bathroom and he made his way back to the kitchen. He didn't remember that he and Kari didn't have but just a few swallows of milk in their jar and he was going to get some from Uncle Marvin's ice box if it was good. Uncle Marvin refused to buy a refrigerator and continued to use the same ice box he had used since he struck out on his own. A.J. warned him that it was going to get harder and harder to find someone that sold those big ice blocks you put in the bottom as they were just going out of style. Uncle Marvin thought that a refrigerator you plugged into a wall was excessive and beside that, he thought that it made the milk taste funny. No, sir, Uncle Marvin was not having anything modern if he could help it, except for his Admiral radio. That was his pride and joy.

When he made it to kitchen, he could see Uncle Marvin sitting at the kitchen table, almost in the same spot he had been last night reading the Bible. "Hey, you old fart, you done went and gone deaf? I said it is time to eat." He laughed as he made his way around the table. When he saw his uncle sitting there, he knew without any more confirmation, he was gone. He felt the lump rise up in his throat and he grabbed both sides of his uncle's cheeks and touched their foreheads together. When his hand touched his uncle's cheeks, he was cold to the touch; more evidence that his uncle was dead and based on how cold he was, he figured he must have died right after they visited.

Tears welled up in his eyes and he began to cry. "God help me, I love this man. Please, God, watch over him now." He cried more than he could remember and was glad no one was around to see him lose control of his emotions the way that he was. He stepped back and looked at his uncle. He looked as peaceful as he had ever seen him. He thought it was remarkable that he was sitting up and still had his eyes open. It was a little eerie, but it was also peaceful. He died doing what he loved to do, reading the Bible. After he thought about it, A.J. got angry that his uncle's last night on this Earth was spent dealing with idiots, but he remembered the conversation about miracles happening right there in his kitchen. A.J. didn't believe in miracles, but maybe this was as close as he would ever get to one. He was thinking about how to go ruin breakfast for Kari and actually dreaded going over there to deliver such bad news when he heard a voice. "It's a damn shame, he was a good man. Tough as nails and sneaky as a cat."

A.J. spun around and was startled to see Ansil Anderson standing in the kitchen doorway. A.J. clinched his fist and took a few steps toward Ansil when Ansil pulled a revolver from his hip and pointed it directly at A.J. "Hold up there, kid, this ain't no time to do something stupid." A.J. stopped the minute he saw the gun pointed at him. He was still angry. His mind was racing now. Maybe his uncle didn't die peacefully, maybe this idiot standing in front of him had something to do with it. "Did you do this to my uncle?" Ansil put the gun back in its hip holster. "I only brought that gun cause I knew you'd blow your stack as soon as you seen me."

Ansil motioned over to his uncle who was still sitting at the table as peacefully as he ever was. "It's time I filled you in on things." Ansil walked into the kitchen and grabbed a glass out of the cupboard. He reached into the ice box and poured some of the milk that A.J. intended to use for breakfast. "Never could

## Chapter 28

get my fill of the stuff. I could keep a milk cow workin' nonstop if you'd let me." A.J. turned so that he could keep his shoulders squarely pointed at Ansil Anderson. "I asked you a question and I don't give a shit about your milk craving." Ansil took a drink of the milk and shook his head as he swallowed. "No, I reckon you don't." He took another drink of milk then walked over and sat down at the kitchen table directly beside his uncle. "I found out what those hooded assholes was planning yesterday and sent some men out here to keep it from happening, but they were just a little too late. My boys scared off that pack of pussies and was about to take down their calling card when you came outside." He looked up at A.J., who was now standing directly in front of Ansil, but on the opposite side of the table. "Go on and sit down, Marvin here ain't going nowhere and neither am I, at least not until you get to hear what I have to say." He motioned for A.J. to sit down, but A.J. was not in the mood to sit with Ansil Anderson or his uncle at the moment. "I didn't see nobody when I came out." Ansil took another drink of his milk. "No, they knew you might try to shoot them so they backed out across the field so you couldn't see them."

A.J. could feel his fists clinching at the end of his arms and he did nothing to try and hide it as he had done on the sidewalk in front of the store the day he first met Ansil Anderson. "You better quit lying to me and start making sense, you old horse killing fool." Ansil reached down toward his pants where he had placed the gun and A.J. thought for sure he was going to pull it back out, but he didn't. Instead, he pulled a handkerchief out, slung it around until it had unfolded from its crumpled state, and blew his nose. As he was blowing his nose, he said, "Kid, I am a lot of things, but a liar ain't one of them. I tell you the truth even when it hurts, that's why I am here now. Sit down and quit acting like a shithead. There ain't but one white person in this town that got the stones to come sit here at this table with you and get you up to speed on what is going on in this backwards ass town, and that's me. So, sit your ass down and listen!"

He slammed his milk glass down on the table as he said it, which caused some of the milk to spill out over the top and onto the table. There was still some agitation in his voice, but he calmed down and wiped the milk off his hand and off the table. "Your uncle was dead when my boys finished cleaning up that mess out front. I know cause they told me. They peeked in through the back window; the oil lamp was still burning on the table then and from the window they could see he had gone on to meet the Man, if you believe in that kind of shit." A.J. was still having a hard time understanding why this man was here, now, sitting at the table talking to him. "Oh, so your men can tell by candlelight if a man is dead?" It wasn't a question as much as it was A.J. being as sarcastic as he could. "Man, I ain't got time to listen to your horseshit, I got to go tell my wife that my uncle is dead."

Ansil Anderson leaned back in his chair and let out a deep breath. "No need, I got some folks over at your house eating breakfast with her, probably the boys, too. Cute little devils, they are." A.J. took a step towards Ansil Anderson and before A.J. knew it, he was staring at the barrel of a gun again. "You do anything to my family, and it will take way more than a gun to stop me!" A.J. was furious, while he was over here, there were men at his home! "I told those boys that are simply watching your family while we talk that if you came over there by yourself to assume that you got the best of me and they were to send you all to meet your uncle, including those two adorable little boys." A.J. could not believe this man could be so calm while describing killing the way he did.

Ansil slammed his hand down on the table and since he didn't have the milk glass in his hand, he grabbed it and threw it at the ice box where it shattered. "Now, sit your ass down! I am sick of this shit already! You want to see a hot head go to work, then just keep trying to press my damn buttons! I will splatter your sorry ass all over Uncle Marvin here and then I will go cook those little boys in a frying pan and make me a sandwich out of them! Don't fuck with

Chapter 28

me!" The room got quiet and the two men just stared at each other for a few minutes. Ansil still had the gun pointed at A.J. as they played the staring game. "Fact is, those men last night came here to hang your uncle from that tree in the front yard and they were going to make you watch while they did it. I ain't about to tell you what they had planned for your wife. Instead of being home with their families celebrating the holidays, they showed up here. They been bragging about it for days now." His voice became calmer as he said it. He certainly had a way of getting a man's attention and he had A.J.'s attention right now. "I stopped it all, you hear that, kid, I stopped every bit of it."

He put the gun back in the holster for the second time. "In their simple minds, your uncle here was causing trouble with the help of the NAACP and he needed to be removed. Fact is, ain't none of them worth a pile of donkey shit." He paused and rubbed his forehead. I told you on the sidewalk that we were living in a messed-up world, you remember what I said about it?" A.J. could think of nothing but his wife and boys, his jaw was clinched as tightly as his fists, but he tried to focus. "You said, 'Fuck 'em.'"

Ansil Anderson laughed again as he had done on the sidewalk that day. "Yes, sir, that is exactly what I said then and that is what I am saying by being here now." A.J. relaxed his hands, took a breath, and sat down. He was confused, but obviously there was some truth to what this man was saying. "Ok, you have my attention, I want to get to my babies, so let's hear it." Ansil leaned forward and put his elbows on the table then folded his arms together as if he was leaning forward to share a big secret. "I told you, I got no beef with anyone. Skin color don't mean shit to me as long as you drink. Hell, it's Christmas! People should be drinking and having fun, but instead they pull this crap."

Ansil proceeded to tell him that Uncle Marvin was arranging meetings and was in heavy communication with some of the folks in Atlanta. He spoke very highly of his uncle, which caught A.J. off-guard a little. He said he had known his uncle for many years and that Marvin was the only man he trusted in this whole town and that whatever Marvin said was as good as gold and he always kept his word. What he told A.J. next almost made A.J. jump from the table again and run over to Kari and the boys, and not because he thought any of Ansil's men would hurt them.

# Chapter 29

ANSIL WALKED WITH A.J. FROM Marvin's home to A.J.'s, but they really didn't walk. After Ansil finished filling A.J. in on the pulse of the local idiots, A.J. practically ran to his house with Ansil pacing close behind. When they reached the back door, A.J. could see through the screen that there were two men sitting at his table and Kari was standing against the cabinets. She had her arms crossed and a look on her face that A.J. had seen before. It was the look of anger that always scared him. There was no doubt that she was beautiful, but when she was angry, she was scary to A.J.

When he stepped into the kitchen, he went straight for Kari and hugged her. She may have been angry, but she let some of her stress go when she felt his arms around her. He turned to look back at Ansil as he had now entered the kitchen. Ansil understood the look. "Let's go, fellas." He turned to look back at Kari and A.J. "Ma'am, I am sorry if we frightened you, but I assure you it was necessary to do it this way, we didn't want your husband shooting us." The two men at the table stood up and walked out the back door, leaving just Ansil. A.J. and Kari in the kitchen. Ansil tipped his hat to Kari then looked at A.J. "I don't know what you can do about it, but at least you know. I've done about all I can do." He didn't exit through the back door like the other two. Ansil Anderson never entered or exited a back door of any place, he wanted to make sure that people knew he didn't sneak in or out of anywhere.

After the kitchen was cleared, he turned back to Kari, pulled her close to him, and squeezed her as tightly as he could. Even with all that had transpired, with armed men breaking into her house making her and the boys stay in the kitchen without saying much to her as to why, and worrying about her husband out facing those pathetic men hiding behind masks and in the cover of darkness, she was confused, but never once did she ever think for a second that her husband was not in control and would not be able to handle whatever was thrown at him, but this hug he was giving her at this very moment was different.

Kari could tell that there was something very wrong. She pulled away from him and put both her hands on his face. She held his face in her hands and stared deeply into his eyes. It was a stare that A.J. loved and hated. He loved it because he believed that when she stared at him this way, he could see straight into her soul and he knew that he loved her with every fiber in his body, but he hated it because he knew she could see right into his soul and he hated being transparent to anyone, even her. He felt like it made him weak and if he was weak, he thought he would be vulnerable.

He could feel the tears streak down his cheeks as they stared at each other and could do nothing to stop the flow. He tried to mouth the words that his uncle, their uncle, had gone on to meet the Man, but the words came out screechy, which made him mad. Kari must have understood his screechy words as he explained that Uncle Marvin had simply passed away on his own and not at the hands of those men because she began to cry, too. She hugged him tightly and whispered in his ear, "He is with God now, and there, he will have peace." He felt some of the stress of the night leave his shoulders, but not all of it. He regained his composure, pulled away from her enough to see her face and said, "There's much more to the story, baby."

# Chapter 30

BUDDY TRIED TO LAY DOWN and rest after reading the letter, but he couldn't sleep. He laid there on the floor where he had every night since Doris had died. The floor was cold, but he really didn't feel it. The three shots of Old Fitzgerald were keeping him warm at the moment. He let the words of the letter appear in his head as if they were floating above him. He would snatch one out of the air and hold it in his hand, which led to another, and then another. Each time he grabbed a word, he slid further towards his days in the war, and he hated it.

Sleeping with Doris helped him get over the nightmares, but sometimes even her soft touch and the way she would drape her arm and leg over him to settle him when he would scream was not enough. He would often have to get up, go out onto the porch, and look at the stars. The wonder and awe of the stars and universe actually helped him remember the war was over and he would go back to bed. Doris was always there, pretending to still be asleep, but he knew she wasn't. Just as soon as he slid back into bed, she would wrap herself around him and he would soon be asleep. He felt guilty sometimes because she always woke up when he had bad dreams and had to get up, but sometimes she would slide out of bed and he would never know it.

He missed her more than he knew he would ever miss someone. She made him a better man and now he was on his own. He tossed and turned and continued to grab the words of the letter from Corporal Jerome Mack from the air that floated around his head. Words like desperate, justice, help, protect, and the words that lingered the most were *Semper Fi*.

He got up, lit the oil lamp that sat beside his and Doris's bed, sat down on the bed, and opened the letter again. As he was opening the letter, he heard little footsteps and looked up to see that both Janie and Jimmy were standing in the doorway rubbing their eyes. Both had bed heads; he almost laughed when he saw them with their hair going in a million different directions, but he didn't. Truth was, he had never seen anything more pleasing to the eye than his kids standing in that doorway, in their sleep shirts. "What's the matter, kids, ya'll need to go back to bed. We have a lot of work to do tomorrow." Jimmy took his hands away from his eyes for a minute and said, "Can we sleep with you?" Buddy put the letter back down on the night stand, realized that his bed was still made because he hadn't slept in it since she died, turned and pulled the covers back and said, "Come on, jump in before you catch a cold."

Both Jimmy and Janie ran to the bed and jumped in, taking their spots with Jimmy on the outside and Janie in the middle. Once they were in their places, he pulled the covers over them, looked down at the pallet he had been sleeping on for the last few nights, turned the oil lamp off, and crawled in next to his babies. As soon as he pulled the covers over himself, he felt Janie put her little arm on his chest and scoot up really close to him. The emotion of that touch brought tears to his eyes and he felt guilty again. He should be the one making his babies feel better and here was Janie, in her own angelic way, comforting him. In the quiet dark room, he heard Janie whisper, "The bed smells like mommy." He choked back the tears and was grateful that it was dark and they couldn't see him crying.

## Chapter 30

He rose quietly after a few hours of sleep, there really was a lot of work to do, but he couldn't stop thinking about the letter. He grabbed it off the night stand and headed into the kitchen where he would need to figure out how to make some coffee. Doris always made the coffee while he went to the barn and checked on Agnes. It was the same routine every morning, he would go out with the intent of yanking a little milk from Agnes, but she would kick up a fuss and he would simply throw some new hay at her and head back into the house where Doris would have the coffee already made.

She would also have put some old coveralls on with her rubber boots because she knew that every morning, Agnes would not let him draw any milk and Doris would have to go out and do it instead. He had watched her do it and he didn't see that Doris handled Agnes any better than he did, but it would nearly make him angry because the minute that Doris pulled up the stool and sat down next to Agnes, that silly cow would act like she was the sweetest thing on the planet. He remembered this morning that even in old coveralls and rubber boots, Doris was the most beautiful woman in the world. Some mornings, he would grab her before she headed out to draw from Agnes and squeeze her tightly. He would tell her that she was the sexiest woman he ever saw. And every time he said it, she would blush and try to shoo him off as if he was being silly. She would say things like, "In these old coveralls! Heavens no!" It might have been a simple and silly routine every morning, but it was their routine, and now it was over.

He dropped some more kindling in the stove, but he was happy that it was still relatively hot. The flames flickered inside, and he released the damper for one of the burners. He took the coffee pot to the sink and pulled the pump handle just once and water began to fill the old blue ceramic pot. Once the pot had plenty of water, he stuck the stem back down and filled it to the top with coffee grounds. He was pleased with his work since he wasn't really sure how it all worked. He capped the top and set the pot on the slightly open damper and decided it was time to go let Agnes know who was boss. When he got to Agnes, she gave him a look that he didn't like, so he decided that the two of them needed to have a little talk.

"Now, look here, you stubborn hunk of leather. You'll just need to get used to me, my hands, and the way I do things, otherwise that milk you got will fester, your teats will swell, and then you'll end up in that big dairy farm in the sky, so you just might as a well relax and try and enjoy it." She bellowed a little then looked away as if she heard him but was having none of it. He found the stool and sat it beside her back right hind quarter. He slid the bucket under her then patted her on the flank. He was surprised to see that she didn't move, but she did manage to whack him a good one with her tail. "Now that was uncalled for. I haven't even touched you yet." He rubbed his hands together to warm them up because he remembers that Doris told him that no woman liked cold hands, especially in such a sensitive place.

He reached under her to grab a teat and to his surprise, he started whistling one of his favorite tunes, which was a Tommy Dorsey tune called *Boogie Woogie*. Buddy had no musical talent and couldn't sing a lick, but he knew how to whistle, and he loved Tommy Dorsey. Apparently, Agnes liked Tommy Dorsey, too, because the minute he started to squeeze and pull, she started to produce. It then hit him that every time Doris sat down next to Agnes, she would sing to her. At the time, he thought it was silly, but he never complained because Doris had a beautiful voice and he loved to hear her sing anytime she decided to cut loose. Now, he was putting two and two together and figured out that this cow liked to be courted a little before she would participate. He continued to whistle and shook his head. He thought to himself, *Women...*

Proud of his work, he placed the milk bucket on the table along with the eggs he collected from the hens that morning. He searched for the cast iron skillet and found it. He really hadn't cooked anything since he and Doris married. He knew how to

## Chapter 30

from his days in the war, but he really didn't care for it and was certain that no matter what he cooked, it wasn't going to taste as good as hers. He had little mouths to feed, so he pushed his culinary insecurities aside and went to go wake up the kids. They would both have to help him with the chores this morning so that he could go into town and make arrangements for the trip. As he was about to go wake them up, he saw the letter on the table again and opened it.

*Dear Sarge,*
*It took me a little bit to find your location, but with the help of a kid that works here, I managed to do so. I hope you made peace after the war as I have. I'm afraid I have a piece of bad news, well, bad for me. I have been accused of something I didn't do, and I fear I might be in a desperate spot and could use some help. I'm sitting here in this God forsaken jail cell in Montgomery and, just so you know, I ain't no killer and I didn't do what they say I did. I certainly don't trust the justice system in this part of the country. I'm afraid I don't have many more places to turn right now, but my main concern is my family. If anything happens to me, I would be obliged if you'd look after and protect them. Semper Fi!*
*Respectfully,*
*Corporal*
*Jerome Mack*
*U.S. Marines*

## Chapter 31

HE SCRAMBLED THE EGGS FOR Janie and made them sunny-side up for Jimmy. He knew how they liked their eggs and he considered himself a pretty fair hand at making eggs, but as far as the bacon, he let that cook just a little too crispy. When he had the plates on the table, he started to turn and go get the kids, but Jimmy was already walking into the kitchen and Janie was trailing right behind him. Both were still rubbing their eyes but were awake enough to offer a good morning to him.

There wasn't much talking at the table, so Buddy used the time to think through what he needed to do. When he had it straight in his mind how he would handle the letter, he cleared his throat. "Jimmy, I am going to have to take a trip and I need you to look after your sister." Janie dropped her fork on her plate and lowered her head. Although her hair now covered her entire face and hung down in what was left of her eggs, he could see her back heave up and down and knew she was crying. "Janie, look at me, baby." She didn't look up at first, but then slowly raised her head. "I will be back, but I have to help a friend." She nodded up and down and then lowered her head again. "Daddy." Jimmy sat his fork down on his plate; his face was stern and as grown up looking as Buddy had ever seen.

*Chapter 31*

The look actually caught Buddy off-guard a little. Buddy sat his fork down, too, and gave his son his undivided attention. "How long will you be gone?" Buddy drew in a breath because he had a feeling he knew why Janie was crying, it was simply too soon to leave them after their mother had just left them. The emotional strain was just too much. Buddy smiled and put his hand on Jimmy and reached across and put his hand on Janie as they were both in arm's reach from the table. "You know, I was just thinking, it's winter, the crops aren't due to be put in for a while yet, maybe all three of us could take a train ride to Alabama and see some friends. What do you think about that?" Immediately Janie raised her head up and smiled, but the tears were still streaming down her face.

Jimmy smiled, too, but Buddy could tell there was something else on his mind. "Son, are you not wanting to go?" Jimmy glanced out the kitchen window toward the barn and then he looked back at his daddy. "Agnes can't stay by herself, daddy. The chicken will need some scratch every day." He stopped for a second as if he was scared that he was talking too much, but then he looked down at the floor next to the heater where Betty-Jean had curled up for warmth. "And she needs looking after, too." Buddy smiled even bigger and his heart swelled. He was so proud of his young son for thinking about the responsibility of being a farmer and caring for things that could not care for themselves. "Well, son, you know I hadn't thought of that. I sure am glad I have you around to help me remember such things."

Buddy already had worked out a plan for the animals while he tossed and turned in bed with the kids last night, but he wanted Jimmy to feel like he had a stake in what happened around the house. He would need that attitude from both of his kids if he intended to make a go of things without his wife and their mother. He could see Jimmy swell with pride for this was the first time he had been able to contribute to the decision-making of the Patton household. The one thing that Buddy found amusing was that Jimmy was not concerned about missing school.

*Choice of Honor*

"Well, Jimmy, I reckon I need to get someone to look after the place while we are gone. I think I need to go into town today and work that out." Buddy leaned back in his chair, looked up at the ceiling, and showed some worry on his face so that the kids could visibly see it. "I reckon that means you'll have to stay here today and look after your sister and the animals. I'm not sure I can heap that much responsibility onto you." Jimmy nearly jumped straight up. "I can handle it all, daddy, I promise. Everything will be just fine! Really, me and Janie know how to do everything, including draw milk from Agnes this evening!" Buddy laughed, sat forward, and then touched his babies on the arm again. "Well, then, it's settled, you two stay here and handle the chores and I will find us someone to look after things while we are gone."

Breakfast the rest of the morning was quiet, but happy. The kids polished off everything on their plates and Jimmy snatched the last two pieces of bacon from the stove before anyone else could. They all cleaned up the kitchen, which Buddy found amusing, they usually didn't clean up so easily. Even Betty-Jean did her part by licking the floor under the table. That part really wasn't that abnormal for Betty-Jean as Janie always dropped a few things under the table for her. Buddy realized that his plan of trying to get back into a routine around the house after the funeral would just have to wait. Maybe a trip for the kids was what they needed.

Buddy knew of only one person he trusted to look after his place, and he would go visit Clancy Biggars before he got busy slotting mail. He cleaned up and made sure that Janie's hair was combed the best he could. He would never do it as well as Doris and honestly never wanted to. Janie seemed to know this as he was combing a particularly bad section of tangled hair and she let out a little yelp. Buddy apologized and actually tried to blame the roughness on the brush he was using when Janie interrupted, "It's ok, daddy, you'll never do it as good as mommy, but I wouldn't want anyone else to do it but you." He smiled as he continued to brush, but he could feel the water building up in his eyes. He

## Chapter 31

quietly thanked the good Lord for giving him kids, these kids. He wasn't much of a praying man, but at that moment, he felt like he needed to square up his gratitude with the Man.

Ole Blue kicked up a little fuss that morning and didn't want to start, but after a little sweet talking and few pumps into the carburetor, she kicked over and was ready to roll. He covered up in the blanket as best he could and vowed to get the heater in that truck fixed just as soon as he got back. He pulled in front of Clancy's repair shop and left the truck running. He didn't want to risk her not starting in town.

"Hello, Buddy! I didn't expect tuh tuh tuh tuh see you so soon." Buddy couldn't figure out why Clancy stuttered because there was no one else in the store and no reason for Clancy to be nervous, or at least he thought, until he heard a voice behind him. "Hello, Mr. Patton, are you and the children all right?" Buddy turned to see Miss Ellen Conner holding some mail in her hand. "Uh, hello, Miss Conner, we are all fine, I just needed to ask Clancy for a favor this morning." Buddy had no idea why he shared his reasons for being in the store that morning because he certainly didn't owe her any explanation, but it just came out. She must have noticed a little anxiety in his facial expression. "No need to explain, Mr. Patton, I was merely inquiring." She blushed a little when she said it and now Buddy felt like a heel for being so transparent.

"The children will be back in school after we commence from Christmas break, I take it?" Buddy tried to answer without telling a lie because he knew there was no way they could take a trip to Alabama and be back in time for school. "Uh uh uh uh I am not sure, we decided we are going to visit some family in Alabama." He stuttered almost as bad as Clancy and immediately understood what Clancy goes through with every conversation with people he was uncomfortable around.

He didn't understand why he was so nervous talking to this woman. She was genuine, he had already figured that out. She wasn't nosey like the rest of the people in this town. She was

*Choice of Honor*

pretty, but she was not nearly as pretty as his Doris, so he just decided that there was no answer to this question. He turned to look at Clancy and said, "I was wondering if you could look after the place while we are gone. There ain't much to it, just throw some new hay at Agnes, throw down some scratch and gather all the eggs you can eat, but you might have to bring Betty-Jean into town with you because she just gets too cold outside."

Clancy was about to answer when Miss Conner interrupted, "Not to pry, Mr. Patton, but the children and I will be studying Animal Husbandry when class resumes, and it would be a delight to have Betty-Jean stay with me so that she can be in class with us." To Buddy, this didn't seem as much of an offer as it did a command. Buddy could tell when he needed to say yes, Doris had trained him in a somewhat similar fashion. "I think that would be just fine, ma'am, and I thank you." Miss Conner thanked both men for their time and inquired with Clancy as to when her heater would be repaired. Apparently, the classroom needed some extra heat.

Buddy stood patiently and let the two discuss business. When she exited the store, Buddy turned to Clancy. "Well, what do you think, can you swing it?" Clancy put some things away under the counter and said, "Of course I can, I will even tote Betty-Jean over to Miss Conner's place tomorrow morning. I assume you are going to leave in the morning?" Buddy was pretty sure he would leave with the kids in the morning, but had toyed with the idea of leaving that night because they were going to have to drive to Lubbock to catch the train because the train that carried people instead of cows that direction ran out of Lubbock, but he decided to let the kids have a good night's rest.

He finished the last of the instructions for Clancy and shook Clancy's hand. The two vowed to go turkey hunting soon, which to Buddy sounded like a pretty good idea. He loved to hunt and fish, but he knew now that Doris was gone, he would have to either take the kids hunting or find someone to help watch the kids for a few days. It was stuff like that that continued to pop

## Chapter 31

into his head, and it was making him tired. He never knew how much Doris handled to make his life easier until she was gone.

He stepped out of Clancy's store and headed for the truck when he heard his name called again. "You come into town to give me my five dollars?" Buddy turned around to see Bob Boatright walking toward him. "Don't owe you five dollars, Bob." Buddy had no idea what Bob was talking about and really didn't care, he didn't even care if he skipped the cordials with Bob, so he just stepped off the sidewalk without so much as a hello or even an inquiry as to this mystery five dollars. "Hey, don't walk away from a man when he is trying to talk to you, that's just down right rude."

Buddy reached for the door handle of Ole Blue when he felt a hand placed on his forearm. Buddy knew it was Bob Boatright without even turning to see. Buddy looked slowly down at the hand that was gripping his forearm, but never looked up, he just continued to stare at the hand and said, "You'll need to take your hands off me." Bob reacted by tightening his grip on Buddy's forearm. "Your dog killed my dog after I'd paid five dollars for him over in Snyder and I am here to get my money back." Buddy never looked up, he just continued to stare down at Bob's hand. Without uttering any words, Buddy grabbed Bob's wrist with one hand, spun around and grabbed Bob by the throat and slammed Bob backwards onto the hood of Ole Blue. Bob immediately resisted but he was no match for Buddy.

Buddy was a hand-to-hand combat expert and instructor in the military, and he was good at it. When Bob realized he couldn't get loose, he started making gurgling sounds, but couldn't string any words together. Buddy kept the grip on his throat but leaned in close to Bob. "Bob, you're as dumb as a bag of bent hammers. I asked you nicely to take your hands off me and you chose not to. Your dumbass Hitler dog got his ass kicked, which is what I will do to you the next time you try to collect on money that ain't yours." He let go of Bob's throat and Bob slid down the hood of the truck until he was sitting on the ground next to the driver's side front wheel. He held his throat, gagged a little, and tried to catch his breath. "Oh, and if you ever touch me again, the undertaker will collect five dollars from your family. You have my word on that."

Buddy jumped into the cab of the truck that he had left running. Bob was still leaning against the wheel when Buddy started backing out. Bob panicked and lunged away from the truck fast enough to hit his head on the steps in front of Clancy's store. Buddy smiled and waved at Clancy who had come out to see what was going on. Clancy waved back and smiled because he knew that whatever Bob had done, he deserved it.

Buddy put Ole Blue in first gear and eased off the clutch. Just as he was about to shift into second gear, he saw Arthur Lee Henry waving at him from the sidewalk in front of Arthur's office. His office was right on the corner of Littlefield Drive 6th Avenue and he was there almost all the time. He seemed to be trying to say something, so Buddy slowed the truck down and rolled down the window. "Arthur Lee." Arthur Lee stepped off the sidewalk and approached the passenger side of Buddy's truck. It was cold, but Arthur didn't have a coat on. The cold didn't seem to bother him, but Buddy sure hated it. "I'd like to come out and visit with you when the time is right, Buddy."

Buddy thought that was a strange request because the whole time Buddy had lived in Littlefield, Arthur Lee never visited him. "What about, Arthur Lee?" Arthur Lee reached up like he was looking for something in a breast coat pocket, but he realized he didn't have a coat on. It was actually comical-looking to Buddy. He thought to himself that even rich folks are absent minded. "Well, shit, I left it in my coat pocket!" He looked back at his office but seemed to realize that it would be improper for him to ask Buddy to wait while he ran back inside.

Arthur Lee was rich, for sure, but he did not lack for manners. "Just want to visit with you about your property, Buddy. Times are changing here in West Texas and I think your property can produce more than cotton, my friend." He looked back at

## Chapter 31

his office again and decided to end it at that. "Time just ain't right now, we all still mourn for the loss of your missus, but when you have a chance, I'd sure like to visit with you." Just like always with Arthur Lee, he smacked the inside of the truck door with his hand, turned on his heels, and headed back inside. He hadn't even given Buddy time to respond. Arthur Lee spoke his peace and moved on. Buddy had no idea what he was referring to, but he knew that Arthur Lee was right about one thing, now was not the time.

# Chapter 32

THE TRAIN WAS QUITE AN adventure for Janie and Jimmy as neither had seen nor done anything like it. Buddy knew that the trip would take their little minds off the pain of losing their mother, but it did nothing to help ease his mind. Janie nearly pinched a hole in his thigh when the train made its first lurch forward as they began the journey East to Montgomery. After a few minutes and the train picked up more speed, things smoothed out and she relaxed. Jimmy had to sit by the window, and he sounded like a radio show as he called out everything that he saw. He was fascinated with the view from the window.

After a few hours of nervous energy, both Janie and Jimmy succumbed to the motion and the rhythm of the train and they both fell asleep in his lap. Buddy placed his hands on both of their backs and felt their little chests rise and fall as they slept. He wanted the same peace that they had at that very moment, but he knew it would never be that way for him. He wondered how he could possibly help the man who had saved his life so many years ago. He didn't know the area, but he certainly understood the racial divide that still existed, despite the fact the country had gone to war to stop a man named Adolf Hitler from taking over the world.

## Chapter 32

It was going to be a long ride, so he leaned back in his seat, stoked Janie's beautiful hair, tilted his head back, and before he dozed off, he thought of his lovely Doris. He missed her and he regretted never taking her on a train ride somewhere, anywhere. He took everything for granted, especially his kids and his wife. He promised himself that he would never let that happen again. He was not wealthy by any stretch, but the crops had been very good the last few years and he was smart with money.

Even though he tried not think about it, his mind reflected on the events of the war that could be attributed to this train ride. *Semper Fi* was not just a catchy term to him, he believed in its meaning and its core. He understood that without the sincere commitment that went along with the simple utterance of those words, everything he stood for meant nothing. He really didn't know Alvin Jerome Mack, their brief encounter only lasted a day, but he was certain that without the help of Corporal Mack, Janie and Jimmy would not have come into this world because he would not have survived that day.

He sat there in the seat of the passenger car thinking about his run in with Bob Boatright and how he had stopped by the Army recruiting station to see if maybe they could give him any information on anyone from his Marine unit that may be living in Alabama, or preferably Montgomery, since that was where he was headed. Buddy thought that the guy at the Army recruiting station didn't try to help very much and he also thought he was smarmy and arrogant. If Buddy hadn't just throttled Bob Boatright, he might have done the same to that smarmy little fart, but he decided that he would just let it go and try to figure it all out when he got to Montgomery. He would deal with the smarmy Army guy when he got back to Littlefield. He laughed to himself when the words Army and smarmy came out.

Janie shuffled and moved her head on his leg from one side to the other, but when she lifted her head, he could see that she was leaving a nice little puddle on his pants. He never understood how such a little girl could drool so much. Some mornings her entire pillow would be soaked. It never seemed to bother her, she would simply sleep in the puddle.

The porter nudged him on his shoulder, which spooked him a little. He hadn't realized he had fallen asleep. He remembered looking down at Janie's head in his lap and the drool that she was leaving. He remembered looking at Jimmy with his head leaned against the window and he was sound asleep. The window was dark as the night had snuck up on him, which might explain why he dozed off. "Sir, I am sorry to wake you, but we will be stopping in Dallas shortly." Buddy tried to sit up, but the position he was sitting in with Janie on his lap made it difficult to move and he found that his back was stiff now. "Uh, ok. Did you need to wake me for that?"

Buddy was slightly perturbed about being told they were going to stop, Buddy would have been just fine sleeping through the stop. "I am sorry, sir, but we will be adding passengers to this car. The three seats across from you will be occupied." Now he understood. That wasn't a big deal to Buddy. The kids would sleep most of the way, so they wouldn't be a bother and he would more than likely snooze along with them. It was a long ride. "Ok, thanks for letting me know." The porter turned and walked back out through the door. Buddy put his hand on Janie and leaned back to almost the same position he was in when the porter nudged him awake. It wasn't long before he was sound asleep.

He heard the door to their passenger car open. So, he opened one eye and tried to sit up straight again. The pain in his back was worse now than it was when the porter woke him. He had no idea how much time had passed, all he knew was that he was sleeping soundly right now, regardless of the uncomfortable position he was sleeping in, and it all surprised him. He hadn't slept well in a very long time, but there was something about this trip that was giving him a small amount of peace. Janie and Jimmy didn't budge when the two men and a lady entered the small compartment that now just got smaller. The two men were

## Chapter 32

quite large. He estimated that one of the men had to be six and a half feet tall, for sure, and the other was quite a bit shorter, but stocky. The woman was petite, smelled like roses, and smiled as she walked in.

The two men waited for her to be seated in the middle and then they both wedged her in snuggly between them. They all seemed to respect that the children were asleep and made whispered gestures to Buddy as they settled in. The lady pulled a Bible from the big bag she was carrying and placed it on her lap. She didn't open it but took her hands and stretched them out so that they were in front of the two men. Both men seemed to know what to do and they grabbed her hands so that they were all connected by holding hands. Once they were firmly locked together, the lady bowed her head and began to pray. The men bowed their heads and remained silent. Buddy wasn't sure what to do, so he just stared straight ahead. The lady kept her voice low, but Buddy could hear what she was saying: *"Lord, watch over us as we embark on our journey. Give us the strength to see it through to the end, the patience to endure the hardships, and the wisdom to solve our problems. In all these things we pray. Amen."* The men said *Amen* when she was finished and they all three looked up and seemed to stare straight at Buddy.

Buddy didn't flinch, he felt for a second that he was about to get chastised for not praying along with them, but he was never one to pray and he certainly didn't flinch when it came to intimidation. The stare lasted for a few seconds when the lady cracked a smile. "Beautiful little angels you have there." Buddy drew in a breath and hadn't realized that Janie had woken up and shifted her little body as closely to Buddy as she could. She was trying to hide behind Buddy but was doing nothing more than wedging her face between his back and the back of the seat. Before she got her face completely wedged between him and the seat, she tried to whisper to him, but it didn't come out as a whisper. "They are a different color."

The lady looked up and down at the two men sitting beside her, then looked back at Buddy. "My goodness, she's right you

## Choice of Honor

know." Buddy couldn't help but smile at that comment. One of the men, the small stocky built one said, "You do realize you are in the colored section?" Buddy tried once again to slide upright and this time was successful, despite the objections from the small of his back and his now completely numb backside. "Does the colored car not go to Montgomery?" Buddy sort of grunted as he straightened out his posture. The two men smiled as did the lady. The really big man started to say something, but she interrupted him, "It's just unusual to share the car with a person of a different race. We are happy to have the company."

By this time, Jimmy had woken up and he was now trying wedge his head behind Buddy, which was getting really uncomfortable, so Buddy leaned forward, reached behind himself on both sides, got a firm grip on the two children, and positioned them so that they were sitting straight up and straight forward then said, "This is Janie, this is Jimmy, and I am Buddy Patton." The lady stuck out her hand, which was still covered in a silk white glove. Buddy took her hand and said, "Ma'am." When she let go of his hand, she said, "I am Ms. Cecilia Adams, no relation to the late two past presidents." Buddy almost laughed out loud, but she continued with the introductions. "This is Mr. Paul Leigh." She pointed to the stocky man that was sitting to her left. "And this tiny fellow is Mr. Sherrill Jackson, no relation to the late president." Buddy couldn't help but chuckle at that one. This was obviously a style of introductions that she had done many times over. Each man stuck their hands out as they were introduced, and Buddy shook each man's hand. He was struck by the size of Mr. Jackson's hand when it was their turn to shake. The man's hand was as big as a baseball glove and his grip was like a vice.

The porter timidly stuck his head in the car to check on things. He seemed to expect some kind of ruckus and when he found nothing but calm, he smiled. "We will be pulling out of the station shortly." He turned and closed the door behind him. When the door was closed again, Miss Adams turned her

## Chapter 32

attention back to Buddy. "Mr. Patton, the children are lovely, it is unusual for a man to be traveling with such small children without the company of a lady. Is there a Mrs. Patton?" Buddy was about to answer when Mr. Leigh interrupted, "You never stop, do you." Mr. Leigh shook his head as if he was bewildered by something. "You hush! I am just having a conversation with the gentleman that will be sharing a car with us for the next several hours." She smacked Mr. Leigh on the leg playfully and returned her stare to Buddy. "Is there a Mrs. Patton?"

Buddy looked down at both Janie and Jimmy then looked up at the three people across from him. "She passed away." Buddy wasn't sure what to expect in the reaction category, but it sure wasn't what he got from her, a complete unchanged expression. It was almost as if she hadn't heard him say that his wife had passed away. In fact, he convinced himself that she hadn't heard him and was about to repeat it when she replied, "I am very sorry to hear that, Mr. Patton, children." And once again, she never changed her expression. Mr. Leigh shifted a little in his seat. "See, you've gone and stepped in it again. For once, you might turn off that lawyer beacon you have in your head and just be the girl I've known my whole life." She turned to look at Mr. Leigh again. "And I told you to hush, the fact that I know that his wife and these two beautiful children are in mourning will help me more easily navigate the conversational direction the rest of the trip." She turned and smiled at Buddy again. "Are you going to visit family in Alabama, Mr. Patton?"

Buddy was really not in the mood to talk, but he figured out very quickly that with the woman, not talking would not be an option. The best he could hope for was that they all fell asleep and just had a nice quiet ride. He was optimistic that his plan would work when he noticed that giant Mr. Jackson was already dozing off. "Uh, no, ma'am. I have never been to Alabama. I am going to help a friend." She nodded her head, "Must be a very close friend." Buddy felt like she was asking more questions than she needed to, but he didn't let on like it was bothering him. He didn't want to get into the history and he certainly didn't want to tell her that he had only known this man for a total of about twenty-four hours, even though he knew they were the most important twenty-four hours he may have ever spent in his life. "Yes, ma'am."

The train shook a little and they could feel the wheels turn beneath them. Jimmy jumped up from the sitting position and leaned up against the window so he could see the people at the station in Dallas all waving at the people departing on the train now. Janie wanted to see, too, so she nudged her face against the window next to Jimmy's and then both began to wave at the people waving back at the train as if they knew them. "You're a lawyer?" Buddy heard the words come out of his mouth but couldn't believe he actually said them. He did not want to have a conversation with these folks and now he had pushed the door for pleasantries wide open. The look on his face must have sent some incorrect signal to Miss Adams because she immediately replied, "There are women lawyers these days, Mr. Patton." He sat up and crossed his legs and pretended to brush out a wrinkle on the thigh of his trousers and tried to be as nonchalant as possible. "That's not what I meant."

He could see that Mr. Leigh was now looking at him with a smile as if he knew something was about to happen. "Oh, I see," she said, "Then your question or confusion must stem from the fact that I am a woman of color and a practicing attorney? This confuses you, Mr. Patton?" Buddy could tell that she was trying to toy with him and didn't like it one bit. He didn't like people that tried to twist his words and trap him, and it looked to him that this lady was looking for a fight of some kind. "No, ma'am, I am not confused, I am a dumb ole farmer from Littlefield, Texas who is on a train with his children two days after burying his wife and headed to a place I've never been to help a friend that I met in war under extenuating circumstances."

She started to return words with him, but Buddy wouldn't let her as he continued, "My question merely stemmed from a

## Chapter 32

respectful, conversational standpoint, since you seemed dead-set on having one. From what I can see," Buddy nodded over to the very large man sitting next to her that was now fast asleep, "you prefer your conversations to be merely one-sided, so if that is the case, the children and I will go back to sleep and you can talk to the sleeping giant for all I care." Mr. Leigh burst out laughing, tilted his back then side to side and shouted, "Finally!" She smacked him on the leg again, but this time she returned her stare to Buddy with a less hostile and noticeably kind, beautiful smile. Before she could say anything, Mr. Leigh said, "You see, Mr. Patton, Miss Adams isn't happy unless she is fighting with someone and she is even less happy if she isn't flirting with someone, and the best I can tell, she has tried both on you and failed both times." He laughed again. "I've never seen her get knocked out twice in the same day. Well done, Mr. Patton!" He laughed as Buddy tried to understand what the man had just said.

Mr. Leigh continued, "Why are you in this car, Mr. Patton? The cars up front are much nicer and have more room." Buddy shook his head. "I am not particular, and this was the first train I could catch to Montgomery. I'm not one to squabble about a person's skin color or where they sit. I figure that ain't up to me." Miss Adams smiled, leaned back, crossed her legs in a slow drawn out fashion, then took both her hands and locked her fingers around the top of her knees. "Oh, I think you are more than just a dumb ole farmer from Littlefield, Texas, Mr. Patton."

# Chapter 33

BUDDY, MR. LEIGH, AND MISS Adams ended up chatting for quite a while, longer than Buddy expected; Janie, Jimmy, and the giant slept most of the way. As it turned out, the three of them would be getting off the train in Tuscaloosa. Miss Adams was going to speak at a youth gathering just off the campus of the University of Alabama. By all indicators, they expected there to be some trouble, but according to her and Mr. Leigh, it was nothing that they hadn't seen before and nothing they couldn't handle.

Buddy was fascinated with the stories they told as the train rolled along. Mr. Leigh and Miss Adams had met in college in Albany, New York and had been romantic for a while, but realized that they weren't compatible in that regard, but were very compatible in the court room. They remained friends and partners and it appeared that they had done quite well in their professions. They were quick to point out that Mr. Jackson was kind-hearted but fearless when it came to confrontations, and for that reason, he was being brought along on this trip. His mere presence usually tipped the scales in their favor when needed.

When the train stopped in Tuscaloosa, Miss Adams scribbled her name and number where she could be reached through her office in Washington, D.C. and she scribbled the name of

## Chapter 33

the hotel where she would be staying for the next two weeks in Tuscaloosa. Mr. Leigh did the same thing. During the trip, both Mr. Leigh and Miss Jackson tried to extract more information from Buddy as to the true purpose of his journey, but he would never divulge all the details. He simply told them that a friend of his had hit some hard times and had requested his help. He never really went into any specific details. She was happy that he got to talk to someone that he didn't know. He liked some of the folks in Littlefield, like Clancy Biggars, and enjoyed talking to him, but he didn't dare tell anyone anything he didn't want repeated. There were no secrets in Littlefield. He didn't mind telling these folks the story of his wife; how they met and how they ended up where they were. It felt somewhat good to discuss his wife's illness and how quickly from the time of the first noticeable cough to the time he was holding her hand and watching her take her last breath had passed.

It was all a flash in his mind, but it was one week to be exact. She started coughing one night and it never seemed to stop. It just got worse to the point where she would cough up blood. When it got so bad that he couldn't take it anymore, he summoned the doctor against her wishes. She was stubborn and believed up to the day she died that she was going to get better. She would never complain and would simply say, "It's just a cold."

The doctor came out to see her, checked a bunch of stuff that Buddy didn't understand and when he was finished examining her, he asked Buddy to step out into the kitchen where they could talk. Right there in the kitchen, the doctor told Buddy that his wife had cancer and that it was so far advanced that there was nothing he could do. He told Buddy that he should try to make her as comfortable as possible and suggested that he send for family. He gave Buddy a bottle of laudanum and told him to give her a spoon full about every four hours and he would bring another bottle out in a few days. Buddy remembered that the doctor was so matter-of-fact in the way that he told him of his wife's condition that it sort of pissed him off.

As the doctor was talking to Buddy about his wife, the doctor had the nerve to reach into the ice box, grab the milk jar, and drink straight from the jar. "Did you tell her she was dying, doc?" The doctor took another drink of milk, wiped the dribble on his sleeve, and replied, "She already knows. I didn't need to tell her anything." He put the milk jar back into the ice box and closed the door. "Now, Buddy, I will tell the church ladies what you are going through out here and they will come out and help." The doctor looked around the kitchen and saw a bowl of fruit; he walked over to the bowl, picked through the bowl, and came out with an apple. He rubbed the apple on his sleeve and then took a bite. He chewed as he continued to speak. "Try and make her as comfortable as you can. She is fading pretty fast, so tell her you love her and that kind of stuff. I will be back out to bring you the laudanum." With that, the doctor spun around, looked for something that he didn't find, turned back to Buddy, patted him on the shoulder and said, "Sorry for your loss, Buddy."

Buddy stood there in the kitchen, dumbfounded, trying to process what the doctor had just said. He was crushed and pissed. He couldn't believe the doctor had been so flippant about announcing that his wife was dying of cancer. Before the weight of the doctor's words could completely sink in, the doctor was already out the front door and gone. If Buddy hadn't been so shocked by the news he had just heard, he would have punched the doctor right in the nose for the way he behaved in his home with such rude manners.

When he gathered his composure, he went into the bedroom to see his wife. She was laying there on her back sleeping, so he just sat in the kitchen chair he had moved into the room a week before because he found he was spending more and more time just sitting with her. He had done everything he knew how to do to make her feel better, but he could tell she was in pain. At least now, after the doctor had given her some of the medicine, she was sleeping peacefully. He sat there and stared at her, at her beautiful face and her

*Chapter 33*

pale but flawless skin. He wondered how she had maintained her beauty on the farm.

Farm life was tough, and she never let it show. She went to great pains to dress and look like a lady whenever she could. Even when she would help in the fields, she always stood out because she looked like she didn't belong, but she did. She was as tough as anyone he'd ever known. It tore him up that she was in so much pain and he wasn't man enough to stop it. He cursed the God that would do this to her, even though deep down he knew that things like this happened and God had nothing to do with it. At least that was what he told himself to keep from being so angry. He never wanted her to see the worry or anger on his face, he hoped that when she looked at him in her last few hours that all she would be able to see written on his face was love. Love for a woman that he wondered how he would ever live without.

# Chapter 34

THE PORTER CAME IN TO tell him that they would be arriving in Montgomery in approximately forty-five minutes. No one else had joined them in their car after Miss Adams, Mr. Leigh, and Mr. Jackson got off the train. Jimmy took advantage of the empty seats across from them and made himself a nice little bed. Janie was not about to venture away from her father, so she had stayed in his lap and she was small enough to stretch out and get comfortable enough to sleep all the way to Montgomery. He eased himself out from under Janie's head and gently laid her head back down on the seat. He reached above them for the small amount of luggage that he brought along with them and opened the case that had just his things in it.

He opened the case and reached into the bottom underneath the two shirts and two trousers he packed and found it. He pulled the Colt M1911 from the bottom for no other reason than to make sure he had put the gun in the case. He brought that pistol home from the war and put it in the tack room in the barn where it stayed until he received the letter from Corporal Mack. He cleaned it thoroughly and wrapped it in an old towel. He slid the .45 back into the small little suit case and latched it.

## Chapter 34

Buddy left the suitcase on the floor and then reached up and grabbed Janie and Jimmy's things. When the train stopped, he wanted to make a quick exit, grab something to eat, and find a place to stay for the night. The porter stuck his head in the car and announced to Buddy that they would be rolling into the station in five minutes. "Thanks. Say, do you know where I could find a place to stay this evening?" The porter scratched his chin as if he was thinking and then said, "I really don't, sir. I would imagine that there are some hotels downtown that would put you up for the night." He started to turn and walk away, but he turned back and said, "I will check with the hospitality station before you and the babies get off the train." Buddy looked at him and then back to the kids. "Thank you."

The porter gave him the name of three hotels in downtown Montgomery and one that was just on the outskirts of the city limits. The porter told him that the one on the outskirts was probably not suitable for kids, although the hotel claimed that they were. He said it was near a juke joint called The Quarters and sometimes had some unsavory customers. The porter whispered the information to him as if he didn't want people to know he knew so much about the place. He did say that the music was fantastic, but he just didn't think it was a proper place to stay. He said the loud music might keep the babies awake. Buddy could tell that the porter wasn't a phony, so he took his advice and hailed a two-toned crimson and gold painted cab to the Monarch. He remembered thinking that he liked the colors. They reminded him of the Marines. Even Janie noticed the colors.

"Daddy, that looks like that suit you have at home." He smiled. "Sure does, baby." The cabby jumped out of the car, picked up the two pieces of luggage and put them in the trunk. "Where you folks headed?" He closed the trunk and quickly moved around to the passenger side where he opened the door to the front and the back doors. Buddy was impressed with the speed that this guy moved. "We are headed to the Monarch by way of the county jail." Before the cabby could close the door behind Janie and Jimmy, he stopped. "You want to take these kids into the jail?" He seemed a bit unnerved by the prospect of taking two kids to county lock up. Buddy understood his concerns, some of the jails he had seen in his lifetime were no place for kids, but his choices were limited. He didn't know anyone in Montgomery, so he had to take Jimmy and Janie wherever he went.

"Yeah, the jail. Let's go before I get hungry and spend your tip money." After everyone was in the cab, the cabby jumped into the driver's seat and adjusted his mirror first so he could see Janie and Jimmy and then adjusted it so he could see out the back. "The county jail it is." After he had the Packard pointed in the right direction, Buddy said, "Good looking Packard, is it a '38?" The cabby didn't know what year it was, he was only able to confirm that it was Packard. Buddy didn't think the cabby was too bright, but who was he to judge? Buddy himself wasn't much of a conversationalist, but since he was a stranger in a strange town, he felt compelled to strike up the small talk.

"Town is gearing up for a big fight, are you and the kids here for that?" Buddy was looking out the passenger window when the cabby asked him the question and he turned to look at the cabby. "Don't know anything about a fight, just here to try and help an old Army buddy. Is it boxing?" The cabby laughed, "I sure wish Old Rock would come whip someone here in Alabama, but this is the black folks and the white folks arguing about who can use what shitter and whatnot." He shook his head as if he was confused about the whole thing. "Sure wish folks would just forget it, black folks need to use their privy and things would be just fine." Buddy hadn't asked for the cabby's opinion and didn't offer much of a rebuttal other than, "I think it's about more than just a toilet." The cabby didn't say anything but wouldn't have had much time to say anything because no sooner than Buddy threw his opinion into the ring, the cabby pulled the Packard into the only available parking spot in front of the courthouse, which was also doubled as the county jail.

# Chapter 35

BUDDY COLLECTED THE LUGGAGE FROM the cabby, paid the man, and shook his hand. "Smells funny here, daddy." Buddy hadn't smelled anything and was about to tell Janie that, but Jimmy piped up, "Yeah, it smells funny, kinda stinky-like." Buddy chuckled, he didn't smell anything stinky. "Well, I don't smell anything." Buddy knelt down so he was looking in both Janie and Jimmy's eyes. Buddy hated to be talked down to, and for that reason, he always tried to make a point to get eye-to-eye with his kids so that they could see into his eyes. He guessed he figured he was trying to train them on how to spot a phony when they got older. "Now, when we go in here, don't kick up a fuss, don't wander off, and keep to yourself. You two understand?" They both nodded, and with that, Buddy picked up the luggage and started inside the courthouse.

Buddy checked in with the woman at the window just inside the entrance of the jail. The place was somewhat quiet with just a few people filing some paperwork and one guy who was working on a light switch. It was amusing to watch because the best that Buddy could tell, this guy had no business messing with electricity. Twice the guy jumped back from the spark he created with the screwdriver he was holding. The lady at the window pointed down the hall and she said to take the stairs on the left and that would lead to the jail. She warned him, as did the cabby, that the kids should not go downstairs, and he thanked her again for her concern, as he did the cabby. The building had a hollow sound to it and Jimmy found it amusing to double click his shoes on the tile floors just to make more noise that bounced off the walls. He giggled as they walked, so much that Janie decided to try and make the same noise, but hers just came out as stomping. It was annoying to Buddy, but he decided to just let it go.

They did as the lady at the window instructed and took the steps down to the jail. Once they reached the bottom, the area opened up and was not what Buddy expected, at least this part. This area was well-lit, almost brighter than the upstairs area was. There were more people down here than there were upstairs. Most of the people here were jailers and they all had uniforms. Buddy stopped at the check-in desk and introduced himself. "Sir, I am Buddy Patton and I am here to see Alvin Jerome Mack." Buddy looked around as if maybe he could spot Alvin and felt kind of stupid for making the gesture since he was certain that Alvin was locked up.

"Are you a friend?" The man behind the desk stopped what he was doing, took his reading glasses off, and sat them down on the papers that were in small piles all around him. He raised up from his seat just a little and looked over the counter at Jimmy and Janie. Before Buddy could answer his first question, the man said, "The kids can't go any further. They will have to stay out here." He settled back down in his seat and picked up his glasses. He looked around the piles and found what he was looking for. "Fill this out. When you are done, I will have someone escort you back."

Buddy did as he was told, sat down in the nearest chair and filled out the form. Buddy sat the little clipboard and paperwork on the attendant's desk. He turned and sat with Jimmy and Janie. "You kids are gonna need to stay here while I go see a friend." He patted Jimmy on the knee. "You look after your sister and keep an eye on our things." Just as he was about to say

## Chapter 35

something to Janie, he heard his name. "Uh, Mr. Patton?" Buddy looked up to see a tall, skinny kid, at least he looked like a kid to Buddy. "Yes?" The kid didn't offer to shake hands, he simply asked Buddy to follow him, which he did.

They walked down a long hall that seemed to get darker the further they went. When they hit a dead end with nothing but a yellow door, the kid turned to Buddy. "Inside here you will be searched, and you will need to empty your pockets and do as the jailer says." He pulled some keys from his belt and inserted them into the lock. Before he opened the door, he turned and brushed against Buddy. It was subtle, but Buddy felt the kid's hand go into his coat pocket. He quickly whispered into Buddy's ear, "Just put that in the tray when you empty your pockets." Buddy didn't know what to think about this little exchange, but he wasn't completely gullible. "Hey, what the hell, kid?" The tall, skinny kid gave Buddy a sharp look and then a crooked smile.

After the crooked smile he winked at Buddy. "Sir, I repeat, once through the door, you will need to empty your pockets and consent to search." He turned and opened the door, let Buddy walk in first, and then he went behind Buddy and closed the door. They were in a small room with two more doors; one that went to the right and one that went to the left. There was a table in the middle of the room that had a silver tray right smack in the middle of the table. "Mr. Bobby!" The tall, lanky kid yelled, and it was just a few seconds that Buddy could hear the clank of more keys and the door to the left slung open. In stepped a very short man with huge jowls, and from what buddy could tell, no neck and no chin. It just looked like a large lump on a man's shoulder. He had a huge plug of chewing tobacco in his left jaw and he spit a big wad of something in the corner of the room as he walked in. Buddy thought maybe that was what Janie smelled outside the building because this guy was as fowl-smelling as he had ever smelled, post-war.

The fowl-smelling man wiped the spit dribble off his chin with his shirt sleeve. "Empty your pockets, boy, and don't miss nothin' or I will find it." He coughed a little as he glanced at the table, a signal as to where he wanted Buddy to empty his pockets. Buddy fumbled around and took everything out of his pockets as he was told and was beginning to fume a little about this guy's arrogance. Mr. Bobby, the fowl-smelling man, sifted through the things that Buddy emptied out into the tray. He grabbed the folded-up piece of paper. As he was reading whatever was on the paper that Buddy had been slipped earlier, he lifted his leg ever so slightly and farted.

Without missing a beat or seemingly embarrassed for such crude and fowl behavior, he said, "Don't get many white folks want to see the coloreds." He read the paper out loud. "Mr. Robert Patton, Esq., appointed council for Mr. Alvin Jerome Mack." He crumpled the paper and threw it back down onto the table where it took a slow roll and fell off the edge of the table. Fowl Mr. Bobby made no effort to pick it up. Buddy was shocked at what was on the letter, but never changed his expression. His mind was racing at the moment, but more than anything, he wanted to take old fowl-smelling Bobby to the courthouse square and let everyone watch him beat some manners into this piece of shit.

"Mister, I don't care if that dumbass President Truman appointed you the title of king shit of all colored, you are in my jail now and you will lock step and cow tow, or I will put my boot up your Texas ass. You got that?" Buddy stared straight through the man; if he could figure out a way to drill holes in this guy's head with a stare, he would do it. Buddy had made peace with most of his demons after the war, but tolerance for bad manners was something he absolutely couldn't stand. He took a deep breath and tried to steady his rage. He had no idea where the letter came from, but something told him that in the larger scheme of things, he needed to placate this moron enough to get beyond this point and see about Corporal Mack. "Yes, sir, your jail, your foot. Understood."

The fowl-smelling man spit another wad of tobacco juice in the corner of the room and wiped the dribble with his sleeve

## Chapter 35

again. "Good, law says I gotta let a lawyer and his so-called client have some privacy, but mind you…" He stuck a little chubby finger in Buddy's chest and poked him. In any other part of the country, that would have been enough for Buddy to beat this man to death, but he simply breathed heavily again. "You try any fancy lawyer shit in my jail, I will…" Buddy interrupted before he could finish and said, "Put your boot in my Texas ass." Mr. Bobby stopped in mid-sentence. Buddy could tell that this man wasn't used to being thrown off his routine and being interrupted probably caused him to forget his well-prepared lines. "Us Texans catch on to the rules pretty quick."

Buddy didn't wait for any more banter. He started gathering his things and putting them back in his pockets, walked around the table, and picked up the crumpled letter he had been given. Fowl-smelling Bobby laughed a little, turned, and opened the door to the left. The keys clanked and he had to jiggle the lock a little with the key before it would turn. He led Buddy down the long wide hall where the smell and the lighting got worse the further they went. For good measure, Mr. Bobby decided to cut loose a few more farts as he walked and led Buddy to their destination. Buddy tried to move to the side in hopes of not having to inhale this man's gas, but it was impossible. This man was like a walking outhouse. He stopped when they got to a room on the right, opened the door, and simply said, "Wait in here and I will bring the sum bitch to you."

# Chapter 36

THE DOOR OPENED AND BUDDY could hear the clank of leg irons dragging on the ground. When he saw Alvin Mack's face, he did everything he could to keep from wincing. A.J.'s left eye was swollen shut and had dried blood coming from both ears. His hands were cuffed, and the cuffs were attached to a chain that went around his waist. He was somewhat hunched over, but when A.J. saw Sergeant Major Buddy Patton sitting in the chair waiting for him, he managed to smile. A.J. hop stepped over to the chair that was across from Buddy, but the jailer gave him a slight shove, which caused him to lose his balance.

Buddy could see that A.J. was about to hit his head on the table, so he jumped up quickly and caught him, then eased him into the chair. "Take the chains off his wrist." Buddy presented it as an order, not a question. "Can't do it, boy. Jail regulations." Buddy decided he had had about enough of this man's rude behavior. "It wasn't a request, Mr. Bobby. As counsel for the defendant, you are aware that it is written in the constitution that I have the right to confer with my client without the burden of restraints." The smelly man started to say something, but Buddy interrupted, "And as experienced as you are at your job, I assure you that any interference with my requests will leave

## Chapter 36

you in contempt of the constitution and subject to imprisonment of up to but no more than one year." Mr. Bobby swallowed his tobacco juice instead of spitting it. Buddy was sure that he had scared him a little. "Unless you want me defending you at a later date, Mr. Bobby, I suggest you remove the shackles. NOW!"

Buddy slammed his hand down on the table for good measure and he could see that it worked. The smelly jailer started fumbling with his keys and started mumbling under his breath, loud enough for Buddy to hear, but as he was mumbling, he was also unlocking A.J.'s hands. "It's your own hide, boy. This sum bitch would just as soon cut your throat as to look at you. It would please the ever lovin' piss out of me to come back and find your Texas ass fileted all over this cell." Buddy decided that this guy took great delight in having the last word and thought it best not to deprive him of it, even if he was mumbling his last words.

Mr. Bobby grabbed the shackles and threw them in the corner, then turned and walked out the door. He slammed it for good measure, obviously to let Buddy know he was still in control of his jail. Buddy waited for just a bit before he started to speak, but A.J. spoke first. "Is that true, what you said about the law and these cuffs and stuff?" Buddy looked around the cell as if he was expecting someone else to be there and said, "Not a word of it. For all I know, I may have just broken the law, but what's important is that HE doesn't know it." A.J. smiled and leaned back in his chair, but then realized he hadn't presented a proper greeting. He rubbed his wrist, stood straight up, and saluted Buddy.

Buddy waved his salute down. "What? You want a court's marshal, too? You know I am a non-comm and retired at that. You don't salute, Alvin." A.J. sat back down in his chair. "Friends call me A.J., sir." A.J. stuck out his hand and Buddy immediately took it. A.J. leaned forward and whispered, "So, you aren't a lawyer, sir?" Buddy just shook his head, reached in his pocket, and pulled out the crumpled piece of paper he had been given earlier. "Know anything about this?" A.J. read the small memo but shook his head no. "Somebody must

*Choice of Honor*

have known they wouldn't let you talk to me in private if you weren't a lawyer and ain't no lawyer around here wants to take my case, especially a white one."

Buddy took the paper and folded it up neatly and put it in his pocket. He figured he would have to track down the kid that gave it to him later. "So, what exactly is your case, A.J., and what the hell happened to your face?" A.J. leaned back in the chair and touched his swollen eye. "Fart master there tries to get me to confess to the killings every day. He enjoys his work very much, especially when I'm cuffed and can't do shit about it." Buddy nodded his head in agreement. "Look, Corporal," A.J. interrupted him, "A.J." Buddy put up a hand in a stopping gesture. "Look, A.J., I have no idea what happened or how I can help you. I made a commitment to you on the island that day and I am here to prove my loyalty was true then and it is true today."

A.J. stopped, looked down at the table, then looked back up. "All I know right now is they came and got me in the middle of the night, said I killed a kid and white lady. They ain't even told me who. I just know that my boys and my Kari are by themselves and I can't protect them from here. That's why I sent for you. I don't expect you to help me get out of jail, but I'd be beholden to you if you could see to it that they are taken care of and the boys get a fair shake in life." Buddy tapped his finger on the table where the two sat.

The two men sat in silence for what seemed like an eternity to A.J. Buddy broke the silence, "Look here, man, I will do what I can to help your family, but if you didn't kill anyone, then why are you sitting here now?" A.J. thought about it and didn't really have an answer. He told buddy about the night that his Uncle Marvin passed away and how Ansil Anderson had told him that his men were planning to come for him soon and take his business from him. The way Ansil put it was that they were going to do things to his wife and that he wouldn't ever see her or their boys again. He told Buddy that for the first time since the war, he was scared, and that while he was arranging to bury

## Chapter 36

his uncle, he started making plans to get Kari and the boys out of Montgomery, and that's when he thought of Buddy.

Buddy didn't tell A.J. about losing his wife, maybe when the time was right, but right now he needed to figure out how to help A.J.'s family. He knew for sure that tomorrow he would send a telegram to the attorney on the train. Maybe she could help out somehow. A.J. gave Buddy the directions to his house before Buddy left. Mr. Bobby came back into to room after Buddy let them know he was done speaking with his client. As Mr. Bobby was putting the cuffs back on A.J., Buddy moved in very close, uncomfortably close to Mr. Bobby.

"Mr. Bobby, find a cold steak or some ice for my clients swollen face, that should get the swelling down." Mr. Bobby took a step back from Buddy. "Don't count on it, lawyer man." Without any warning to Mr. Bobby, Buddy reached down and grabbed the man's hand so fast that Mr. Bobby didn't know what to think, and in the split second he was trying to decide what to do, Buddy dislocated his pinky finger. The man screamed in pain for a second, but Buddy didn't move a muscle. It all happened so fast that even A.J. wasn't sure why the smelly jailer was screaming in pain. "When you are trying to find some ice for that little pinky, maybe you can get some for my client." Then Buddy leaned in so that he was whispering in the man's ear. "Punch my friend again and I will do more than just yank that pinky out of its socket. Trust me. Now go take a damn bath, you filthy piece of shit."

Mr. Bobby didn't know what to do. At first, he hunched over and held his hand like he had burned it. A.J. turned quickly since he had his back to the action and saw the Mr. Bobby's pinky pointed in a different direction. The jailer had left the exit door open, so Buddy took a step through it, but before he exited, he turned to speak to A.J. "I will be back in the morning." Buddy said it loud enough so that the jailer could hear it and hopefully understand that he would be back to check on him, too.

Janie and Jimmy were sitting on the bench just across from the check-in station, right where Buddy left them earlier. "It smells funny here, daddy." Janie said it as she slid off the bench and grabbed the little bag she was carrying. Buddy grabbed the big luggage and Jimmy grabbed the rest. "I know, honey, that's why you never want to go to jail." He paused for a second, looked around the building, and said, "Let's get out of here."

# Chapter 37

THE THREE OF THEM CHECKED in at the Monarch Hotel. Buddy was shocked at the price per night. He asked to see the manager because he thought that he was being gouged or played for some out of town fool. The manager came down a dollar on the price, but it still didn't set well with Buddy. He was on a limited budget and this was really taking a bite out of his funds.

After he was done haggling with the manager over the daily price of the room, he hauled the kids and the luggage upstairs to the room. He was getting tired and needed to rest, so he put the luggage in the corner, laid down on the bed with Janie on one side and Jimmy on the other, and the three took a quick nap. He was dreaming of riding the train with his wife. She was drinking tea as she smiled at him and crossed her legs like the lady she was. In that dream, she looked as beautiful as he had ever remembered. He was lucky to have her as his bride. He knew that she was not a farm girl and she probably could have married better, but somehow, he had managed to get her attention and even better, he had managed to get her to love him.

She came from an industrial family. Her family hailed from Fort Worth, Texas and had made a small fortune making propeller shafts for most of the planes that flew in the war. She came from the country club crowd and was as beautiful as any woman could ever be. He knew she should have found someone from her own circle instead of picking a rough-edged soldier who wanted nothing more than own his own land and a quiet spot to farm it. He had no regrets about choosing her as his wife, despite her father's objections. Her father wanted nothing to do with him at first, but he warmed up a little as the kids came along. He didn't like his daughter wearing coveralls and driving a tractor or milking cows, but he knew there was nothing he could do to change it. He and Buddy got along, and Buddy never showed him any disrespect, in fact, he went out of his way to show his father-in-law that he was worthy of his daughter's love.

In his dream, he was about to lean over and kiss her when the porter knocked on the door. He mumbled for the porter to go away. He was in the mood for some of his wife's loving and did not wish to be interrupted when he realized it was not the porter on the train but someone knocking on the door to their hotel room. He opened his eyes and stared up at the ceiling for a second, then looked left and right to see that both Janie and Jimmy were still asleep. He eased out of bed, which was no easy task being wedged in between Janie and Jimmy. Janie had already created a huge wet spot on his shoulder where she drooled all over him. Bless her heart, he wondered how she kept from drying out completely when she slept because she drooled more than anyone he had ever seen.

When he was free of the bed and the grip of the children, he made his way to the door. He looked down to realize he was barefoot, but he figured he was in a strange place and nobody knew him, so he didn't bother. The cold floor felt good on his feet. He opened the door to a somewhat stocky man with a five o'clock shadow in a police uniform. "Can I help you?" Buddy said as politely as he could while he looked the man up and down. The man on the other side of the threshold did the same thing to Buddy, and when his eyes got to Buddy's feet, the man snickered a little and started to step into the room. Buddy immediately put

## Chapter 37

his hand on the man's chest and offered the stranger some very firm and deliberate resistance. "Mister, I haven't invited you in, and your chances of me extending that invitation are somewhere between slim and none."

The man looked down at Buddy's hand then looked back up at Buddy. "Just wanted to chat, Mr. No need to get cranky." Buddy let his hand drop, but he was still firmly blocking the door. "Where I am from, we extend an invitation first." Buddy now crossed his arms only because he couldn't figure out what to do with his hands. He didn't want to put them in his pockets because he didn't know this guy and he wanted his hands ready. He was certain he could take this guy easily, there were few men who Buddy couldn't take. Years of war, hours and hours of drilling and combat training, and a natural grit that very few people had made Buddy tough as nails and dangerous when provoked.

"I understand you went to go see a killer today?" The officer took a step back. He sensed that Buddy was ready to strike him at any second, so he was trying to give himself some distance. "I also understand that you left one of my jailers with a badly disfigured pinky finger." The officer smiled and crossed his arms. Buddy took it as a sign that the officer was getting comfortable with his surroundings and that was the last thing Buddy wanted. His training was to always keep the aggression going, take the high ground, keep your opponent off balance, make them nervous and keep them wondering what you are going to do.

Buddy took step out of his room and crossed the threshold into the hallway. Now he was standing nearly nose-to-nose with the officer, which immediately caused the officer to step back, but unfortunately, there was no more room and he backed right up against the door across the hall from Buddy's. Buddy knew now that he had this guy off balance. "Mister, I left your jailer in wonderful shape. I have no idea what happened to him after I left. He seemed addle and a little clumsy, so maybe he tripped on his own feet." Buddy inched just a little closer, which caused the officer to try and back up further. Just as the officer was pressing himself against the door, the occupant in the room across the hall, a lady in curlers, opened the door, causing the officer to fall backwards on to her and then on to the floor. They both sprawled out on the floor and both tried to scramble to their feet. It was embarrassing to both of them and Buddy tried to help the lady up and did so.

Now that Buddy had tossed this guy's humility to the side, secured the lady, and apologized to her for the intrusion, he pulled the door closed to her room and was now in front of the officer. "Officer?" Buddy looked all over the uniform for a name, but he couldn't find one, so the officer answered without any hesitation. "Moore, Officer Mickey Moore." Buddy took a step back because the man's body language had changed from confident and aggressive to weak and placid. "Ok, Officer Moore, did you have anything else you wanted to discuss with me? Any more jailers sick or ailing in some way?" Buddy knew he sounded like a smart ass, but he couldn't help it. This guy just assumed he would intimidate Buddy and then leave. Buddy turned the tables on him in seconds, which was something that Buddy had done well for most of his adult life.

Officer Moore stood in the hallway looking around as if he was waiting on someone to help him, but no one came. He drew in a breath and put his hands in his pockets. "I just think for a man that don't hail from around here you might want to slow down and not make any trouble for yourself. We can generate enough trouble ourselves without outsiders coming down and giving us a dose of their own." He looked down at his feet and shuffled a little. "That's all I was gonna say." Buddy could tell the officer was nervous and probably regretted making this visit, so he decided it was probably prudent to not make any more enemies than necessary.

# Chapter 38

BUDDY GOT JANIE AND JIMMY up and dressed them the best he could. Jimmy was easy to dress; he had a nice pair of trousers and a shirt, but Janie fussed about everything he tried. He was not cut out for this, for sure. He missed his wife badly and thought about how much easier this would be if she were here helping. When they finally settled on a dress that Janie could tolerate, he sent for a runner from Western Union and dictated a telegraph. Once that was complete, he ordered a cab.

"Where to, Mac?" Buddy helped Janie and Jimmy get into the back seat and he took the front seat. The cabby looked a little surprised when he sat up front. Buddy could tell he was about to say something about the seating arrangement, so he shot him a look that he used to use on his platoon. It worked every time. His men told him after the war that it was like staring death right in the face. They said they would much rather charge a machine gun nest with just a field knife than have to deal with his stare.

Buddy softened his stare a little, but if it helped the cabby relax any, Buddy couldn't tell. The man looked genuinely scared. "County Road 1413." The cabby was lifting the clutch when Buddy told him where he was going, and the cabby pressed the clutch back down and put his foot on the brake. "Uh, Mac, you and those babies don't belong in that stretch of town. It's best you stay on our side of the tracks." Buddy shot the look back at the man, which struck fear into him again, so he turned straight ahead, nodded, and simply shifted into first and dumped the clutch. Just as quickly as he accelerated, he slammed on the brakes. Jimmy and Janie spilled onto the floorboard of the back seat but giggled as they thought it was funny. Buddy hit his head on the side window and then on the dash in front of him.

Buddy was looking at the local paper just to familiarize himself with what was going on and didn't see the police car pull in front of them, blocking them from going any further. "What the hell!" The driver said out loud, then realized that he had children in the back seat and quickly apologized. "Sorry, sir, I plum forgot that there was babies in the back seat." Buddy shook his head and brushed it off. "They've heard worse, but why is he cutting us off like that? Did you run a stop sign?"

Both men were still confused when the policeman got out of the car. He was a tall man who took his time adjusting himself as he was finally out of the car. He fiddled with his belt just a little to get it centered around his waist, but Buddy caught the slight little motion of the policeman unsnapping the holster. Buddy knew you only unsnapped a hammer when you wanted to pull it quickly, which caused Buddy even more confusion. There were very few hardened criminals in the world traveling by cab with two small children. Before Buddy could process the policeman walking towards their car now, he heard a tap on the window. He turned to see the barrel of a snub nose .38 tapping on the window. Janie saw it, too, and she screamed.

Buddy didn't care much for this little show of force. He pulled the handle on the door and opened the door as quickly as he could. He was out of the car and standing in front of the policeman that tapped on the window with his pistol faster than the policeman counted on and actually showed some fear on his face which Buddy immediately noticed and seized upon the advantage, despite the fact that this cop was already holding a

## Chapter 38

gun. "I don't appreciate you scaring the hell out of my daughter, officer, and I would like to know what the hell ya'll think you are doing!" Buddy took a step toward the policeman and the policeman took a step back. As he was stepping back, he tripped over something and fell backwards. Buddy was one step ahead in his thought process and realized that the cop was falling backwards with the gun in his hand and it was pointed directly at him. Buddy quickly side-stepped the cop and it turned out to be the right move because the cop managed to squeeze the trigger on his .38 and it fired above Buddy's head and up in the air, but not quite high enough. They all heard the glass break in the building across the street. Buddy turned to look at where the shot hit the building just in time to see the tall officer pull his night stick and act as though he was going to use it on Buddy.

Buddy made a quick step again and took away any angle the tall cop may have had in order to hit him with the stick. "Hell fire, Matt! You better not have shot anyone over there at Woolworths or I will tan your sorry hide, you dumbass!" Matt took offense to the public berating and jumped to his feet with the gun still in his hand, and he obviously didn't realize that he was pointing the gun directly at the tall cop now. "Don't yell at me! I tripped, or maybe this dumb hillbilly pushed me!" The tall cop stepped to the side out of the line of fire, but for some reason, Matt followed him with the gun still pointing at him.

Buddy found all of this amusing, but the tall cop didn't. "Dammit, Matt! Put that gun in your holster before you shoot me!" Matt then realized he was still pointing the gun at the tall cop and his face went red. He slid the .38 back into its holster then turned his back to everyone. Buddy could see him wipe his sleeve across his face and for a brief moment, Buddy thought that officer Matt was actually crying. The tall cop turned his attention to Buddy, but Buddy was sure that he only turned his attention toward him to take the attention off the other cop. "Word has it from County that you assaulted one of their jailors." Buddy looked the tall cop in the eye then looked down at the silver plate above his left pocket that had his name on it: Laine.

"I am afraid the only assault that took place in that jail, Officer Laine, was the assault on my nose from that jailor's smell." Buddy looked back over to Matt, who had now turned back around. Buddy could see that he had wiped some tears out of his eyes. "However, things must be mighty slow for you to cut us off like you did just to hear that the jailor smelled like a smoldering pile of horse manure." The expression on officer Laine's face slowly changed to a smile. "It's pronounced Lane, no emphasis on the E, and I know the jailer you are speakin' of. He does smell pretty damn bad. Not sure why they don't just shove him in a shower and give him a scrub, but it ain't none of my business."

Buddy peeked in on Janie to make sure she was okay. She was still heaving a little, but she wasn't full-on crying like she was, which was a good thing. It always tugged hard at Buddy's heart when his little girl was crying. He'd do anything in the world to fix whatever ailed her if he could and he would do the same for Jimmy. It was just something about his little girl that could make him as soft as a floating cloud and mean as a rabid dog if he felt like someone was threatening her. "Sheriff, is there something I've done wrong? Because I have business to attend to. "It's chief, the sheriff handles the jail and some other stuff in the county, but inside Montgomery, it's me. Chief Beauregard Laine, but most folks just call be Bo."

Bo walked over closer to Buddy and stuck out his hand for Buddy to shake. Buddy would never refuse a man's handshake, he had been taught that even when you weren't sure about a man's motives, you still accepted the gesture. He shook Bo's hand and gave it a very hard squeeze, one that can hurt if you aren't careful.

Buddy had very large rough hands. He was a champion boxer in his battalion back in his service days. He was a good athlete in high school, but he never realized he was a good boxer until he

## Chapter 38

went into the Marines. He loved the sparring and the technique and the workouts. He just felt like there was something exhilarating about stepping into a ring with another man trying to defeat him with a little strength and a lot of tactics. Buddy had only been beaten once during his Marine boxing days and that should have never happened. Even though the other guy was bigger than Buddy, he was much slower than Buddy.

Buddy jabbed away at this guy for nearly ten rounds. The other guy's eyes were nearly swollen shut when they entered the tenth round, but he answered the bell. That was the day that Buddy learned to never let up on an opponent, never feel sorry for them until they have been counted out. He learned that then and only then can you show compassion. Since it was Marine boxing, and simply something to keep troops entertained, the fight was never judged; the last man standing decided the winner. Buddy was sure that this guy couldn't see his punches coming and if Buddy kept pummeling him, he was seriously going to get hurt. He decided that he would try and get the guy in a clinch, then maybe whisper in the guy's ear to drop before he went blind, but just as he was about move in to grab the guy, the guy landed an uppercut that caused Buddy to see stars. No, sir, never let up.

"They say you are a lawyer, is that right?" Buddy made one last squeeze of the chief's hand and then let it go. "That's what they say, huh?" Buddy looked over at the crying cop and then back at the chief. "Again, Chief, have I done something wrong or is this the normal welcome wagon for Montgomery visitors?" Buddy looked at the cabby who had not budged from his seat. "I, we've got things to do." Bo smiled again, looked into the back seat of the car then back to Buddy. "No, sir, you haven't done anything wrong yet. I am sorry my officer scared the little missus. I will cover protocol with him again."

He looked over at Matt with an angry look on his face. "Come on, MATTHEW." He strengthened his voice when he said the officer's name. "We gotta go see if dumbass here shot anybody over at Woolworths." He started to walk back to his car and Matt started to walk back to his car, but the chief yelled at him again. "Leave your car right there, Matt! You ride over with me." Matt shrugged his shoulders and walked over to where the chief was standing, although it wasn't much of a walk, it was more of shuffle with his feet making a dragging noise as he walked.

Buddy took a look across the street at the window on the second floor of Woolworths that now had a bullet hole in it and smiled. He opened the door to the cab and looked at the cabby, who was still frozen in position with his hands gripping the steering wheel so tightly that his knuckles were turning white. "Hey." Buddy tried to get his attention, but it didn't work. He had seen guys like the cabby in combat. They would get scared and freeze up, which was dangerous to the other men because they couldn't function. At this moment he couldn't figure out why the cabby was so scared, and he really didn't care, he just wanted to get on with the business of helping his friend. He reached up and put his hand on the cabby's hand.

When the cabby felt the touch, he loosened his grip on the steering wheel and looked at Buddy. "Let's go, please." The cabby still hadn't said anything, but he depressed the clutch, shifted into first again, and slowly let off the clutch. It either wasn't slow enough or he didn't press the accelerator enough because the Packard lurched forward and stalled. Buddy smiled and shook his head. "Want me to drive?" The cabby shook his head and started the car again. This time, he got the proper acceleration mix with the clutch release and they were smoothly back on the road.

# Chapter 39

∽

"STATE YOUR BUSINESS, MISTER, AND make it quick." Buddy could easily hear the gruff voice on the other side of the door. It didn't sound pleasant at all and he could feel Janie and Jimmy each grab his legs. It reminded him of the funeral, and he hated that feeling. Buddy put his hands on the heads of his kids, but sort of shuffled to the side of the door. He wasn't sure what the man on the other side of the door would do, but he didn't want his kids to be in the line of fire if someone on the other side had a gun.

"I am here to see a Mrs. Alvin Jerome Mack, is she available to talk?" There was silence on the other side. Buddy turned to make sure the cabby was still waiting as he instructed, he didn't want to be stuck out here without a way to get back to town. He heard the distinct sound of a shell being chambered in a pump shotgun and he took a step back from where he was standing and moved the kids directly behind him. I am here at the request of Corporal Mack. He sent me a letter and asked me to help him."

A few silent seconds passed, and he heard the door beginning to open. He instinctively took another step back as far as he could without sending him and the kids tumbling off the porch, although if he got the slightest hint that he was about to be shot at, that would be his first course of action. It was cold standing there on the porch and he could feel Janie begin to shake. When the door opened, he could see a beautiful young woman through the screen door that she had not opened yet. There was no smile on her face, and she looked tired, like opening this door took all the energy she had left. Even with the puffy eyes and weary look, Buddy could tell that she was as beautiful as A.J. had described to him earlier. She didn't say anything as she stood in the doorway. "Uh, ma'am, I am Buddy Patton, and these are my kids, Janie and Jimmy. I personally kind of like the nip in the air, but as you can see, the kids are a little cold. May we come in?"

Kari looked down at the kids when he said that, and Buddy could see the expression on her face change. It was almost as if she hadn't seen them until Buddy made mention of it. Buddy could tell that this woman had been through a lot. When she saw the kids, she smiled and then Buddy could truly see what A.J. was describing. "I'm afraid I have lost all perspective of my manners, Mr. Patton. Won't you and the children please come in out of the cold?" She reached up and undid the latch on the screen door and opened it. She made a gesture for them to come inside. Buddy took a few steps forward, but nearly tripped because he hadn't realized how tightly both Janie and Jimmy had gripped him. He stopped long enough the pry their little arms loose from his legs and held their hands as he ushered them inside.

"Mr. Patton, I am delighted to finally meet you. I have heard so much about you. You left quite an impression on my husband, he tells me that you saved his life." She stopped as she was about to say something else and changed course, "I apologize again, my manners are simply dreadful these days." She made a sweeping motion with her arm that began from her hip and ended up pointing at the man standing in the hallway that led back to bedroom and kitchen area. "This gentleman holding the shotgun he is about to put away is our long-time family friend, Mr. Curtis Freehold."

She squinted her eyes at Mr. Freehold, which clearly was designed to get him to put the gun away. He complied but didn't do it with glee. Buddy could see that this man was very

## Chapter 39

apprehensive about disarming. It was clear to Buddy that tensions were very high in the house and despite the calm and grace that Kari had shown them initially, Buddy was not about to let his guard down. "Uh, ma'am, I believe it was the other way around, A.J. saved my life, and it is very nice to meet you, Mr. Freehold." He stuck his hand out to Mr. Freehold, but Mr. Freehold made no effort to accept it. Buddy let his hand stay out in mid-air for a few seconds but retracted it when he realized it was causing some more tension in the room.

"Uh, these two trouble makers are my children, Janie and Jimmy." He put his hands on their heads that were looking down at the floor. He used his big hands to clamp down on their heads just tightly enough to force their little heads to look up. "Say hello to Mrs. Mack and Mr. Freehold, please." Both Janie and Jimmy mumbled a hello and as a reward, he released his grip on their heads. Simultaneously, they returned their heads to their earlier positions and continued to stare at the floor.

"Would you like some coffee, Mr. Patton?" He realized he still had his fedora on and quickly removed it. "Uh, yes, ma'am, that would take the chill off my cheeks." Just as she was about to turn around, the twins stuck their heads out from behind Mr. Freehold. "These are our boys. Alvin Jerome, A.J. for short, and this one is James Robert." She looked at the boys and then back to Buddy. "A.J. would like us to call him Buddy, but I ain't havin' none of it." Buddy's face felt hot when he heard the second name. "I'm sorry, ma'am, did you just say that boy's name was James Robert?"

Kari suddenly realized what she had said about not allowing him to be called Buddy and that the man standing in her living room now had introduced himself as Buddy. "I'm so sorry, Mr. Patton, I have no problem with Buddy as a name." He could see that she was struggling to correct her mistake and he wanted to relieve her of any stress she was causing herself. "Ma'am, it is quite all right. It's actually kind of a silly name when you get right down to it."

He looked around the room, which was a habit he had. He took in everything; every detail about the room, the green sofa, the wood floors, the loose plank in the far-right corner, the lamp with a frayed cord, and the rabbits foot laying on top of the huge Bible laying on the coffee table that had some very noticeable chew marks on every corner. He wasn't sure if it was a dog, but since he didn't smell a dog, he assumed it was one or both of the little boys that he had just been introduced to. "Mr. Patton, I should be asking you to sit or offering you something to drink and here I am, making you and the children stand awkwardly in my home while my friend points a shotgun at you."

She put both hands on her face to cover her cheeks and shook her head at the same time. "You've come all this way and I treat you like an intruder instead of the man my son is named after!" It appeared as though she was about to break down in tears, which was the last thing Buddy wanted to happen, since he considered himself terribly inept at consoling a woman's tears. Janie must have sensed the same thing Buddy did because she let go of Buddy's leg, stepped out from behind him where she obviously had been watching the awkward introductions, and made a few quick steps toward Kari and put her arms around Kari's waist. Buddy thought if it was Janie's intention to stop Kari from crying, it didn't work.

When Janie wrapped her little arms around Kari's waist, Kari felt the emotion of all she was enduring bubble up from where she had been suppressing it and it came out in the form of tears. Buddy was surprised at how strong Kari apparently was because she cupped her hands under Janie's arms and lifted her up easily. The only two women in that house found an emotional connection and both Janie and Kari cried as they embraced.

Buddy was proud of his little girl for her ability to read the moment so well at such a young age and be able to act on it. Janie was definitely shy and up until that moment, Buddy had never seen her make such a move toward a stranger. The room was quiet and all you could hear were the two ladies' soft

## Chapter 39

whimpers as they buried their heads in each other's shoulders. Buddy could feel Jimmy tighten his grip on his leg, so he put his hand on his son's shoulder. He could immediately feel Jimmy relax. Obviously, the tension in the room was higher than Buddy realized, which made Buddy feel awkward.

Mr. Freehold must have also sensed it and made his way down the hallway back to the kitchen. He and the shotgun stayed out of view of everyone for quite a while. Janie released her grip slightly on Kari and leaned back in Kari's arms so she could see Kari's face. Janie put her little hands on both sides of Kari's cheeks. "You're pretty." When Janie said that, Buddy could see a smile appear on Kari's face and he knew for certain that it was probably the first time Kari had smiled in a very long time. Kari ran her hand through Janie's hair and then gently touched her face. "Thank you, young lady, and so are you." She pulled Janie close again and gave her another tight hug. While she was hugging Janie, she looked at Buddy. "Mr. Patton, would you like some coffee? I believe we should talk."

# Chapter 40

THE SUN STARTED CREEPING UP over the horizon, but Mr. Freehold, Buddy, and Kari didn't notice. Kari talked all night. Buddy lost count of how many pots of coffee she made, but he did realize that she made one hell of a cup of coffee. He had no idea what she did to it, but he loved it. He had to excuse himself to go outside and rid the coffee from his body. He knew for sure the minute he met Kari that she was not a phony, not even close. She was beautiful and soft spoken, but he thought she had a grit to her that came through in the way she spoke, the way she breathlessly and flawlessly spoke of the night that Uncle Marvin died and of the men who stood in her kitchen and kept her from seeing her husband. She didn't hold anything back from her fear of the night and the dreadful day A.J. was arrested.

Buddy was careful not to interrupt her; he knew she needed to release all the emotion she had been holding inside her. When she was finished, or at least when he thought she was finished, he asked for a few more details, but not many. He was intrigued by her story of Mr. Gibson and his relationship with A.J. Mr. Freehold added the details of A.J.'s arrest. It was clear that Kari did not want to talk about it, so he told the story as best he could. He wasn't actually there the day A.J. was arrested, but he

## Chapter 40

came as soon as he found out. Even though he added some crucial details that Buddy tried his best to process, he really didn't speak much throughout the night, only enough to fill in some of the gaps that he thought Kari was not elaborating on some of the details around Mr. Orville Gibson. By the time the sun came up, Buddy was sure that Mr. Freehold was not a phony either.

Kari had laid out a pallet in the living room floor for Janie and Jimmy and the two slept like they have never slept before. Buddy had too much work to do to sleep. After listening to the story of Mr. Gibson and his shenanigans, he was glad that he had taken the time to send the telegrams that he had sent. He just hoped that the runner would find each of the targets. "Mr. Freehold, do you think you could loan me a car for the day?" Buddy was certain he knew where to start and what to do. Even though he wasn't familiar with the territory, he was familiar with the people and the players. Out of all his travels, through the war and then back home to Texas, the places changed, but the people were the same. There was always a town bully, a town power broker, a town know-it-all, and a town busy body.

He had formed several categories of people over time. He wasn't judgmental by any stretch, but he didn't have time for games or phonies. Through Kari's words, he had carefully placed each person in one or more of his categories, and the one person that stuck out the most was Mr. Orville Gibson. Holding court with a woman of color on the side, having a child with the woman, then extorting time and money from A.J. placed him in a few of Buddy's categories: town sleaze, town know-it-all, town web master. The web master was probably the best fit. Buddy despised that one more than the others. The web masters always thought they were smarter than everyone else and they took delight in the thinking that they were steps ahead of everyone else's moves.

"Of course you can, Mr. Patton. I can take A.J.'s one remaining cab he had parked here before they took his cars and you can have mine for as long as you like. I don't expect to stray too far from Mrs. Kari, though." Buddy smiled, he knew from that statement on that he could trust and count on Mr. Curtis Freehold. "Thank you, and I would appreciate it if you would just call me Buddy, all my friends do." Mr. Freehold smiled. "Okay, Buddy, in that case, you gotta call me Curtis." He was smiling when he said it.

Buddy was about to respond, but he wasn't given any time. The smile on Curtis's face evaporated as quickly as it formed. "Mr. Patton, uh, I mean, Buddy." He rose from the table and took a long look out the back door, then turned to Buddy, who was half in the kitchen and half in the hallway holding another cup of coffee. "This ain't none of your concern really, and there just ain't no need in you getting' tangled up in this spider web. These people won't give two shits about your code or where you are from." Buddy walked over to the small table where they had all spent the night listening to Kari. He sat his coffee down on the table and walked over and stood beside Curtis, except Buddy was staring out the back door and Curtis was facing the kitchen. The two men were shoulder-to-shoulder.

Curtis continued, "In fact, the fact that you are not from here will make it worse, much worse." Buddy crossed his arms across his chest as he breathed in heavily and turned to look at Curtis. "I understand, I really do." He paused for a second, turned back around and looked out the window, and said, "Curtis, if I don't help him, he will probably die, that much I know." Curtis turned to look out the window. Neither men looked at each other, but Curtis spoke as he placed his hand on Buddy's shoulder. "And if you ain't careful, so will you."

## Chapter 41

"WHATS YOUR BUSINESS?" THE MAN in the front room of the grain warehouse that Ansil Anderson owned and kept an office belted his question out like he was some kind of authority figure. He was dressed in overalls that were unbuttoned on the sides to accommodate his sizable beer belly. After Buddy had thought things through, he felt like Ansil Anderson was the best place to start. He knew he would cross swords with some folks, but according to Kari, Ansil was the one man he should check in with. She felt that everything of importance in town ran through Ansil Anderson.

Not only did the man try to have an authoritative-sounding voice, he had a cocky attitude that Buddy couldn't stand. "If I wanted you to know my business, I'd ask to see you, now wouldn't I?" The man took a step towards Buddy, but in true Buddy style, he had already anticipated the man's actions, so Buddy took two steps towards the man, cutting off his aggression and surprising him. The man reached behind his back. Buddy wasn't going to wait to see what he was reaching for, so he reached up quickly, grabbed the man by the throat with his left hand, and with his right hand, he stopped the man from reaching behind his back. Then in one quick motion, he kicked the man's feet out from under him, which sent him to the floor on his back with a huge thud.

He hit with such force that it knocked the wind out of him, and he gasped for air. Buddy kept his hand wrapped around the man's neck and was about to let go when he felt the thump in the small of his back. He released his grasp from the man's throat and spun around to see three men behind him. One was holding a baseball bat, which through quick deductive logic was the reason why the small part of his back hurt like hell at the moment.

The man with the bat made three quick steps toward Buddy, apparently to try and finish the job, but Buddy ducked and came up quickly with an uppercut to the baseball player's chin. There was a crunching sound and the man dropped like he had been shot. That left just one man and he was very skinny. Tall, but skinny. He looked like a teenager to Buddy and he also looked scared. "Kid, I can snap you like a twig or you can tell me where Mr. Anderson is. I wasn't looking for trouble, just a polite conversation." The kid was about to answer when he was interrupted.

"I'm Ansil Anderson and you must be the fella pretending to be a lawyer for A.J. Mack. Would that be correct?" Ansil didn't shuffle his feet, he walked with confidence, as if he didn't have a care in the world. When he stepped out of a side hallway door clearly within range of being able to hear the scuffle going on outside, he chose not to investigate the cause. Buddy knew the type. He stayed in the office to measure the strength of his enemy, or what he considered to be a potential enemy. "No, I am just a cotton farmer from Texas trying to help a friend."

Buddy put his hand on his back where the bat had surely left a mark. "I take it you are Ansil Anderson, or do you have another baseball bat for your guest?" Ansil put his hands up to show that he had nothing in them. He smiled and made his way over to Buddy. As he approached, he stuck his hand out to offer a shake, which Buddy took. "You should teach your boys to fight better, or at least tell them the war is over." Ansil laughed. "You've kicked up a fuss, pissed off some folks already." He laughed again and shook his head. "You know what I say, though?" Buddy shook his head and shrugged his shoulders. His

## Chapter 41

back still hurt from the baseball bat and he knew he would have trouble sleeping tonight. "I say, 'Fuck 'em.'" He let out a huge belly laugh.

"Wish I could have been there to see you scare that dipshit little Matt Moore into shootin' a hole in the Woolworths! I bet that was a sight to see!" He bent over laughing. Buddy felt a little awkward because he didn't find anything funny about it when it happened, but it was kind of funny to know that people were already talking about it enough to reach this man who was now bent over laughing about it. "Sure did piss off Beauregard, though. That isn't a good thing. That man has a mean streak in him. Some folks say he mutilates puppies for kicks." Just as quickly as he started laughing, he stopped laughing and got serious. "Well, cotton farmer from Texas, why are you knocking on my door?"

Buddy rubbed the small of his back the best he could as he spoke, "I don't want trouble from the wrong people and help from the right ones. A.J. saved my life in the war and I intend to help him if I can. He's not a killer, not within a country mile." Ansil bent over to help one of his guys up off the floor. "No, I'd have to agree with you, but Ole Man Gibson swears that A.J. killed his wife out of hate and pure meanness. Says he choked the life out of her because she hated him."

The man he was trying to help off the floor obviously wasn't putting enough effort into helping Ansil get him up, so Ansil dropped him to the floor with a thud. "Jesus, you damn sissy. Get your ass up on your own, I ain't doin' all the damn work." Ansil turned and looked at Buddy. "Ole Gibson ain't the problem anymore, though. The problem is Old Beau." Buddy walked over to where Ansil had dropped the man and proceeded to help him get to his feet. "Why's that?" Ansil shook his head when he saw Buddy helping his man up. "Why, you say? Well, because Old Beau ain't ever gonna let A.J. stand trial for anything. He's gonna transport him to county tomorrow night. Actually, he will get his orders from the circuit judge to transport him tomorrow morning, but he we will delay for some bullshit reasons and when night fall comes, he will transport your buddy right into the arms of those morons that dress up in their finest sheets and howl at the moon."

Buddy pushed the injured man toward a wall so that he could hopefully hold himself up. "How the hell do you know all that, Mr. Anderson?" He stared at Buddy for just a few minutes, as if he was searching for a good way to answer. "Hell, I guess there ain't much I don't know around here. Hell fire, I guess sometimes I'd rather not know what I know." He turned quickly and started walking back toward the door he came from. "Want some coffee, cotton farmer? It's damn good stuff if I do say so myself." He turned to look back at Buddy when he reached the door. "Perk your ears up, cotton farmer, you better hear what I got to say. Come on back." With that, he disappeared into the doorway to his office.

Buddy tried his best to make sure the guy he helped up could stand on his own, but he was pretty sure that as soon as he let go of the man, he would fall back on the floor, so he used the wall to ease the man back down to the ground where he then released his grip and the man slumped over. *At least I didn't drop him,* he thought. It was the best he could do under the circumstances.

Buddy took a step through the door that Ansil had disappeared through. It opened up into a pretty big room, bigger than Buddy expected. The room was equipped with a pool table, a huge desk, two overly tall winged-back chairs, and a giant leather sofa. The incredibly giant fireplace in the room was designed to overwhelm and awe people, but Buddy could not have cared any less.

The wood creaked beneath his feet as he walked past Ansil, who had taken a spot leaning against his desk with his arms crossed. "Mr. Anderson, I don't want any trouble with anyone, but my friend is not a killer and I think you know by now that I am not about to sit around twiddling my thumbs while your friends try and get their jollies inflicting pain." He was about to continue when Ansil interrupted him. "First off, they aren't my

## Chapter 41

friends, and secondly, they aren't planning on inflicting pain on your friend, they are planning on killing him. There's a big difference, cotton farmer."

Buddy took a breath and steadied his pulse as he used to do in combat. "Well, Mr. Redneck, if you'll go along with deplorable behavior right under your own nose, then you are as dumb as you look." Ansil started to speak, but this time Buddy interrupted him by picking up a pool ball off the table and tossing it in the fireplace. "Thing is, Mr. Redneck, as far as I'm concerned, you ain't no better than the ignoramuses trying to pull this shit brained stunt."

He reached down, picked up a pool stick from the table, broke it over his knee, and then gently placed the broken sticks in the fireplace. "Looked like your fire was dying, and I hate pool anyway." Ansil was visibly amused. It had been a very long time since anyone showed that kind of moxie towards him and no one had ever shown that kind of nerve in his own office. He was about to say something, but he found he was kind of speechless. Buddy walked past him without saying a word and left the office. It was time for him to visit the second person on his list.

# Chapter 42

HE FOUND A NICE STRETCH of oak trees that provided some good cover and parked the car behind them. He made his way across the field to the little house that Olivia Compton resided. He couldn't believe how cold it was. He walked and rubbed his hands together thinking about the gloves he left back in Texas and how handy they would come in now. His feet crunched a little in the spots that had snow that had not melted yet. The weather was weird here in Alabama as far as he was concerned, one minute it was sunny and the next minute there were snow flurries. At least in West Texas, the wind blew, and it was cold; no tricks from Mother Nature and no false spring, just damn cold and sure damn windy.

Even though the sun was setting more quickly than he had expected, he could see the house in the distance; it was just as A.J. had described it when the two met at the city jail. It had a porch that wrapped all the way around it. It wasn't anything special, but it was nice home. The smoke stack was in the center of the house and it was belching out a nice consistent plume of gray smoke. He chose to walk in because he didn't want her to see him coming, especially if she had a visitor, but from what Buddy could see, there were no cars in sight, which meant there were no visitors.

## Chapter 42

Buddy didn't want to frighten her or her son in the least way, he just didn't want her running off into the fields around the house and potentially hurting herself. He quietly walked up the steps to the front door. The steps creaked as he put his weight on the boards. He didn't realize that ice had formed on the top step and when he placed his foot on the ice, he completely went sprawling down the stairs and back to the ground.

The pain in his back was enough to make him wince, but not shout. He wasn't sure if the pain was a remnant from the baseball bat or from the stupidity of the fall. He was extremely upset with himself for giving away the surprise because she came busting out of the front door and she was armed. From what Buddy could see from his current position lying flat on his back looking up at her, it was a Mossberg 16 gauge over and under. If she pulled the trigger now, he would certainly not see tomorrow. "What the hell are you doing sneaking around on my property? And you damn sure better not lie or I will pull this trigger and take your damn fool head off!"

He placed his hands up over his head as if he was being arrested but remained on his back. "First off, it ain't your property. It belongs to Orville Gibson and I work for him." He could see her cock the hammer on the shotgun. "He sent me here to check on you." She pressed the shotgun harder against her shoulder as if she was preparing to pull the trigger. "Bullshit, he would have told me he was sending someone to check on me. You better come clean, cowboy, or you're gonna be missing a head." Buddy thought to himself, *what was it with all these names people were calling him*? He didn't for one minute think he looked like a cowboy and he didn't think he looked like a farmer, but Buddy was impressed by her. He had misjudged her wits and she was tougher than he thought. "Fine, L.C. asked me to find you."

This must have struck a chord with her because she lowered the shotgun. "Dammit! Tell that old fool to leave me alone!" She turned and went back inside without saying another word. Buddy was perplexed at how quickly the mention of her father's name would send her back into the house. He was somewhat impressed with his ability to think on his feet, or in this case, on his back. He heard the door lock after she slammed the door; so much for his original plan of just knocking on the door and forcing his way in.

He sat up, dusted himself off and made his way up the stairs, mindful of the ice at the top this time. When he reached the door, he heard the gun go off and instantly felt a sting in his right hip. He knew immediately what had happened. She had shot through the door! "I've had enough of this shit!" With that he kicked in the door. He knew from the sound of the blast that she had pulled the trigger on both barrels. He didn't want to give her time to reload.

When the door flung open, she was standing there trying to jam another shell in the breach. He took three quick steps toward her and yanked the gun away from her and shoved her back at the same time. He wanted to smack her upside the head for shooting him, but he showed a great deal of restraint. "Geez, lady, you just put a damn pellet in my hip!" She started crying. "I'm so sorry. Please tell my daddy to leave me alone." Buddy was in no mood for tears. He could feel the blood running down his hip and down the front of his thigh. He took the shotgun and threw it outside, then pulled the door closed to let the house warm up again. The door wouldn't close completely now that Buddy had kicked it open.

Once he had the door closed, he had no other choice but to pull his pants down to check on his hip. "Mister, I ain't doing that with you so you can just pull them pants right back up!" Buddy shook his head; I guess she wasn't as smart as he originally thought. "Lady, you just shot me in the hip, if you don't help me get the hole plugged and the bleeding stopped, you just might go to prison for murder!" She must have just now realized that she indeed had shot this man and she started screaming. "Oh, my God! I'm so sorry! I didn't mean it! I swear! I was just scared and trying to scare you off! Please don't die, mister!"

## Chapter 42

Buddy rolled his eyes as he was inspecting the little hole in his hip and the blood slowly seeping out of it. He was lucky, if she had aimed a little further to the left, she just might have shot him right in the dingus. "Calm down for Christ's sake. I am not going to die, but I have to get this pellet out before it causes an infection. You got any tweezers?" Olivia continued to cry, but she got up and founds some tweezers and handed them to him. "I need some alcohol or something to clean it out." She looked around and found a bottle of Old Fitzgerald and handed it to him. He laughed out loud, "Finally something you got right." It was his favorite.

He took a drink then poured some on the hole in his hip. It stung like hell, so he took another drink. He poured some Old Fitzgerald on the tweezers and took out his lighter he carried home from the war and lit the tweezers to be sure they were clean. When he was satisfied he had disinfected everything enough, he started probing for the pellet. It hurt like hell, too, but he needed to find it. "What kind of shells did you put in the gun?" She shook her head as if to say she didn't know. "Grab me one, please." She reached in the coffee table drawer and handed one to him. Buddy could see that it was a birdshot. "Too small, I can't bend over enough to get it out. You need to help me." She stopped crying and started shaking her head violently.

"I am NOT pulling that thing out of you!" Buddy grabbed his pants to keep them from falling down as he walked and took a few steps toward her. "You put it there, you take it out. NOW!" She quieted at his raised voice, almost as if he had flipped a switch in her; she calmed down, grabbed the tweezers, and kneeled down in front of him. In less than a minute, Buddy calculated, she had the pellet out of him. He was surprised that she managed to do it with very little discomfort. When she had the pellet in her hand, she got up and tossed it in the trash bin, grabbed a towel from the sink and cleaned the blood around Buddy's hip. She handed him the towel.

"I don't have any bandages. Keep the towel on it." Buddy was surprised now by how calm she was. "You better leave. If Orville finds you here, he will probably kill you. He's very jealous." Buddy laughed. "You won't laugh if he catches you here." Buddy laughed again. "First off, he will come here to kill you, not me. You know he's already killed his wife and now that he is free of her, he will play the field again and you ain't gonna be in the picture any more. He can't have his black girlfriend and bastard son running around spoiling his fun." She looked shocked. "He didn't kill his wife, mister! It was that cabby that he used to drive him around. His wife hated him, and he hated her. Orville said she must have got under his skin and he choked her to death right there in their kitchen!"

Buddy finished cleaning his hip wound, gently pulled his pants back up, and buckled his belt. He was careful not to buckle it too tight, his hip hurt like hell. "Lady, you are being stupid. You have a couple choices, stay here and die or come with me and live. It isn't any more complicated than that. You and that boy will never be heard from again." She crossed her arms and looked at the ground. She shuffled her feet just enough to make a scratching sound on the hard wood floor. "I know you think I am stupid, but I love him. I just don't believe he would ever hurt me or our son."

Buddy was about to speak when he caught a flash of light way off in the distance, a flash in a place that shouldn't be where it flashed. It was coming from the entrance to the property. Luckily, the entrance to the property was almost a half-mile drive. This Orville fellow didn't want anyone to see his mistress easily. "Get your son and let's go. Now." She looked up and could see the seriousness on his face. "What's wrong?" She looked around the room to try and help explain the worry on his face. "You get a lot of visitors at night? Cause if not, my guess is Old Orville has made up his mind that tonight is the night."

Buddy looked around the room and threw all the blood-soaked rags they had used on the floor in the kitchen. He kicked

## Chapter 42

over a trash can and flipped the dining table over on its side. He threw some dishes against the wall and they all shattered. Olivia stood perfectly still, but she had a shocked look on her face. She could not believe this man was destroying her home. "Go get your son. Leave your coat but bundle him up." She started to move, but she rebelled. "Mister, I told you I ain't goin' nowhere." Buddy grabbed her by the arm. "I will make a deal with you. If you come with me, we can find a nice spot to watch who comes up to the house. If Orville has a driver, I will let you go do what you do with him, but if he drove himself, which I know for a fact that he never does, then you come back with me. He will not want any witnesses. It's a simple plan and certainly not unreasonable."

She thought it through but was taking too long. "Lady! We are out of time. Let's go!" She was startled into reality by the tone of his voice and she took off to go get her son. When she had him bundled, the three went out the back door where buddy was sure to close it behind him. They made their way across the South field into a patch of gum trees until he felt they couldn't be seen but could clearly see who was coming to see Olivia.

The car pulled around to the back of the house up next to the porch and turned its headlights off. The car continued to run, though. Buddy couldn't make out what kind of car it was, but he could see that there was only one man. The man realized he left the car running, so he reached in and turned the car off. Buddy had excellent hearing and he could hear the keys jingle in the man's hand as he walked around to the back of the car and opened the trunk. Buddy looked at Olivia and whispered, "Who is it?" She shook her head and shrugged her shoulders. She was holding the toddler and shifted him as she shrugged.

Luckily for them both, the boy was sound asleep and had been since she scooped him up and left the house. The man made his way around to the side of the house. He peeked in a window and then moved back to the back of the house. Buddy was thinking that if this were Orville, he wouldn't bother to peek in a window. Perhaps it was someone that Orville sent, but he knew guys like Orville and even though they were sleazy, they were smart. They knew better than to allow too many people to have secrets they could use against them. He thought that if it wasn't Orville, he had no idea who it could be. He watched the man enter the back door of the house and could see his shadow move through the house. It seemed as though he was checking every room. When the man made his way from the back of the house to the front, he came back out and got in his car. He started the car again and drove off towards the entrance of the property without his headlights on.

"You see! It wasn't Orville! You were wrong!" He couldn't argue with her, but he knew the man that came to the house was not there for a good reason. He didn't know what reason, but he was still glad that they left the house when they did. "You're right, but I get the feeling that the man who did show up had some bad intentions." She held her little boy close to her. "Can we go back now?" He was about to say yes when he heard gravel crunching down the long road that led to the house. He thought the man must be coming back because he hadn't turned his headlights on. This time, the car stopped right in front of the house, but something struck Buddy odd about the car. It wasn't the same car. It was getting so dark now that he couldn't see a lot, but he knew cars, and that car was a Cadillac, for sure.

The man got out of the car and walked up the steps and went right into the house. Buddy looked at Olivia and he could immediately see that she was struggling with the moment and the expression on her face gave it all away. It was Orville. After Orville walked up the steps and opened the door without any introduction, Buddy looked at Olivia and he could see a tear well up in her eye and then roll down her cheek. "Does he ever come to see you at this hour?" Buddy knew the answer already, but he wanted to make sure that Olivia understood completely that she would probably be dead right now if he hadn't forced

Chapter 42

her and her son out of the house. He figured the first car must have been a scout for Mr. Gibson, they simply came too close together to be anything else.

# Chapter 43

"MY CAR IS ONE HUNDRED yards straight that way." Buddy pointed in the direction of where he parked the car. "Do you know how to drive?" She shook her head yes. "Take the boy and go sit in the car. Wait for me, I will be there shortly. Go ahead and start it and run the heater and get warm. I will be there shortly." Buddy made his way back to the house; he was quiet about his movement. He took a second to look inside the car and he could see the keys hanging there in the ignition. He quietly opened the door and took the keys.

He made his way to the back of the house, taking time to peek in the two windows along the side wall. He could see the man looking through the mess that Buddy created in the kitchen before they left, and that man was definitely Orville Gibson. Even though Buddy had never seen him before, he was just like he had imagined. "You must be Orville Gibson." Buddy had already snuck in the back door, careful to not make a sound because he was certain the man would have a gun. Orville spun around, clearly startled by the voice in the room that he was not expecting.

Orville fumbled in his coat pocket but didn't have time to find what he was looking for before Buddy cracked him in the jaw with a swift uppercut. Orville dropped quickly but wasn't

## Chapter 43

knocked out. Buddy intentionally held back his punch. He knew this guy would be fragile. While he was down on the kitchen floor, Buddy went through his coat pockets to see what he was fumbling for. "You planning on doing something with this .22, Mr. Gibson?" Orville made a grunting sound that Buddy had never heard before. Buddy's best guess was that Ole Orville had never been punched in his life.

"Who are you and why are you in my house?" Orville said it in a way that sounded like he was badly constipated. Buddy could hear the pain in each word. "Well, I come to tell you what you owe me for my cab company. I heard this is where you like to, uhhh, hang out." Buddy laughed when he said it. "No pun intended." Buddy helped Orville up off the floor and sat him down on a chair in the kitchen. Orville was still grunting and holding his jaw. "You are crazy, and I am going to have you arrested for assault." Buddy smiled. "Are you sure? I understand that you are using my cabs as your own personal service and have collected income that is mine." Orville was completely confused and let it show on his face. He stopped rubbing his jaw long enough to reply, "I did no such thing! I don't even know who you are, bub." He rubbed his jaw again and started to get up, but Buddy shoved him back down in the chair. "Alvin Jerome Mack sold his company to me yesterday. I have the signed bill of sale right here." Buddy patted his jacket breast pocket for dramatic flair.

"Who in the hell is Alvin Jerome Mack?" Buddy drew in a breath and shook his head in a sarcastic way. "A critical mistake in business is to not get to know your business partners. You know him as A.J." Orville stopped rubbing his jaw and looked up at Buddy. "Yeah, that's right, the man you've been blackmailing for the last few years sold out to me." Orville looked around the room as if he was plotting an escape. Buddy held up the car keys and jingled them so Orville could see them. "If you are thinking about leaving, you'll have to do it on foot." Buddy smiled.

"Okay, how much do you want for the company? I am sick of this little game you are playing. Price it and let's be done with

- 275 -

this shit." Buddy pulled up a chair and sat down next to Orville. "Well, I like the way you cut right to it, a sincere business man! It is so great to watch in action." Buddy reached into his pocket and pulled out a pen and folded paper. He scribbled a number down and slid it over to Orville. "I'm not good at this business stuff, but I understand that's how they do things." Orville shook his head, clearly disgusted that he had to deal with this. He looked down at the figure Buddy had written down on the paper. "You're crazy! I wouldn't pay that for all of Alabama!" Buddy laughed, I wouldn't pay that for all of Alabama, either, but you will pay that for my cab company."

Orville wadded up the paper and threw it back at Buddy. "You're nuts, mister, absolutely nuts." Buddy picked up the paper, uncrumpled it, pressed it out neatly, and laid it back on the table. "Understand that I will have you arrested for possession of stolen property, extortion, and unreported income, which I think leads to tax evasion. Because it's Alabama, you probably won't serve any time, but it will cost you a ton of money, which I know you love, not to mention what it takes to defend your sterling reputation." Orville slammed his hand down on the table, once again trying to be dramatic, but it didn't faze buddy. "What the hell is that supposed to mean and who the hell are you?"

Buddy smiled again, he could tell that Mr. Orville was rattled and was trying his best to act tough. "Well, your wife is dead, and you have a mistress, a bastard son, and your mistress is a young naïve woman of color who thinks you love her. I am not sure how Montgomery is going to handle all that news." Orville bowed his head and looked at his hands that were now clinched together tightly. He raised his head and looked at Buddy, his bravado was now gone, and he seemed to be distraught. "I will pay you that sum if you leave me and Olivia alone." He reached into his coat pocket, took out a bank book, and wrote a draft for the amount that Buddy had demanded he pay. When he finished, he removed the draft from the book and slid it over to Buddy.

Buddy looked down at draft and did everything he could to keep from smiling. "You're going to be very happy with the condition the

## Chapter 43

company is in. The balance sheet is healthy, and business is booming, I believe." Orville interrupted him. "Where is she?" Buddy was about to answer when both men were startled by another voice in the room. "Her mother has taken her to the church so that God can cleanse her wickedness and flush the evil that flows through her bloodstream." Both men looked towards the sound of the voice, which was coming from the front of the house. Buddy knew this was trouble and he eased the Colt M1911 from the back of his belt where he intended to keep it, but something told him that he might be wrong.

The voice he was hearing had to have been the first car that he saw earlier and had now returned. A very large man stepped into the kitchen where both Orville and Buddy were sitting. At Buddy's best estimate, the man had to have stood 6' 6" and was probably tipping the scales well past 300 pounds, for sure. "Mister, I got no beef with you, you can leave." The man was holding a shotgun in his hand and was pointing it at the table where they were sitting. "Don't even think about pulling that hammer you got behind your back. You might as well ease it back into its saddle." The man was looking directly at Buddy when he said it. Buddy slid the Colt back into his belt and placed his hands on the table so the man could see him. "You must be Mr. L.C. Compton." As soon as Buddy said the name out loud, he could see the expression on Orville Gibson's face turn to fear. "I said you can go."

Buddy very slowly rose from the table and kept his hands up. "I'm afraid I can't do that." Buddy was deliberate in his words. He figured Mr. Compton was already burning a short fuse and he didn't want to get shot, nor did he want Orville Gibson to get shot. He might be a sleaze, but he didn't deserve to die. Besides, Buddy had a feeling that Orville Gibson really did have deep feelings for his mistress. In a twisted way, it made sense to Buddy. "You don't want to do this, Mr. Compton. This man ain't worth the repercussions and you know as well as I do what those repercussions are."

L.C. walked around the table and when he got almost beside Orville, he smashed the butt of the shotgun against Orville's

## Choice of Honor

chest, which sent him flying backwards, chair and all. Buddy didn't flinch, he knew this was not his fight and he needed to tread lightly. This giant man was enraged and was there to extract revenge or discipline or retribution for his daughter. L.C. racked the shotgun and pointed it at Orville as he lay on the kitchen floor. Orville put his hand up to guard his face, however, if L.C. had pulled the trigger, he would have lost the hand and still been dead.

"She was a baby and you abused her! She ain't all right in the head and you took advantage of her! Hell has a special place for despicable men like you! I am sending you to meet the devil, you worthless son of a bitch!" Orville started crying, "Please! Please! I'm sorry, but I love her!" L.C pointed the gun toward the kitchen ceiling and pulled the trigger. The sound was deafening. The blast sent little pieces of ceiling falling on all of them. "You don't love her!" He pointed the shotgun at Orville again and racked another round in breach. "You wanted her sweetness as a woman, and you took it from her!" He pointed the shotgun at the ceiling again and pulled the trigger and again, more debris fell from the ceiling.

L.C was so focused on his revenge and Orville that he didn't notice that Buddy had picked up a rolling pin off the counter and had eased behind him. L.C dropped to the floor directly on top of Orville. Buddy felt bad about hitting him, but he really didn't have any choice. If he let the man kill Orville, which he cared nothing about, then he would not be able to deposit the draft that he held in his pocket.

# Chapter 44

"WHAT THE HELL HAPPENED?" L.C. rolled over and grumbled. "Where did that child rapin' son of a bitch go?" Buddy decided to stay with him until he came around because he only wanted to deal with this man once. He figured if he left him, L.C. would show up somewhere else and probably at the wrong time. He also decided to let Orville leave as a gesture of good faith. Orville was happy to get the hell out of that house, but not before he gave Buddy some handy information. Buddy was certain that Orville Gibson had flirted with death enough for a lifetime and he wouldn't cause him any more trouble. If he did, he would deal with Orville Gibson appropriately.

Buddy put his hand down to offer L.C. a hand up. L.C. took a long look at Buddy's hand, as if he was deciding whether it was safe to touch him. After he decided that Buddy's hand was safe, he took it and got to his feet. Buddy strained considerably trying to help this man up. Buddy couldn't remember seeing anyone quite this big in his entire life. He thought the man on the train with the lawyer lady was big. He tried to remember that man's name, but it wasn't coming to him, nor was it important at the moment. Buddy was certain that if L.C. decided to beat the crap out of him, he could do so and there

*Choice of Honor*

wasn't much Buddy could do to stop it. Buddy was quite a fighter, but he wasn't up for this challenge.

"I asked you a question, where did that child molester go? It is my mission to send him to hell where he belongs." He looked around as if he hoped that Orville Gibson would just pop into the kitchen where he now stood looking down at Buddy, who remained seated that the table. "You let him go?" Buddy shook his head in agreement. "Then I should send you to hell, too!"

Buddy shook his head then yelled, "Sit down!" L.C. jumped back like he had just heard a gunshot. Buddy had always had a presence about him that got people's attention. Buddy had been careful his whole life to stay in the background as much as he could, but when it came time to lead and handle things, Buddy always stepped up. Now was the time for that. "Look! I have had about enough of people threatening me and waving guns in my face, so sit down and hear what I have to say!" L.C. quickly grabbed a chair, spun it backwards so that he could rest his arms on the back of the chair, and looked at Buddy with a curious look. "Who are you? Where were you taking my daughter, mister?" He paused for a second. "She's my baby and he took advantage of her. He put a baby inside of her for Christ's sake!"

Buddy tried to think of how he would feel if the tables were turned and it was Janie the two were talking about, but he hated the thought and put it away quickly. "I can't deny any of that. I was afraid that your daughter and your grandson were in some trouble and I was trying to help." Buddy could see that L.C. was tensing up and was about to finish the story when L.C. leaned forward so that he was very close to Buddy's face. "He ain't my grandson!" Buddy leaned forward even more, closing the distance between his face and L.C.'s face so that their noses were almost touching. "Then whose damn grandson is he?"

Buddy had a little spittle fly out and hit L.C. in the forehead, but L.C. didn't notice. At least if he did, he didn't act like it bothered him. "You think that boy asked for this? You think that boy picked who and how he came into this world? What

## Chapter 44

the hell kind of preacher are you that would condemn a child of his own blood line before he is ever given a chance to even know why he's being condemned!" Buddy leaned back into his chair and let that settle in the quiet room for a minute. L.C. also leaned back, but he crossed his arms. "You damn Bible-thumpers are all the same, every one of you preach forgiveness and acceptance and love, but when it comes down to the nut cutting, you're just full of shit." Buddy got up. He grabbed the shotgun that L.C. came into the room with, racked a shell into the chamber and tossed it at L.C.

L.C. caught it with one hand, which sort of impressed Buddy. That man had some huge hands. "Do what you want, I ain't got time for your two-faced preachin'." Buddy opened the back door and stepped out into the yard. He took a few steps. His hip was still hurting pretty badly, so he was trying to walk in a way that eased the pain. He heard the back door open; he had his back to the door and was certain that L.C. would not shoot him, but he didn't bother to turn around to find out. He kept walking, "What kind of trouble?" L.C. shouted.

Buddy stopped but didn't turn around immediately. "I was certain that they were going to be taken away or worse, either way, you would never hear from them again." Buddy turned around after he said it and looked at the giant man that was still standing on the back-porch steps. L.C. didn't say anything, he just continued to stare at Buddy. Buddy was tired of this little game and he turned and headed back to where he had parked the car.

## Chapter 45

"WELL, THE JUDGE SAYS I got to turn you over to county now and from there you'll probably be handed over to the feds." Chief Beauregard Laine stood in front of A.J.'s cell. A.J. had just returned from the cafeteria where he endured another welcoming party. In the few days that he had been in city lock up, he had become a regular punching bag to all kinds of different folks. Guards, inmates, both black and white all took a few shots at him. The guards would just claim he was being unruly, and they would beat him with their sticks. Those sticks hurt the worst because when they started, he could only protect his head, leaving his body exposed to all the blows they reigned down on him. They didn't last long, but they sure seemed to enjoy it. The white inmates would beat him just because they were allowed to do what they wanted when they wanted. It was the black inmates that puzzled him. They beat him, too. He tried to rationalize it, but he couldn't. In fact, he hadn't done a damn thing wrong, so he couldn't rationalize any of it.

"We will get you a nice pretty transport and have you out of here tomorrow morning bright and early." Chief Laine laughed as he said it. "My God, it might be just in the nick of time too, you ain't got friend one in this joint. Everybody wants a piece of

## Chapter 45

you, son. It's a damn shame really." A.J. stood up from his bunk and walked toward the bars that separated him and Chief Laine. "I didn't kill that woman and you know it. Mr. Gibson killed her because she was mean, and she definitely didn't like the fact that…" The chief cut him off. "Mind your next words, boy. I will turn you loose in the mess hall again and this time you won't be so pretty when they are finished with you." A.J. started to finish what he wanted to say, but he thought better of it.

He knew they had no intentions of handing him over to county and wondered if all the things that he and Buddy had talked about during Buddy's visit was helping or not. He couldn't be sure. Buddy had asked a thousand questions about everything during their meeting. He was nearly exhausted when Buddy was finished with his questions. He had never been through anything like that. He could not believe some of the questions that Buddy asked. He remembered Buddy asking him to describe Kari and the twins, to describe their facial expressions when they laughed or when they cried. He asked to describe Orville Gibson and every time A.J. would talk, he would mention another name of another person and Buddy would ask him to describe them, and not only describe their physical appearances, but to add anything he could think of that described the way they walk or any nervous ticks or anything that he could add. "Once you get to county you will see that they don't have any lush accommodations like we do here. Lotta queers in county that are just hard as a rock and waiting on some new meat." He laughed as he started walking away.

"Chief." A.J. tried to say it with confidence, but he was worn down and didn't have much fight left in him. "Chief, can I have something to write with?" Beauregard stopped laughing. "Why in the hell would I do that? You already wrote a letter to that redneck lawyer friend, illegally, I might add, and now you want to write another letter? Boy, you are crazy as a shit house rat." A.J. placed his hands on the bars and wrapped his fingers around the cold steel. "Please, sir, it's a letter to my wife. I want to tell her I love her. You know she can't come see me here. Please, Chief." A.J. leaned his head against the bars. He could feel the cold steel against his forehead. He wanted to slide down these bars and just sit on the floor, but he held himself steady.

He needed to scribble out words to his beautiful Kari Rae. He didn't know what to say other than maybe write *I love you* over and over, but he knew he had to get it down on paper. She may never see it, but it would sure make him feel better if he could just write down what he was thinking.

He didn't think the Chief would accommodate his request for one minute, but at least if he asked, he felt like he was doing something to help her as opposed to feeling useless behind bars. He didn't care how many times he got beaten, he needed to write down what he was thinking.

"All right, good grief, don't start crying on me now, A.J. I will get the jailer to give you some paper and a pencil. Keep in mind, though, I will read every word, so mind your manners." He turned around and took a few steps toward the bars that A.J. was leaning on. He patted A.J. on his forehead as he was leaning on the bars. "And don't you worry about that wife of yours because I promise you that if anything happens to you, I will personally take care of her." He laughed, then turned and walked down the hallway of cells that led out of the basement.

The echo of his shoes was deafening. A few minutes later, the jailer on duty brought A.J. a sheet of paper and a pencil. A.J. sat down on his bed and began to write. He fought back the tears as he wrote, but every now and then a tear would splat right down on the paper.

## Chapter 46

JANIE AND JIMMY MET BUDDY at the door, as they were understandably very excited to see him. Although Kari kept them busy all day doing everything under the sun, they were still in a strange place with strange people and their daddy had been gone most of the day. Buddy had stopped by the hotel, sent one more telegram that evening, and picked up all of their things.

"Daddy, look! Mrs. Mack showed me how to paint a tree in front of a lake with a reflection of the tree!" She grabbed her paper and was holding it in front of Buddy. He bent down to look at it so that he could be eye-to-eye and on her level. He never once wanted to be intimidating to his kids, so every time they talked to him, he would bend down on one knee and let them talk. "See! It even has a reflection of the tree on the water!" She was pointing at the tree. Buddy thought he could make out what she was talking about, but decided it was just best to embrace the beauty and the pride of her painting with gusto. "Holy smokes, baby, if you hadn't told me it was a painting, I would have thought we were looking out a window at such a beautiful tree and pond!" He hugged her tightly. "It's not a pond, daddy, it's a lake!" He laughed and squeezed her even tighter. "You are so right!"

Jimmy was holding something behind his back and was grinning. "Son, what have you got behind your back?" Jimmy grinned even wider. "You'll never guess! I made something for you! Mr. Freehold showed me how to make it..." He pulled his hands from behind his back and was holding a leather strap. "Look, daddy! It has your name on it!" Buddy let go of Janie in order to inspect the leather strap that Jimmy was so excited to show him. He held it in one hand and reached out to pull Jimmy close to him so he could hug him like he had hugged Janie. He didn't hug Jimmy near as much as Janie, but that was ok. He chalked it up to the whole father son thing and that daughters just gave dads more hugs. He didn't figure there was any more to it than that.

"We all worked on projects today, even Mr. Freehold." Kari stood there in the middle of the living room with Mr. Freehold in the doorway that led to the kitchen. "I see that, I have never seen so many beautiful hand-made presents. I don't even know what to say. Janie with her painting skills and Jimmy works wonders with leather and a stamp kit. I love them all." He could see Janie and Jimmy smile from ear-to-ear as he lavished praise on their hard work. He knew he was seeing the kids smile for the first time in quite a while. They had only been with Kari a day and she was making them happy again, all the while dealing with the struggles in her own life.

Buddy could easily see why A.J. lit up like a Christmas tree when he spoke of his beautiful bride when they met at the city jail. Buddy started to rise from the kneeling position he had taken in front of Jimmy to inspect the leather strap he had given him when the back window blew out and Mr. Freehold fell forward. Kari screamed something and instinctively shoved both kids to the floor in one sweeping motion, then yanked Kari's arm, forcing her quickly to the floor. He could see blood on Mr. Freeholds left shoulder, so he belly crawled to him, but realized the twins were in the side bedroom, so he continued quickly to where they were.   Little Buddy was sitting up rubbing his eyes and was oblivious to the noise the blast made.

## Chapter 46

Buddy quickly pulled him and his brother to the floor, which scared them both, and they began to wail. The room filled with a fine dust that made it look like there was a winter fog inside the home. Buddy didn't realize it, but she had not only made her way to the twins, but she had practically dragged Jimmy and Janie along with her. Buddy stood up and went directly to Mr. Freehold, who had managed to sit up but was holding his shoulder. "How bad is it?"

Mr. Freehold looked up at him with a dazed look on his face. "What just happened?" Buddy knelt down to look at Mr. Freeholds shoulder and snapped his fingers in front of his face to try and snap him out of whatever state he was in, but it didn't work very well. "How bad is your shoulder?" Buddy said it very slowly in hopes that he would get it this time, but that didn't work either. Buddy figured he would live, so he moved towards the back kitchen door. He could see that the kitchen table had turned over and the chairs were scattered all over the kitchen. The doorframe had been blown off and was in splinters all over the floor. Other than that, the damage was minimal.

He pulled the M1911 from his belt and slid along the wall leading to the back door. He slowly peeked around the side of the doorframe. He could feel the cold night air on his skin now, so he knew his adrenalin was wearing off. He stopped and took a breath, thought to himself that just a few weeks ago, he was happily married and besides A.J., he didn't know a single one of these people, nor did he care to.

He could see two figures approaching the house. After the explosion that ripped off the back door, he wasn't about to let anyone get close enough to try again. "Stop right there!" The two figures that were barely visible in the dark stopped. "Duh duh don't shoot." Buddy recognized that distinct voice and stutter. "Clancy?" He hoped that Clancy got the telegram in time to react to it and it was obvious he did. Buddy sent him a telegram after he met with A.J. in the city jail. He felt like he was in over his head and he wanted someone to help him if the need arose and the need seemed to rise every few hours for Buddy. He knew Clancy now, but he sure didn't send for anyone else.

As the two men approached the back door, Buddy could see that the man walking with Clancy wasn't really walking, Clancy had a grip on the guys back collar and was sort of dragging him along. "Huh huh hope you weren't expecting the puh puh puh Pope, were you?" Buddy shoved his gun back into the back of his pants and reached out to help Clancy pull the man he was dragging up the steps and into the kitchen. "Man, am I glad to see you, Clancy." He smiled and looked Clancy directly in the eyes. He still had an adrenaline rush from the blast and the shock of it, but like he had always done, he steadied himself quickly. "Damn, I must have sent the wrong telegram. I damn sure asked for the Pope." He chuckled but couldn't resist. "Who did you bring with you here?"

Clancy released the man he had by the neck, which caused the man's knees to buckle and fall to the floor in a sloppy heap. "I have no idea. I watched the house for while like the telegram said and I started to come up on the back door and I see this guy come running out of them wuh wuh wuh woods throwin' somethin' at the back door." He paused and looked up to see Curtis Freehold limp into the kitchen holding his shoulder. He could tell that the man he hadn't met yet was bleeding from the shoulder. "Damn fool nearly blew himself up when he threw it, lucky as hell he still has all his fingers. Man can't throw for shit. Throws like a damn sissy if you ask me." Clancy stepped around Buddy, who didn't see Curtis entering the kitchen behind him. Clancy grabbed Curtis by the arm and ushered him to a chair. "I take it that hole in your shuh shuh shuh shoulder is from sissy pants here throwin' that hot rock.

Buddy turned his attention to the man that was now crumpled on the floor. He was moaning and holding his right leg like he was in pain. "What happened to him, Clancy? Clancy didn't answer but kept his attention on Curtis Freehold's shoulder. He grabbed a towel he saw on the counter and pressed it against

## Chapter 46

Curtis's shoulder. "He didn't get out of the way fast enough. He was a victim of his own han han han handiwork." Kari came into the kitchen holding a twin in each arm. Janie and Jimmy were walking right behind her. Buddy could tell the children had taken to her very quickly. He was surprised at how calm everyone was, considering their back door had just been blown off.

The kitchen wasn't big enough for everyone to congregate, so he quickly introduced Clancy to everyone. "And that fella with the hole in his shoulder is Mr. Curtis Freehold." He was about to say something else, but Clancy interrupted him, "It's just a big ole splinter from the door frame." Clancy stood up straight as he said it and was holding a splinter that Buddy thought looked more like a ten-penny nail. "Good Lord, did you just pull that out of me?" Curtis Freehold had a shocked look on his face. "I didn't feel a thing!" Clancy smiled. "I'm a juh juh juh jack of all trades."

Buddy thought it was best to get a handle on the situation; things were too ragged for him. A back door had been blown up, a man had a splinter the size of a dart in his shoulder that was removed by someone he didn't even know, not to mention there was a dazed stranger lying on the kitchen floor of a house that was owned by a man who was sitting in a jail cell for something he didn't do, and his lovely wife didn't seem to be rattled by anything. She was as calm as anyone he had ever been around. "Ok, everyone, go back into the living room while I try and get some information from the man that nearly blew himself up. Mrs. Mack, please make sure the children are put to bed somewhere and if you don't mind, I would like some coffee. Mr. Freehold, put some alcohol on that shoulder to keep it from getting infected and Clancy, help me sit this worthless piece of cow dung at the table."

Everyone scrambled as ordered, just as they had done when he was in the Marines; the entire house came alive with shuffling feet and chairs being scooted around the hard wood floor. Once the kitchen was cleared of everyone but himself, Clancy, and Mr. Sissy Pants, he could smell the coffee brewing. The intruder was now slumped at the table, but Buddy had a suspicion that he was now pretending to be knocked out or playing dead. "Clancy, can you go out into the shed and see if you can find a hammer and two nails?" Clancy didn't hesitate, despite not knowing where the shed was located or even if it contained a hammer and nails.

"Clancy, lay his hand on the table with his palm down and spread his fingers out real wide so I could easily play mumbly peg if I wanted to. I am pretty good at it, you know." Buddy held up his hand that was missing the tip of the pinky finger he lost in war so Clancy could see it. "I only had this one little mishap." Buddy had a suspicion that his guest was simply pretending to be out of it in order to try and escape when no one was looking. "Give me that nail you brought. I want to make sure he is out. We can bury him in A.J.'s South pasture later." Clancy could tell that Buddy was playing, so he went along with it quickly. "Buddy, let me pound that nail, I uh uh uh always wanted to do that. I really can't buh buh buh believe anyone could stand that kind of pain." Buddy winked at Clancy. "Sure, partner, pound away." Clancy took the nail from Buddy and placed the point of it on the back of the intruder's hand so he could feel the point. "This is a damn good hammer; this damn thing has weight and it feels good in muh muh muh my hand."

Buddy tried to keep the laughter down and disguised one that was about to escape with a cough. "Smack that hell out of it, Clancy, it will be kind of fun to watch." Clancy smiled and choked back his own laughter. "Count to three fuh fuh fuh for me, puh puh please. I ain't sure I got the juice for this." Buddy got up from his spot on the table and started counting, but right before he could get to three, the man yanked his hand back and tried to jump up from the table. Buddy was there and anticipated he would do just that and shoved him back down. "You sum bitches are crazy as shit house rats! I ain't lettin' neither one of you damn hillbilly's pound a frickin' nail into my God damn hand!"

Buddy quickly slapped the man across the face. The man started to say something else, but before he could get another

## Chapter 46

word out, Buddy slapped him again, only this time much harder. The man nearly lost his breath and could only stare at Buddy with a scared and shocked look on his face. Buddy leaned down quickly and pushed his face as close as he could to the intruder's face. "You just blew a door off and maybe killed a man, we don't know yet, so you are in no damn position to tell me what I can and can't do!" He slammed his hand down on the table, which made the intruder and Clancy jump.

"Mister, you can bury me anywhere you want, but there were two other fellers with me, and they are already on their way to tell..." He caught himself before he said their names. Buddy slapped him one more time with a little less force than the second time he hit him, but more than the first. The man's face changed from defiance to defeat and for a second Buddy thought he was going to cry. "Better finish what you started, mister, otherwise the ending ain't gonna be good for you. Who are the other two going to tell?"

The man looked up from the table directly at the light overhead, then back down to the table. "It is my cousin, Matt." Buddy looked at Clancy, who shrugged his shoulders to indicate he didn't know, and Buddy almost laughed because how in the world could Clancy know anyway? He had been in town for less than an hour. "Who in the hell is Matt?" Buddy sat back down at the table. "My cousin, I told you that already, dipshit!" Buddy slapped the guy right in the forehead, which popped his head back quickly. "Forgive me, dipshit, I missed the moron family reunion. Who the hell is Matt!"

It was the first time that Clancy hadn't stuttered all night. "He's a cop in town. He doesn't care much for this Texas redneck here and wanted to send a little message." He paused and continued, "That's all, I swear!" Buddy couldn't believe what he just heard and had to take a second to process it. He was about to speak when the man let out a big sigh and lowered his head. "Weren't nobody meant to get hurt. Didn't know all these kids was in here." Clancy pulled up a chair and sat down.

*Choice of Honor*

    Buddy was still thinking. "You throw dynamite at someone's door and you don't eh eh eh expect anyone to get hurt? The man let a tear roll down his face. "It wasn't no dynamite! It was just a few cherry bombs strung together, I just lost count of how many I strung together." Buddy leaned forward in the chair so he could get a little closer to the man that had just blown a back door off its hinges and injured himself in the process and now he was sitting here crying like a little girl. Buddy laughed out loud. "I understand now, your brother is that skittish, weakling cop in town." He laughed again. "The cop that shot a hole in a store today." Buddy looked at Clancy, then down the hall. "My cousin didn't like you embarrassing him the way you did."

# Chapter 47

BUDDY CONTINUED TO PEPPER THE intruder with questions. He found out quite a bit more than he learned from Mr. Gibson, but the two stories seemed to line up. It was good information and he would need it the next night. He had some decisions to make regarding Jimmy and Janie and if things went South, Kari and her boys. He knew he had to have a plan, but it really hadn't come to him yet. He looked through both houses for things that could help him, but he really didn't find anything. He thought about his wife and tried to think about what she would say to him now, knowing what he was doing. He was standing in a house owned by black folks who he barely knew, trying to pay back a debt that if debated in court, he really didn't owe, but there was something to that *Semper Fi* motto that he firmly believed in. If he didn't believe in its value and meaning, then everything he understood and loved about the life and the Marines was lost.

These people he was dealing with didn't seem to care about the law and made no bones about it. That weasel cop that shot a hole in that store downtown was now sending his relatives to scare him and it made him mad. In a twisted sort of way, he felt he was at his best when he was mad. He felt like he was in touch with all of his senses. He was certainly calmer and more

*Choice of Honor*

focused. He knew that staying calm is what got him through the horror of the South Pacific. When he met A.J. that day he was shot in the chest, he had been resigned to the fact that he was going to die, but he had no reservations about it. He had made his peace, but during his conversation with the Almighty that day, he vowed to send as many Japanese soldiers to stand before him before he went. He remembered thinking that it would be a riot to stand there in the judgment line listening to the soldiers explain why they do what they do and listen to the Almighty deny them access through the pearly gates and send them crashing into a lake of fire.

He saw evil in those men who were fighting a war for their country, but with these men, he saw ignorance. They were scared of change, scared of things that were different from them and scared of anything that threatened their way of life. He wished he was back in Texas and more than anything, he wished he was with Doris. She was the best thing that ever happened to him. She made him better in so many ways.

When he finished getting as much information as he could from the cherry bomb expert, he rose from the kitchen table and slid his chair back in its place. "Clancy, what do you think he should do with this young man?" Clancy looked back down the hallway as if he was checking to see if Kari and the children were out of voice range, then looked directly at the man still sitting at the table. "I don't think we can turn in him into the police, his cousin sure won't do anything." Buddy looked down at the man. "That's for sure."

Buddy looked down the hallway and could see Mr. Freehold standing in the living room looking directly at him. Without saying anything, Buddy motioned with his head for Mr. Freehold to join them, which he quickly did. "Mr. Freehold, you were mentioning to me earlier, before we were rudely interrupted and you injured by those wood splinters, that you had family and friends that could handle certain issues discreetly." Buddy winked at Mr. Freehold, who was unsure of what was going on, but to his

## Chapter 47

credit, he caught on quickly and chimed in. "Oh, yes! I have some cousins that live just a few miles from here that supervise that old meat packing plant on Route 7, and they said they could chop up whatever kind of meat we wanted as long as it was after business hours."

Mr. Freehold showed a very strong and determined face to the intruder, a face that clearly reflected anger and aggression. Clancy couldn't help but jump in as he, too, wanted to see this man get really scared if he wasn't already. "Do do do do you think they could chop up a fella so's nobody could ever fuh fuh fuh find him?" Mr. Freehold rubbed his injured shoulder for effect, grimaced a little, and then leaned down and placed his hand on the table. "Oh, yeah, they said that was their specialty. They said they keep a jar of eyeballs and testicles as trophies. They said they got a special room where they slit a man's ball sack and wrists and watch him bleed out as he tries every which way to stop the bleeding. They say it usually takes about three or four minutes before he passes out. They say the man shits himself right before he blacks out."

Buddy could see that the description that Mr. Freehold just used was causing their guest to squirm in his chair. The man actually put his hand over his crotch as he was listening to Mr. Freehold's graphic description. Clancy had a grimace on his face, too, but Buddy didn't see him cover his crotch like their guest had. It was almost too much, and Buddy really wanted to laugh, but he knew this was necessary to scare this man so that he would not report back to his cousin for at least another day. Buddy needed the time to work out all the details with Clancy, Kari, and Mr. Freehold.

"What's your name, son?" Buddy sat back down at the table and lowered his voice to a calmer tone. The man across the table really wasn't a man as far as Buddy could tell. He looked like he had maybe just gotten out of high school. The man didn't answer and was clearly rattled by Mr. Freehold's imagination. If Buddy had been in the South Pacific during the war, he might have been rattled, too. Mr. Freehold was pretty graphic and was quite convincing. "Son, tell me your name, or I turn you over to Mr. Freehold here. My patience is wearing thin at the moment."

The man's eyes got big and he once again placed a hand over his privates. "My name is Francis, but everybody calls me Frankie." He looked down at his crotch as if he was savoring his last moments with his manhood. "Ok, Francis, here is what you are gonna do. You are gonna disappear for two days. I am sure you can find a spot in the woods to camp out or whatever you want to do." Buddy placed his hand under Frankie's chin and forced him to look at him because Frankie was intent on staring at his crotch. "But you're gonna disappear for two days. If you surface before that time and you talk to your cousin or anyone else for that matter, I swear on everything Holy I will hunt you down and stuff your eyes and balls in a mason jar."

Frankie's eyes once again appeared to be ready to pop out of their sockets. "Do you understand me?" Frankie nodded his head furiously in agreement. "All right, then, you are free to go."

## Chapter 48

"OKAY, YOU ALL KNOW WHAT you have to do, right?" Buddy spent the day going over every detail, right down to what Clancy should wear. It wasn't overly complicated, but he used every scrap of information that he was given by Ance Anderson when he met him at his office. That was decent information, Buddy thought, but it had quite a few missing pieces. It seemed to Buddy that Ance Anderson knew details of past excursions and was simply letting him know what would take place and the generality of where it would take place. It was good information, no doubt, but to Buddy Patton, it left too much to chance.

On the other hand, the information that he got from Mr. Orville Gibson as he sat at the kitchen table out at his little love shack trembling, sobbing, and begging for Mr. L.C. Compton not to blow his head off was much better. Mr. Gibson was very well-connected in town and not much happened without him knowing about it. He had details of the supposed transfer that would take place that he shouldn't have. Buddy felt there was a good chance that Mr. Gibson may have planned to be involved in A.J.'s transfer, but after having to confront the father of the girl he was screwing on the side and more importantly, staring down the barrel of a shotgun for a few minutes, he decided he didn't want any part of what was about to happen. In fact, Buddy was sure that Mr. Gibson planned on leaving Montgomery and taking his mistress and son with him. He figured Mr. Gibson had enough money to pull up stakes, go someplace that was a little more accepting of mixed couples and hopefully find peace.

Buddy didn't condone what he had done to his wife in order to get to this point, but there was no way that a jury was going to convict him of murdering his wife. The jury would damn sure convict A.J. for it, though, and that was why Buddy had to somehow snatch A.J. during the planned exchange with county. He had most of the information about the exchange that he needed, although everyone knew that county wasn't going to be there. A.J. would be handed off to a few private citizens with an axe to grind and A.J. would never be heard from again.

Luckily, the inept cherry bomber filled in all the gaps that he may have had about the exchange. He gave Buddy more details than he could possibly hope for. Buddy was a good tactician when it came to combat, but he was an even better strategist when it came to understanding what needed to be done and how to do it. Now if he could get to the spot where he thought they would exchange A.J. long before they did, he could stop it all from happening. It would certainly be tricky with some serious risks, but he was willing to take them. If he didn't stand for this, then he would never stand for anything. He told himself over and over that if something went wrong, his kids would eventually understand. Maybe they wouldn't understand right now, but as they grew up and took hold to their own convictions, they would hopefully appreciate the fact that their daddy stood for what he felt was right.

As for now, they would soon be on a train headed back to Texas and if everything worked out the way he planned, he would join them later. He paced through the house for a little while thinking things over before he was about to leave when he heard a voice, "Daddy, are you going on the train with us?" He turned around to see Jimmy looking at him with sad and unsure eyes.

## Chapter 48

Buddy remembered why he brought them on this trip; they couldn't stand being left without their daddy. They had buried their mother and the thought of being without their daddy was more than they could handle. Buddy walked over to where Jimmy was standing and knelt down so he could be eye-to-eye with his son. He put his hands on his shoulders and pulled him close to him. "Don't you worry none, son. I am gonna be on the next train after yours, I promise." Jimmy looked back down the hallway and then looked at his father again. "I like Mrs. Mack and so does Janie, but I would stay behind and help you if you want me to."

Buddy smiled, he was certain his son was going to turn out to be a fine man. He was already acting like one. "I would like you to stay and help me, I really would. I am not sure I can do what I need to do without you, but you have to ride the train with Mrs. Mack and the twins, remember? She said she has never been on a train before and you are an experienced traveler now." He pulled Jimmy even closer and hugged him. "Mrs. Mack told me just a little while ago that she was glad you were going because she trusted you." Jimmy looked in his father's eyes with a smile and asked, "She really said that?" Buddy laughed. "She sure did, partner. She needs your help and I am kind of jealous because I need your help, too, but it's more important you help Mr. Biggars look after the ladies."

Buddy could see his son's back straighten up and his chest puff out a little. He knew his son felt good to be needed and to feel important. "Son, it's important that you don't let Mrs. Mack and your sister get lost on this trip. I need them all back in Littlefield when I get there. Can you do that?" Jimmy smiled as if he had just won a medal. "Yes, sir, I can! I know how to get them on the train and in the right car. They won't get lost, daddy. I promise." Buddy felt a lump rise up in his throat and he had to choke it back down. His son was handling difficult circumstances better than he ever could have at that age. "I know, son, we are so lucky to have you helping us. I'm lucky, period."

# Chapter 49

THE DOORS DOUBLE CLANKED AND the chatter stopped in every cell. Despite how noisy it could be in holding, A.J. learned that when there was a double clank, that meant to be quiet and retreat to the back of your cell. There wasn't a rule book or orientation for the men in the cells, it was just something you picked up on. Normal guard checks didn't cause the chatter to stop, but the double clank sure did. That meant that BM was coming to take someone out of his cell. A.J. didn't know where they were taken, but he knew that in the two weeks he had been in this cell, whoever was taken didn't return.

BM was the nickname given to the beast of a man who came through the double clank doors. He was perhaps the biggest man that A.J. had ever seen. He didn't walk with anyone else and he never said anything when he arrived. He would simply walk to the targeted cell, open the cell with his keys and extract the prisoner, and then leave. There was talk that BM stood for Bad Man, or simply Big Man, but he couldn't verify and didn't want to. Something just told him that he did not want BM to stop in front of his cell.

BM did soon step in front of A.J.'s cell and for the first time, he got a look at this giant man, and several other nicknames popped

## Chapter 49

into his head. To his surprise, the first one popped out of his mouth and there was nothing he could do to stop it. "Bald Man" came out loud and clear and he wondered what caused such stupidity to overtake him. It was so dumb that he thought maybe he just imagined it and he really didn't say it out loud, but he could hear a few gasps coming from the other cells, so he knew he had said it. BM stood in front of A.J.'s cell for what seemed like an hour to A.J., but in reality, it was only a few seconds. He reached for the keys that were attached to his hip, unsnapped them from their hook, and inserted the key into A.J.'s cell lock. Either BM didn't hear it, which A.J. thought was impossible, or he chose to ignore it. He didn't say a word to A.J., but he did make eye contact.

When the two made eye contact, that is when A.J. found out that BM heard the comment because he quickly grabbed A.J. by the throat and pushed him against the cell wall. His hand was huge, it engulfed A.J.'s throat and for a second, A.J. thought he was going to squeeze his throat so hard that his head would simply pop off and end up rolling around on the floor. Just about the time A.J. was about to black out, BM loosened his grip on A.J.'s throat, but didn't fully release him. BM leaned in closely and sternly said, "I got no problems sending you to meet your maker right now, you piece of shit." BM fully released his grip on A.J.'s throat. A.J. gasped for a little more air and rubbed his throat with both hands. BM smiled and to A.J.'s surprise, BM had a nearly perfect set of teeth.

A.J. couldn't help but smile. He knew the seriousness of the situation but seeing a perfect set of teeth on a man that he would have had to place bets on wouldn't have all of his teeth, much less a perfect set. He found that amusing enough to smile. Luckily, BM didn't see the smile as he had already turned to start walking out of the cell entrance. "Let's go, dipshit." A.J. did as he was told and followed the giant man, who turned left out of the cell and headed towards the double door that apparently was the source of the double clank. BM fumbled with his keys for a second, found the one he wanted, and inserted it into the solid door.

As expected, when BM turned the key, the double clank was as loud as he had ever heard. A.J. had visions of what would be on the other side that ranged from guillotine to one of those electric chairs that fried you alive to facing six men all pointing a rifle at him with one lone guy holding a blindfold and a cigarette. A.J. didn't smoke, but he figured if he were offered a cigarette, he would take it just to prolong the inevitable and at least make his executors wait impatiently for a few minutes.

He was trying to stay positive at the same time, but he knew what was coming. He felt a great relief that Kari Rae and the twins would be cared for after he was gone. He knew in his heart that Sergeant Major Buddy Patton was a man of his word and would see to it that his family never needed anything. He drew in a breath as he stepped through the door and surprised to see that it was simply a small foyer that led to another glass door that he could easily see that led to the outside world.

It seemed odd to him that the cells were all so close to the outside world. He didn't dwell on it much, though, because BM opened the glass door, turned to A.J. and said, "Let's see your hands." A.J. held up his hands to show BM as requested, but he did it in a way that a magician shows he has nothing up his sleeves, which was obviously not the way BM wanted. "Hold them straight out, dumbass!" BM reached for A.J.'s hands and managed to grab one, then yanked his arm so it was stretched out straight. He then slapped a handcuff on A.J. "Now the other one!" A.J. extended his other arm and BM attached the other cuff. "Your chauffeur will be here in just a minute." BM found a great deal of humor in that comment and proceeded to belt out a huge echo of laughter. He slapped A.J. on the back and as he was exiting through the double clank door, laughed some more as he said, "Have a nice vacation!"

With that last comment, the giant man stepped through the door and shut it behind him, leaving A.J. standing in the small foyer alone. He stood there for a few minutes wondering what he was supposed to do. He pushed on the glass door to see if

## Chapter 49

maybe he was supposed to go outside, but it was locked. It was dark outside and the light in the foyer caused a glare on the glass doors, which made it hard to see through. He cupped his hands and pressed them against the glass like a kid looking into a store shop window display, but he still couldn't see much.

# Chapter 50

OFFICER MATT MOORE'S JOB WAS to pick up the prisoner and transfer him to county, however, there was no intention to transfer A.J. Mack to county. In fact, if you were to ask county, they would be completely unaware of any transfer of prisoners on this day. Officer Moore was so excited that he could hardly sit still. He had to down a few beers in the afternoon just to steady his nerves. He had never been allowed to be this close to real action.

He idolized Bo Laine and wanted nothing more than to be recognized as a good cop by the police chief. He and Bo had been friends for a long time. Bo was a few years ahead of Matt in school and was the guy that always got the girls. He was the best athlete and for all practical purposes, he was the best student. Bo went off to college while Matt stayed and worked at the sawmill. He didn't mind the sawmill, but he loved police work.

When Bo made chief of police, Matt asked him if he could be a cop and Bo helped him get into the academy and then gave him a job. He would have walked through fire for Bo Laine, but he just felt Bo didn't trust him to do a good job. He was hell-bent on picking this prisoner up and delivering him to the checkpoint. He was not about to screw this up. This was the chance he had

## Chapter 50

been waiting for. He knew he screwed up earlier with that redneck from Texas. The guy clearly invaded his personal space and had no respect for the badge. That made him mad, and when Matt got mad, he struggled with his nerves. He felt that no one should ever challenge him because he was in uniform and carried a gun. It was clear to Matt that this Texas guy had no respect for authority and that rattled him. He wished he hadn't drawn his gun and accidentally pulled the trigger. Looking back on the event, he really had no reason to be scared of that redneck, but there was just something about him and the way he carried himself that unnerved Matt. He was embarrassed when Bo made him go to Woolworths and see if everything was okay and to check to see what damage he had done with his stray bullet.

He tried all day to forget that incident, but he couldn't until Bo asked him to complete the task he was about to. He pulled the squad car up to the door that was used for prisoner release. He could see A.J. looking through the window, but he had already shut off the lights and eased to the curb. He sat and watched the guard bring the prisoner into the foyer where he was told to pick him up. He was told that the prisoner would be in handcuffs and the door only opened from the outside, so he had been warned not to go into the foyer and allow the door to shut or he would be stuck.

Bo told him that he once assigned the job to a rookie and he accidently got himself locked in the foyer with the prisoner and the rookie ended up being nearly beaten to death by the prisoner and worse, the rookie had been violated during his stay in the foyer. Matt was not about to get beaten in the foyer, he was way too smart for that, and he damn sure wasn't going to let some prisoner rape him. That would be the worst and most embarrassing thing ever. He got a hold of his nerves and decided it was time to collect the prisoner. He was on a strict schedule and he was not about to deviate one minute from it.

A.J. was looking back at the double clank door when he heard the glass door open. "Step outside, boy, and keep your hands where I can see them." He spun around quickly, and it must have startled the man at the door because he stepped back quickly, and the door closed between them again. A.J. wasn't sure what to do, so he stepped towards the glass door, but it opened again, and the man started yelling at him like it was his fault that the door closed again. "You stupid shit bird, what the hell were you thinking?!"

A.J. was confused about the comment, but since he was confined and handcuffed, he decided it was best that he didn't speak. "Don't you even think about bum rushing me, shithead!" A.J. was even more confused now. He hadn't even thought about bum rushing this man, he wasn't even sure what a bum rush was, but here he was being yelled at for it. "Let's go and don't give me any trouble or you'll be sorry!" Matt pointed at the car and made a motion for A.J. to follow him, which A.J. did. Once A.J. was secured in the back of the car, Matt jumped in the front seat with a spring in his step. He was whistling as he started the car and shifted it into first gear. A.J. sat quietly thinking about his beautiful wife, Kari Rae, and prayed silently that she would be able to handle all that would be thrown at her.

# Chapter 51

MATT WAS GIVEN THE ROUTE earlier that day with specific instructions not to deviate from for any reason. Bo told him that if he screwed this up that there was good chance he would not be a part of the city police force by sundown the following day. Bo was very forceful and edgier than Matt had ever seen him. He even stuck a finger in Matt's chest as he was explaining the options for failure to follow instructions. He was to take Old Route 31 South of town and was to stay on that road until he came to the Lake Edna exit. Once he took the turn, he was to travel for one mile and take the gravel road that lead to the old quarry and wait. No exceptions. Matt was right on schedule and feeling very good about the mission as he cruised down Route 31.

He was whistling as he drove. "This doesn't look like the way to county, officer." Matt continued to whistle and ignored the comment from his passenger. "Uh, officer, I own a cab company here in town and I know my way around. You are heading in the wrong direction." Matt stopped whistling and tapped his hands on the steering wheel like he was playing the drums. "You don't have to do this, you know, sir."

A.J. was calmer than he expected he would be and decided he had nothing to lose in trying to reason with this guy. He didn't seem very old, maybe mid-twenties; perhaps he could reach the kid before it was too late. "This will be something that you will regret. Trust me, it may seem right to you now, but at some point, you are going to see the error in your thinking, and it will be too late." Matt started humming. The humming was slow and deliberate. A.J. thought for just a split second that he was humming *The Old Rugged Cross*, an old hymn his mother used to sing to him when he was a boy and was sick or scared. She would either hold him or just lay down beside him and put her hand on his back or chest and she would hum or sing, whichever she felt was the most appropriate for whatever was bothering A.J. at the time.

He caught himself tearing up and choked it all back down. Now was not the time to get weak with a flood of old memories. Now was the time to toughen up and figure a way out this. "Say, officer, I know it might be hard for you to believe, but I am worth quite a bit of money. I could arrange to put some serious cash in your pocket if you just pull over and let me out." Matt stopped humming. "Bribing an officer of the law is a serious crime!"

A.J. leaned forward in the seat so he could be as close to Matt's ear as he could. "No, sir, it's a minor crime, murder is a serious crime, regardless of whether you are wearing a badge or not." A.J. could see Matt's knuckles turn bright white as he gripped the steering wheel as hard as he could. He wanted to be careful and not anger the man. That would do no good at all; he had a real balancing act to deal with here. "Uh, not that you would ever murder anyone, suh." The car remained silent for a few seconds. A.J. was about to continue, but Matt interrupted him. "Sit your ass back in that seat and shut the hell up! I've got a…" He stopped in mid-sentence. "What the hell is that? Gee zuz Christ." He slowly tapped the breaks and downshifted until he came to a stop.

A car was blocking the road, it had at least one flat tire and was propped up on a jack. Matt thought it was stupid for him to try and fix his car in the middle of the road and he should

## Chapter 51

have pulled over to the side. Hell, he could get run over being the way he was. The man who was working on the tire stood up and rubbed his hands on a towel that was lying on the ground next to him. He walked over to the police car with a smile on his face. "Shu shu shu am guh guh guh glad you all come along. I thuh thuh think I threw a ruh ruh rod and then buh buh blew out a tire."

The man rubbed his hands some more on the towel he had while Matt sat and fumed at the situation. "I uh uh uh could u u use a tow into tuh tuh…" Matt had enough. "Shut the fuck up, you stuttering dumbass, and get that pile of scrap metal out of my fucking way!" The man stopped smiling but continued to wipe his hands on the towel. "Uh uh ok but I cuh cuh cuh can't push it buh buh by myself. Can you help me?" Matt was gripping the steering wheel so tightly that A.J. thought he might bend it if he wasn't careful. "Geez zuz Christ! Fine!" He let go of the steering wheel and fumbled around with the door handle until he finally got it to open. He practically fell out of the car trying to get out too quickly, but he regained his balance and took one step toward the car in the road.

"The car is fine, partner. Don't do anything stupid." Matt could feel something hard in the center of his back pressing against his spinal cord. He started to turn, but the voice piped up again. "You miss that last part about doing something stupid?" Matt stopped and just stood there. He collected himself. "I am a police officer and you are making a big fucking mistake!" Buddy gripped the back of Matt's neck with his free hand.

He kept the clothes hanger he grabbed from Kari's closet in Matt's back. Buddy was not about to bring his Colt with him. He was not a criminal and had no intentions of shooting anyone. All he needed was a little head start and he calculated that he could have A.J. on a train headed to Texas before anyone caught up to them. He knew the charges against A.J. were all bullshit and the chief of police would more than likely not pursue them, but he wasn't sure. If he did pursue them, that would make Buddy a criminal, too. "Hand me the keys to the cuffs, partner." Matt thought about being a little more antagonistic and less cooperative. He felt like he needed to resist, but he simply didn't have it in him to have a physical confrontation with anyone.

He reached into his pocket and pulled out the keys to the cuffs then dangled them over his shoulder without turning around. Buddy took them from him then tossed them to Clancy. Buddy was impressed with Clancy. Clancy was never allowed to go to war because of his stuttering problem, but Buddy had a gut feeling that if he were ever in combat again, he would want Clancy by his side. He was fearless and he never questioned a single thing. He was definitely a square dealer and a true friend. He secretly hoped that Clancy would not get into any trouble for helping Buddy, but he suspected that the thought never even crossed Clancy's mind. Clancy opened the back door to the squad car, leaned in, and took the handcuffs off A.J.

A.J. had a very shocked look on his face as he was unsure of what was going on. It was dark and from the angle he had in the back seat, he could not see the men very well. When he stood up outside the car, he heard a voice say, "I've seen you three times in my life now, two of those in the middle of the night and the other time in jail. Not a very good track record, Corporal." It was difficult to see their faces at night, but Buddy had a smart-ass smirk on his face and A.J. was smiling. For the first time in almost two weeks, he felt like he had hope. "Clancy, take the car and catch up to the rest of them. We will be along shortly."

Clancy took a step towards the car that was used as a diversion and fell. He fell just about the time Buddy heard a pop. He knew what the pop was, and things were about to change quickly. He was now wishing he would have brought his Colt along. He strengthened his grip on the back of Matt's neck and shoved him to the ground. He couldn't tell where the shot came from, but he yelled at Clancy, who did not respond. A.J. had instinctively crouched down behind the back left tire of the squad car.

Buddy knew these guys were unpredictable and counted

## Chapter 51

on it. During the shove to the ground, he pulled Matt's service revolver from its holster. Matt never even noticed. "You hit, officer?" Matt was surprised that this man was even asking him. "Hell no, I ain't hit, but your sorry ass is about to be." Buddy was about to say something, but he was interrupted. "I need for everyone except the stuttering moron to stand up!" Chief Beauregard Laine stepped out of the woods and several lights popped on around them. Buddy let out a deep breath then stood up. He motioned for A.J. to stay down, but A.J. didn't follow orders, he rose up instead. He was not about to cower and let the Sergeant Major stand in front of these guys alone. A.J. couldn't see because of the brightness of the lights being shined on him, but if he could, he would have seen the smile on Buddy's face when A.J. disobeyed the command to stay down.

Buddy knew that A.J. was as tough as they come. He couldn't think of anyone else he had ever met that would have kept his finger in his chest while they were being attacked by enemy soldiers. The kid never flinched, never even turned around to see the soldiers charging them. He just kept his finger in Buddy's chest. Buddy had dreams quite regularly about that night, nightmares was more like it. The outcome was always fatal, and he would wake up in a pool of sweat.

"Mister, I got to hand it to you, you are tenacious and smart, but your luck just ran out." Even though Bo Laine was speaking directly to Buddy, he spoke as if he was speaking to a crowd, which from what Buddy could see was a pretty good-sized crowd. What struck Buddy was the seriousness on everyone's faces. Even from the glare of the lights, he could see that these guys were angry. "Don't believe in luck and I never was much of a gambler anyway." Buddy spoke in a soft and confident tone, it was clear and unmistakable. He had a serious dislike for Bo Laine, but at least Bo was not a phony. He was who he was, a bigot with a badge, and he had no problems letting you know it. He was a lot of things that Buddy despised in people, but he was not a phony.

Buddy was about to speak when it felt like something bashed him on the back of his head and he fell to the ground. It really didn't hurt, but it sure made him dizzy. He dropped to his knees first, but before he could fall completely forward, he caught himself with his hand. He looked like he was trying to do a push up when he felt a blow to his stomach and that one for sure hurt. It knocked the wind out of him and for a second, he thought he would throw up. The force of the kick caused him to flip over onto his back. He laid there for a second looking up at the night sky and marveled at how beautiful the stars were. He had trouble getting air back into his lungs but managed to sit upright with both of his hands on his stomach. He put one hand on the ground and started to roll over so he could get in a standing position when he felt another blow to the side of his head. That one didn't hurt, either, it just forced him to roll over more quickly than he originally planned.

"Damn it, Frankie! That's enough!" Bo's voice came through loud and clear and things went quiet for a second. Buddy rose to his feet and checked his lip that was starting to swell just a little, but he figured he was no worse for wear. He let a small grin come across his face because when he heard Bo's voice, he knew right away who was punching and kicking him. He turned around to see the inept cherry bomber standing behind him with a stupid grin on his face. "This sum bitch was gonna nail my hand to a table, Bo, and I'm gonna kick his ass!" Buddy stood there staring at Frankie then smiled at him.

Even in the dark and with the glare of the lights, Buddy could see that Frankie's face turned white as if he was scared. Buddy had underestimated Frankie. He judged Frankie as a scaredy-cat that would have actually gone and hid for a few days as he was instructed, but he guessed he decided not to. "You hit him one more time and I will nail your ass to Sherman's barn door with a note stapled to your chest explaining what you been doing with his daughter." Some of the crowd giggled a little and Buddy

## Chapter 51

didn't understand the inside joke, but Sherman was Buddy's uncle and apparently Frankie and Mary Ann, Sherman's daughter and Frankie's first cousin, had been experimenting with the birds and the bees for quite a while. They thought it was a secret, but Frankie just found out that it wasn't. All Buddy knew at that moment was that Frankie's face turned from white to red.

Chief Laine walked over to where Buddy and Matt were standing. "Give the gun back to Matt." Matt reached for his gun with a surprised look on his face when all he found was an empty holster. Buddy reached behind himself and extracted the gun from his back belt where he had quickly hidden it when he and Matt went to the ground. He handed it back to Matt without any resistance and smiled as he handed it to him. "Mister, were you plannin' on shooting all of us with his gun?" Bo had a slight grin on his face and made a gesture to the men who were now surrounding them. "Nope, just keepin' anyone else from getting' shot. I have seen first-hand how your deputy handles a firearm." The crowd around them giggled at that, too, but not very loud, just enough to know that they knew how skittish Matt was when he got intimidated. Bo laughed a little then said, "Now that is the first thing that you and I have agreed on so far." Bo walked around sort of circling Buddy, Matt, and Frankie. As he was behind them, Buddy looked at Frankie. "We had a deal. I promise to keep my end of it."

Frankie clinched his fist and made an attempt to punch Buddy again, but this time Buddy caught his fist with his right hand and with his left hand, he hit Frankie with an uppercut that knocked Frankie out completely. Frankie crumbled to the ground right where he stood as if he'd been shot. Matt saw what happened to his cousin and to his surprise, he reacted in an aggressive and angry way. He'd never actually seen a man get knocked out cold with one punch.

He lunged at Buddy and managed to grab him high around the shoulders from his back, but Buddy spun his elbow around quickly and caught Matt square on the jaw. Matt went down in one big heap, landing right on top of his cousin. It all happened so fast that Bo didn't have any way to stop it. The chief stood there staring at his two men knocked out cold on the ground beneath Buddy's feet. He pulled his pistol from his holster and pointed it directly at Buddy. "That's enough, mister." His voice didn't have the same showman style it had earlier. Buddy could tell that he was pissed now.

"Mister, you could have left things well enough alone, but now you have stuck that Texas-sized nose of yours where it don't belong." Bo put his gun back in his holster and blew into his hands to warm them up. Buddy could see his breath explode out of his cupped hands into the cold air. He stopped blowing into his hands and looked directly at Buddy and then to A.J. "Now you've gone and made yourself a criminal by helping a murderer escape from custody."

He looked up into the night sky and blew out another puff of cold vaporized air. Buddy was feeling the cold air against his face when he said, "He's no more of a murderer than I am." Then Buddy felt a sharp pain run through the tip of his pinky finger that was missing. That finger he lost in the war always gave him pains like that when it was cold. He cupped his pinky stump with his free hand to help warm it up. "How the hell do I know if you aren't a murder?" Buddy didn't hesitate to reply, "Because if I was, I would have nailed little Frankie's hand to a table, got what I wanted out of him, and then put a bullet in his head. Instead, I let the little liar go." Bo started to say something, but Buddy continued, "However, if my friend Clancy is dead, I will become a vengeful murderer. I promise you that."

Bo stopped walking in a circle and walked directly in front of Buddy and the men who were on the ground near Buddy. "You know, for a man who is out-manned and certainly out-gunned, you sure are brash." Bo smiled and turned to the mob that he must have collected and brought with him. "Hear that, boys? This man threatened an officer of the law. Now you all heard it and I will be collecting statements from all of you later!" He was

## Chapter 51

once again shouting and playing to his crowd. They all chuckled when he said it. One man even hollered, "I reckon you're within your rights to kill the sum bitch if you have to, Bo!" They all laughed again.

"Couple things you need to get straight real quick is your friend ain't dead, he just got popped in the head with new-fangled rubber bullets we are testing. He will have a big ass headache when he wakes up, if we decide to let him wake up, that is. Two, your time on this precious Earth is coming to a quick end. Three, old A.J. Cab Company executive over there is gonna have to watch you take your last breath so he will know what he got you into and..." He paused and clinched his jaw again. "Lastly, don't ever threaten me, you worthless pile of shit." Bo finished strong with his last statement and then he clinched his fist and took a huge swing at Buddy.

Buddy anticipated that the chief would try to sucker punch him to get the crowd fired up and ready for blood and stepped quickly away from the punch. This caused Bo to wildly miss connecting with his target and he stumbled forward, making him look very uncoordinated and awkward. There was a slight gasp that Buddy heard coming from the crowd of onlookers. "We don't, uh, you don't need to do this, Chief Laine. None of this is necessary." Buddy drew in a breath and was hoping he could get through to Chief Laine, but deep down he knew this was all going to end badly for everyone. The chief just missed on a punch, nearly fell in the process, and his loyal followers all saw it. He would have to recover and save face somehow, and that somehow was A.J. Mack and Buddy Patton dead.

# Chapter 52

A.J. HEARD THE POPPING SOUND as he stood outside the car. It all seemed to happen so fast, one minute he was in the back seat of a squad car and the next minute his handcuffs were being removed by a man he'd never met. He fully expected Buddy to help him, but not this way. It never crossed A.J.'s mind that Buddy would turn himself into a criminal by helping him in such a way. He nearly became sick to his stomach when he realized what was happening. At first when they came up on the car in the road, he really believed that it was a motorist in distress. When the guy came over to the squad car and started stuttering, he really thought it was a blessing in disguise. It was taking this poor motorist so long to explain what was going on that he thought maybe they would get off schedule, whatever that was, and maybe he could think of a way to escape.

During his meeting with Buddy Patton, he told him everything about what was going on: the murder, the love affairs, the death of his uncle, and every detail he could imagine. Buddy told him during that meeting to expect anything and to be ready to roll with anything he saw. He told A.J. that he really had no idea how he could help him, but he would sure make the effort and that he could make certain that his family were taken

## Chapter 52

care of. He also remembered that Buddy would see to it that his Uncle Marvin had been buried properly. He was arrested so fast after his uncle passed away that he was not allowed to attend the funeral. During his stay in lock up, he encountered a few guys that would come in and give him a few pieces of information about what was going on outside, they would tell him that his cab company was being taken over and it no longer serviced certain parts of the city, which meant that the cab now stayed away from the black neighborhoods.

But the best information he got was from Elroy Nebb. Elroy told him about his uncle's funeral. Elroy and his uncle had been life-long friends. Elroy tended to get drunk and would often spend a few days in jail to sober up. He remembered Elroy started to tear up when he spoke of the funeral. He said that it was standing room only in the church and that there were folks standing outside in the cold listening to the preacher deliver the eulogy and what amounted to be a sermon about the love of his fellow man regardless of his color or station in life. This particular preacher never missed an opportunity to save some lost souls and he certainly had a bigger than normal audience for his sermon. Elroy said that he was surprised that the preacher didn't pass the offering plate at the funeral, but he never did. Elroy had a great deal of respect for Uncle Marvin and it came out in the way he relayed the details of the funeral.

All these things raced through his mind as he sat in the back seat of that car, but the minute that stranger leaned in and took the handcuffs off him, he knew it was the work of Buddy Patton. His heart raced, not at the idea of being free, but at the idea of seeing his beautiful Kari Rae and the twins again. When he got out of the car, he saw the lights pop on and his heart sank. He knew right away that this wasn't a part of the plan and he would have to just go with it.

When he saw the stuttering stranger fall to the ground, he was certain that he was dead, and things were about to get really bad. He watched Buddy take down two men with a single punch and he nearly laughed when the chief took a swing at him and Buddy sidestepped the punch and Chief Laine nearly fell to the ground. His humor was abated when the chief got embarrassed and summoned others to help him and that's when all hell broke loose. Men came from every direction. Buddy started taking them down one at a time, but two men got to him at the same time and that's when A.J. decided it was time to ante up.

He charged the two men who had Buddy in a grip and knocked the two men and Buddy to the ground. He connected a few punches to the face of one of the men, who for a second, he thought he heard crying. Both Buddy and A.J. managed to get to their feet again and they stood back-to-back. They were certainly outnumbered, but they were not going down without a fight. This time, A.J. didn't have his finger in Buddy's chest and he could actually help Buddy with the attack.

A.J. was not as good at hand-to-hand combat as Buddy was, but he could certainly remember everything he was taught in the Marines. A.J. eye gouged two men nearly at the same time and he heard them scream. He felt a blow to the back of his head, but not enough to stun him. He slung an elbow to the location he thought the blow came from and he connected. There was a crunching sound and based off the splatter he felt on the back of his arm and neck, he guessed he had broken a nose. He could hear grunts and could see bodies falling, he knew that the Sergeant Major was still standing and doing quite a bit of damage of his own. He was beginning to think that between the two of them, they could beat the whole crowd. That's when he heard the real gunshots.

# Chapter 53

"ALL RIGHT! KNOCK IT OFF!" Chief Laine was embarrassed and in need of a way to re-establish control of this mess. He completely underestimated these two men. They had left a pile of his men in a heap and appeared to have the know-how and strength to keep going. He figured he needed to act quickly, or he just might be standing there alone. Everyone stopped fighting and stood still when they heard the shots and his voice. This made Chief Laine even angrier because he wanted the men he had brought along on this little excursion to take the time and subdue both men. Instead, they all acted like they were under arrest and didn't even make a move to gain control of the stubborn combatants. The chief yelled at two men who were in the background to "handle this shit." Two men came sprinting from out of the crowd. Buddy and A.J. saw them both and prepared to take them down, but what they didn't see were the two men who came up behind them. The blows directed at Buddy and A.J. were almost simultaneous and both men crumpled to the ground.

A.J. tried to shake the cloud out of his head. He looked around and realized that they were not in the same location. He could see that Buddy was right next to him and the stranger that stuttered was next to Buddy. As far as he could tell, all three were sitting on the ground with their backs against a fallen tree with their hands tied in front of them. Buddy and the stranger were still knocked out. He didn't see anyone other than those three, but he knew he was cold. He could see his breath as he breathed and he counted that as a blessing because he could see Buddy's breath and the stuttering stranger's breath, too. At least that meant that they weren't dead.

He tried to nudge Buddy, but it didn't work. Buddy just slumped over more than he already was. A.J. drew in a breath and exhaled very hard; the cloud of air looked like a small explosion. He leaned over and tried to help Buddy straighten up from his slumping position. As he was propping his friend up, he whispered, "I am sorry I got you into this. As God as my witness, I am so sorry." He started to lean back against the stump when he heard a voice say, "You don't need to apologize to Buddy Patton. Nobody tells him what to do, he makes his own mind up." A.J. looked over and he could see Clancy looking at him. He wasn't stuttering.

"Still shouldn't have asked." A.J. took a quick look around and still didn't see anyone, then he continued. "I don't know you, my brother, but I know I owe you. I am sorry." Clancy looked around, too, and could tell they were in a small opening in the woods. Trees surrounded them, but the trees were about twenty yards away. The only thing close to them was the stump they were leaning against and the tree that hovered above them. It was a huge tree, but the tree stood all by itself. "Who are you and why are you here?"

Clancy managed to smile at the question, but he was sure that in the dark, A.J. couldn't see it. "I'm Buddy's friend. I'd like to think I am his best friend. He asked me for help, and I didn't hesitate. Buddy Patton don't ask nobody for help, so I feel lucky." A.J. laughed out loud and had to put his tied hands over his mouth to keep from making noise. He had no idea where the crowd was, and he didn't want to bring them back. As far as he knew, they were alone and he was good with that, very good with that. "We are tied up, next to a stump in the middle

## Chapter 53

of nowhere, it's zero degrees outside, and we will likely be dead in the morning. You call that lucky?" Clancy smiled again and looked up at the stars that seemed brighter than ever. "You have a friend that is here with you tonight by choice and I have friend that asked for my help. He'd do anything for me and vice-versa. Yeah, I'd call that lucky." The words sank into A.J. like a car stuck in mud. He felt his chest heave as he grasped the concept. He knew what *Semper Fi* meant, but he guessed he'd never seen it put to the test in such a dramatic way.

    A.J. let the quiet of the night settle around them and then he started to smile. The smile turned into a low chuckle and before long, it was full-out laughter. Clancy looked at him in a confused way, but before long, Clancy was laughing, too. He wasn't sure why, but the look on A.J.'s face and the accompanying laughter just made him laugh, too. A.J. paused and tried to catch his breath, then said, "You should go into show business with that act of yours!" He laughed again and continued. "That thing you do with that stuttering! That was some funny stuff!"

    A.J. doubled over from his sitting position and held his stomach. "Man, that was some of the best acting I've ever seen!" He raised back up. "You should have heard Matt in the car mumbling under his breath. He called you every name in the book!" A.J. noticed that Clancy wasn't laughing anymore. He was about to ask why when Buddy interrupted. "It's because it ain't an act." Both A.J. and Clancy moved to help Buddy sit up straight. "You just insulted the man. He stutters when he is nervous, and he doesn't trust the people around him." Buddy winced as he said it. He rubbed his stomach and chest. "They must have kicked the shit out of me." Clancy chuckled and replied, "You feel a lump in the seat of your pants, do you?" All three men laughed, but Buddy was guarded with his laugh; he was certain he had some broken ribs and it hurt to laugh. "Where are we, Corporal?" Buddy winced as he said it. "I can't be for certain, but this looks like Ance Anderson's place. It's so damn dark that it's hard to tell, but only Ance has property like this around here."

They all sat there looking around at the surroundings and the night sky. Clancy stood up. "I think they are gonna let us go." Clancy seemed excited when he said it, but then he finished with a question. "Wonder why they go to all that trouble and rough us up then just leave us out here in the middle of nowhere?" Buddy struggled to get to his feet. A.J. could see that he was in pain and his breathing was very labored. Oddly, he remembered that exact sound from the first time they met. Buddy could barely breathe, so A.J. caught him under the arm and helped him to his feet.

They were all still handcuffed, but it was easy enough to reach out and help him. "No, we are supposed to make a run for it. Looks better if we are escapees from the jail. Reads better in the paper." A.J. stood beside Buddy with his cuffed hands, still holding Buddy's arm. "You can let go, Corporal. I am fine." A.J. was not certain that Buddy could stand alone because his breathing was really bad. A.J. didn't feel very well, either, but he knew he was younger and in better shape than Buddy. He also knew that Buddy was one of the toughest men he'd ever met, so he released his arm. Clancy said, "So, what do we do, Buddy?"

Buddy put his hands on his shoulder; since his hands were cuffed, he rubbed his shoulder with both hands. "Well, they want us to make a run for it, which means they will be positioned in all areas of concentration." Clancy looked a little confused and asked, "What the hell does that mean?" Buddy wasted no time in answering, "It means that no matter which way we try to go, we will be met with resistance." He paused for a second, looked up at the sky, and the then scanned the area in almost a 360 motion. "We stay right here. They will get pissed that we don't run and then they will come to us, it's too damn cold to sit out there and wait on three cons to make a run for it." Clancy laughed a little under his breath. "Hell, I ain't no con. I am a postman, they obviously don't know who they are fucking with!" He laughed when he said it, so did Buddy. Buddy was about to respond when the headlights from the North appeared and made their

## Chapter 53

way to them. Buddy saw it like everyone else and said, "I reckon they got tired of waiting sooner than I expected."

There were two cars. Both were Nomad-style with extended back ends. Because it was dark and the headlights were pointed at them, A.J. couldn't quite figure out if they were actually Nomads. The headlights bounced up and down as they approached, which to A.J. meant that there wasn't much of a road to travel on, so they were definitely in the middle of Ance Anderson's ranch. They moved in rather quickly. The doors opened and they piled out of the car like they were arriving at a party.

There was laughter and talking and someone dropped a bottle. It broke when it hit the ground. "You damn idiot! That was the only Wild Turkey we had!" There was grumbling from some of the others. "Well, we can drink the fuckin' beer then!" Matt stepped out from around the vehicle. "All ya'll just shut the hell up and remember what we are her for!" The three men looked at each other and each knew that this was not going to end well. A.J. put his cuffed hands on the back of Buddy's arm and gripped it tightly. Buddy felt the grip and smiled. He thought of all the things he wanted to see and do and knew that these folks were going to make sure he didn't see or do any of them.

He thought of his beautiful wife and how life had been cut short for her. He turned to tell Clancy that he was proud to be his friend and he was sorry he got him into this mess when the headlights from the South came into view. There were at least four cars. His heart sank. This was just more thugs wanting to get their kicks. Clancy nudged him, they both looked at each other. Buddy smiled when he saw that Clancy was smiling at him. There wasn't much that needed to be said between Clancy and Buddy, they developed a bond over the years that didn't need explaining to anyone.

"You fellas are trespassing on Ance Anderson's land and you are escaped felons, that's a bad combination of crimes." Buddy laughed out loud. "And you fellas are uneducated and wrong. That's an even worse combination!" Nobody in the small crowd

## Choice of Honor

of men who piled out of the cars said anything, but Buddy heard a voice pipe up that sounded familiar. "It is my land and you are trespassing." Buddy misjudged Ance from their previous meeting. He had Ance pegged as a man who went against the grain. He was oddly disappointed in the man. "Never figured you for a party man, Ance."

Ance stepped toward Buddy, A.J., and Clancy. "All you fuckin' Texans are all alike. You think you are better than everyone else. You think because you show your ass and break a pool cue you scare me?" Clancy nudged Buddy because he had been nudged by A.J. There were more headlights coming from the opposite direction, but Buddy hadn't seen them yet. "Ance, are you pressing charges against these three?" There was another voice that Buddy knew all too well. Chief Laine was back in the mix. Ance didn't waste any time answering and said, "Hell no, I handle my own business and I don't need help from the law to do it."

The chief laughed and took a few more steps towards the three. "I figured you'd take it that way." The chief took a few steps so that he was standing right in front of Buddy, he reached down and grabbed Buddy's hands that were still cuffed. He fished in his shirt pocket for a key, found it, and swiftly unlocked Buddy's cuffs. As Buddy was looking down at the removal process, Matt took a step toward Buddy and punched him in the face. It knocked Buddy a little off, but he didn't fall. Buddy turned to look where the punch came from when he felt another blow to his temple area. There was no mistaking where that one came from; the chief had thrown his own punch. This pissed off A.J. and Clancy and both went to rush the chief and Matt but didn't make it anywhere near him when they were tackled by some of the other guys. Clancy and A.J. were getting kicked and punched by everyone when they heard the gunshots.

As soon as the crowd was quiet and the men stopped kicking and punching A.J. and Clancy, someone said, "I am looking for Chief Beauregard Laine. Would any one of you gentleman happen to be the noble and honorable chief of police?" That was

## Chapter 53

a voice that Buddy didn't expect to hear, but he knew it when he heard it. It was unmistakably female and there was no doubt that it was Ms. Cecilia Adams, the lawyer he met on the train to Montgomery. "Get the hell off my property, bitch, before I shoot your sorry ass for trespassing, too!" Buddy was sure he heard a slight hint of fear in Ance's voice.

Before she could announce who she was to the assembled crowd, the clear and distinct sound of a gun being cocked broke the silence and a voice from East of where they were came from the woods just a few yards away. "Eye for an eye, brother Anderson!" It was clear to Buddy that Ance wasn't expecting this either. "Who the hell is out there!" Buddy couldn't be sure, but he thought he knew that voice, too. While there was silence and nerves were on edge, Buddy shook his head to clear the residual effects of two consecutive sucker punches.

To his amazement, the clarity of where he was came at the perfect time, he saw the chief as clear as the night sky standing in front of him with a surprised look on his face, more than likely as surprised as everyone else to hear a female voice in the middle of Ance Anderson's property and at that moment, he took his revenge. Buddy smashed his fist into the side the chief's face. He couldn't be sure, but he thought he could hear bones crunching and he hoped he had broken the chief's jaw. At least that way, no matter what happened tonight, the chief would have to eat through a straw for a few months. He turned to see Matt staring at him with a surprised look on his face, too, and he smashed Matt right square on the nose. Buddy's hand exploded in pain, but he didn't care. Matt dropped for the second time that night. A gunshot went off again, but this time a second gunshot went off from the other direction.

The chief was trying get up off the ground and was holding his face as he rose. He mumbled something, but Buddy couldn't tell what he said. Buddy took great delight in knowing that the he had successfully punched both Matt and the chief and the chief was struggling to gather his thoughts or to even assimilate

*Choice of Honor*

the sound of a vowel. Through grit teeth, the chief managed to respond. "I am Chief Laine, who the hell are you?" He paused for a second and said, "And whoever is out there in the woods better come out and show yourself!" There was now a third voice that came from the dark that said, "Lower you weapons and get back in the car and go home and we will." That was followed by another cocking sound as if the person was racking a shell into a shotgun.

"Chief Laine, I am Cecilia Adams." She strode toward the crowd without hesitation. The crowd of men let out a hushed gasp in disbelief that a black woman was so brazen in her approach; even Buddy was surprised by her moxie. She was carrying a briefcase just like she was walking into an office. As she made it face-to-face with Chief Laine and was just a few feet away from Buddy, she stopped. "This is my associate, Mr. Sherrill Jackson, and this is my colleague, Mr. Paul Leigh." She actually stuck out her hand in a gesture to shake hands with him, but as expected, the chief didn't return the gesture. He just stood there dumbfounded. "Lady, you are in over your head here. You and your thugs need to get back in those cars and go back to wherever the hell you came from. We've about had our fill of strangers coming in and telling us what we need to be doing."

Ance Anderson walked up to her and raised his hand like he was going to hit her. She didn't flinch, but her associate certainly did. The giant of a man that Buddy shared a car with grabbed Ance's hand so fast that Ance didn't know what to do, but as soon as Ance felt the pressure of Sherrill Jackson's bear-sized hand crushing his, he tried to pull away, but Sherrill had a death grip on him. With his free hand, Ance swung at Mr. Jackson and connected with the side of Mr. Jackson's head. Clancy actually laughed out loud when he saw that Mr. Jackson barely moved his head. It was as if Ance had just punched an ice box. "Chief, we will be pressing charges against this gentleman later. I am certain you will make a fine witness once we have subpoenaed you."

## Chapter 53

Paul Leigh's voice was deep and smooth without any hint of sarcasm. Ance was holding his hand trying to rub some feeling back into it and managed to say, "You got a lot of sand, piece of shit. You are trespassing on my property and you want to press charges against me! You are fucked in the head." Like a good tag team of lawyers in court, Cecilia wasted no time responding. "That would make you one Mr. Ance Anderson?" Ance stood completely straight, as if he was proud that she knew him, but was slightly confused as to how she knew him. "Chief, I apologize, we will not be pressing charges against Mr. Anderson."

Mr. Leigh nodded his head toward Ance when he said it. Buddy could see a smile cross Ance's face, but it quickly went away when Cecilia continued and said, "We will be arresting Mr. Anderson for kidnapping, extortion, tax evasion, and racketeering, but that is not important right now." Buddy could feel the smile come across his face and there was nothing he could do to stop it.

This lady he was watching had grit, moxie, poise, and certainly courage. She was cut from a different fabric, that was for sure. "Lady, you don't have the authority to do any of that shit in the great state of Alabama, so pack your shit and hit the road." The chief was still rubbing his jaw as he spoke. Mr. Leigh continued and said, "Chief, you have falsely imprisoned Mr. Alvin Jerome Mack and his colleagues, and we are here to return him back to society without any more harm."

Buddy was amazed at the back and forth and how easily Cecilia and Paul played off of each other. "Okay, you two have had your fun." The chief looked around for a second and then hollered for Matt. A.J. took the opportunity to throw a verbal jab at the chief. "Uh, your second is taking a nap." Buddy laughed out loud at the comment. "Shut up! Everybody just shut the hell up!" Ance was now screaming. Buddy thought, *you aren't as dangerous as everyone said. You are scared now and that could work to my advantage, but a scared man is also a dangerous man; it would be prudent to tread lightly under that threat.* More than

## Choice of Honor

anything, though, he wanted to see what the two attorneys were going to do.

"Ignoring Mr. Anderson's outburst of unprofessionalism, Chief Laine, I must inform you that you are now in direct violation of a presidential order and subsequent pardon. Any continued actions against these men will be considered hostile and punishable by imprisonment for up to twenty years in a federal penitentiary." No one moved or said a word. Ms. Cecilia was so profound and forceful in the way she delivered the news to Chief Laine that it sent chills down everyone's spines except Buddy, he was trying to stay a step ahead of what these guys would do if they decided the lawyers were full of shit and take matters a step higher on the ladder.

Mr. Leigh picked up where Ms. Cecilia left off. He pulled a piece of paper from the briefcase that Ms. Cecilia walked up with. "By order of President Dwight David Eisenhower, any and all crimes or potential crimes of Corporal Alvin Jerome Mack have been exonerated by the office of the President of the United States of America. He is to be returned to rightful citizenship afforded by all U.S. citizens post-haste. Signed, Respectfully, Dwight D. Eisenhower, Commander in Chief." Mr. Leigh folded the paper and put it back into the briefcase and Ms. Cecilia picked up again. "Chief, it appears that one James Robert Patton, the man who is trying to assist one Alvin Jerome Mack with his quest for freedom, is very well connected."

She snapped her fingers in front of the chief's face because he seemed to be staring off into the distance. "In other words, sir, it helps to be a direct relative of the late, great General George Patton." There was even more silence in the crowd than there ever was. Buddy tried not to smile and thought he was doing a pretty good job of keeping a straight face. The lawyers were playing every card they had in the deck. He was so impressed with their ability to bluff, tag team, and sound believable all at the same time. Buddy knew he would never get into a poker game with these folks, they were good.

*Chapter 53*

Ance came out of his mini-trance and shouted, "You people are full of shit! The president ain't gonna pardon no..." Before he could finish, Cecilia interrupted him and said, "He can, and he has. I would like nothing more than to stand here and converse socially with all of you, but we have a train to catch. And, oh, one last detail for all of you, we have Mr. Orville Gibson in custody, and he is being transferred to the custody of the Mobile office of the FBI for processing. And just for your information, he has confessed to the murder of his wife and miscegenation with one Miss Olivia Compton."

Buddy could hear a grumble through the crowd, and he could hear the air or steam going out of the entire crowd that sounded like a tire going flat. Ms. Cecilia had played this audience like a good lawyer plays the jury. She was prepared and she was amazing. Buddy, Clancy, and A.J. were left looking at each other as if they had just seen a slight miracle.

## Chapter 54

NOBODY MOVED. THE CHIEF HAD a bewildered look on his face. The two men who Buddy had knocked out earlier were now sitting up trying to get the cobwebs cleared from their heads. Ance Anderson was mumbling under his breath and was walking in circles. He had a wild look on his face, one that Buddy was familiar with. He remembered those looks from the war. It was a look he had seen on faces of men who were confused, scared, and angry. They were the most dangerous because they were unpredictable.

Ms. Cecilia reached out and grabbed Buddy and Clancy by the arms and began to move them in the direction of the car. A.J. felt a hand grab the back of his bicep with a vice-like grip and began to also move him in the direction of the car. A.J. turned to look and see who had a grip on his arm and after a few seconds of processing the information, he should have known that it was the giant bodyguard that had been referred to all night as their "associate."

As best as A.J. could tell, this man was a bodyguard, and a good one. He was soft spoken, always stayed semi-invisible (if that was possible for a man his size), and he was quick to get in the way of any threat to Mr. Leigh and Ms. Adams that he perceived. He took his job very seriously and it showed. Chief

## Chapter 54

Bo Laine pulled his revolver and fired it in the air, and everyone stopped. A.J. felt the giant man move him effortlessly behind him, which would have blocked any gunfire aimed at them. A.J. felt a rush of gratitude for a man who he had never met until this evening who was now so willingly placing himself between A.J. and a man with a gun.

The chief was gritting his teeth and trying to control his anger as he spoke, "Everybody better just put a stop to any movement or I will shoot somebody, and that's a promise." He was still pointing the gun in the air when there were four more gunshots, not all together, but one after the other and they were all from a different direction. Then came the voices, lots of them, one after the other.

"Pull that pistol again and I will drop you with one shot, Chief." Then another voice, "Not before I do," then another, "Me first," then another, "No way, I got this Mother Fucker," then another, "Like hell you do, I do, I got him!" The voices came from every direction and every time they heard one, they heard the sound of a gun being cocked or a shotgun shell being racked into the chamber. It was quite an experience and one that neither Buddy nor A.J. expected. How all of these people managed to show up armed and ready at this time was beyond understanding. Buddy felt like it was the right time to speak up now; he stopped and gently freed himself from Ms. Cecilia's grip. She protested quietly by trying to regain her grip on him, but he took a few steps back towards Bo Laine. "Well, Chief, the decision is yours. I came out here prepared to die for my friend. Did you?"

The chief looked around in all directions. He wasn't confident in his actions anymore. He had clearly lost his edge. He was no longer the ringmaster and Buddy wasn't sure, but he thought he could see fear on his face, but it was too dark to make that judgment for certain. "You used your daddy's name to get you out of trouble. Don't ever come back to Alabama again." Bo tried to look authoritative as he said it, even placing his hand on his holster as if he would do something with it. "I will handle your friend after you and your daddy's pardon are long gone." Buddy smiled and said, "Maybe." Then Buddy leaned in closer to the chief and whispered, "But when you lay your head down tonight, know that I hold a grudge for life. I might just tip-toe into your bedroom and slit your throat and leave your wife with a grieving widow." He leaned in even further. "Times change, change with it, but if you ever cross another Marine, especially a friend, I promise you won't sleep peacefully ever again."

Buddy turned on his heels as if he was in uniform and made his way back to Ms. Cecilia. When he reached Ms. Cecilia and Clancy, she smiled at him, reached up and put her left hand on the back of his neck, got to her tip toes, and kissed him on the cheek. She then turned and kissed Clancy on the cheek. She whispered, "I could stay and take advantage of both of you, but we need to leave." She gripped Clancy with her right arm and Buddy with her left arm. A.J. had already been ushered to the car and was waiting on them. When he was close enough to Buddy, he reached out to him, put his arms around him, and hugged him. "Uh, you're not my type." A.J. released him and Ms. Cecilia once again urged them to get in the car.

Bo Laine stood there beside Ance Anderson without saying a word. They both scanned the woods that surrounded them hoping to catch a glimpse of anyone that might be pointing a gun at them, but they couldn't see anyone. Both men were unsure of what to do. Bo looked down and he could see that Matt was coming around along with his cousin. Both men rolled around on the ground trying to regain their faculties. "This is ridiculous." Bo let his words escape his mouth in whispered tones. Ance wasted no time responding, "Fuck 'em, I told that old fool to quit bangin' that colored girl. This is all his damn fault." Bo nodded as if he agreed but didn't let it go. "A presidential pardon? A general's son?" Both Ance and Bo leaned down to help Matt and Frankie stand up. Both men were very wobbly and needed a considerable amount of help just to stay vertical. Bo

Chapter 54

watched the car pull away with headlights bouncing as it made its way back to the main road. "Somebody come get these two idiots and get them home. The night is over, let's get out of the damn cold!"

## Chapter 55

⁓

"KEEP YOUR HEADS DOWN UNTIL I tell you." Mr. Jackson, the giant bodyguard for Ms. Adams, dropped the clutch on the sedan they were using. In the rush to get into the car and leave, A.J., Buddy, and Ms. Adams were in the back seat. Clancy, Mr. Leigh, and the giant man ended up in the front seat. Clancy was thinking that perhaps they should pull over and let Ms. Adams switch places with him since he could barely breathe. The giant man driving the car was taking up most of the bench seat. He quickly decided that pulling over to attend to his comfort at the moment would be quite selfish and a down right bad idea, so he choked the idea back down.

He still had a whopper headache, but it hadn't knocked the common sense out of him. The car was bouncing up and down from the lack of road. The bodyguard was cursing under his breath that he hated something that Clancy couldn't make out. The car came to a quick stop. Each person lurched forward. Buddy instinctively and protectively put his arm across Ms. Adams and so did A.J. She stayed upright while the two men slammed forward. "Gee zuz, Sherill! What are you doing?" Mr. Leigh was rubbing his forehead that had just slammed against the dashboard. "Mr. Mack, thank you for your chivalry, you may now remove your hand from my chest."

## Chapter 55

A.J. yanked his hand back and turned his head away from her quickly out of embarrassment. Buddy was still trying to figure out why Sherrill had stopped so quickly. "Mr. Patton, you may keep your hand there as long as you like." Buddy didn't realize he still hand his arm across her chest to protect her from slamming forward, but he felt even more embarrassed when he realized his hand was cupping, or seemingly cupping, her breast. He quickly removed his hand and literally stuck it in his pants pocket as if it had a mind of its own and he was locking it away to keep it from randomly grabbing a boob.

He tried to look away, but before he turned, he caught her smiling at him. "My apologies, ma'am, I was merely, uh, we were both merely trying to be pro..." He didn't finish, she finished for him and said, "Proactive, I hope." He felt the blood rush to his face, he felt guilty and all he could think of at that moment was his wife. He missed her. *Protective* came out as he intended it to before she tried to finish the sentence for him. Mr. Leigh was looking in both directions and was straining to see behind them. "What in the hell are you doing?!" He continued to rub his head as he searched in all directions. "I think I ran over a rabbit." Everyone became quiet. Buddy was confused by the comment about the rabbit.

Mr. Leigh stopped rubbing his forehead, then took his left arm and placed it against Clancy's chest so he could push him back in the seat far enough to give him a better view of Mr. Jackson. "Let me get this straight. The six of us just faced down at least twenty men hell-bent on hangin' somebody tonight, the two guys got the hell beat out of them, and Ms. Adams is still trying to dislodge Cupid's arrow from her ass, and you slam on the brakes for a damn rabbit!" The huge bodyguard fidgeted with the steering wheel a little bit, then looked back in the back seat as if he was explaining himself. "I had a bunny when I was little."

Ms. Adams leaned forward in her seat and as she did, she placed her hand on Buddy's thigh to give her balance and leverage, but mainly to try and send him a message. Buddy froze, he looked around as if someone would say something about the poor behavior, but it was too dark in the car and no one saw it. "Sherrill, I promise to buy you a bunny when we get back to D.C. if you like, but right now, I would like you to get us back to the main road and on the train."

The car started rolling again and within minutes, it was back up on the main gravel road that would lead them back to the highway. The ride smoothed out even more considerably when they reached the blacktop highway and made their way back towards town. The noise of the road also diminished enough to reverberate the silence that was now engulfing the car. Clancy turned from his middle position in the front seat. "You never told me you were related to General Patton." Buddy smirked just a little and said, "I was happily ignorant of that fact until just a few minutes ago, too."

Buddy turned to look at Cecilia Adams and could see her teeth just as white as anything he had ever seen. She was smiling as if she had just won the biggest poker game ever with nothing more than a busted straight. Clancy started to turn and face forward, but stopped and turned back to say, "So, there is no presidential pardon for A.J.?" Without hesitation Cecilia replied, "They don't know that and by the time they find out, you all will be in Texas and we will be back in D.C." She laughed as she said it; Buddy and A.J. could hear Mr. Leigh laughing in the front seat.

Clancy turned and faced forward. A.J. leaned forward and turned enough so he could see both Buddy and Cecilia. "So, I am an escaped prisoner now!" He rubbed his forehead and looked as though he was about to throw up. Cecilia put her hand on his shoulder. "I guess you could say that." A.J. sat back in his seat and shook his head. "Just let me out, that way you guys aren't in any trouble. I couldn't handle it if you all got in trouble." Mr. Leigh burst out laughing and when he finished laughing, he said, "Mr. Mack, pursuant of Section 752 under Title 18 of the United States Code Service, whoever rescues or attempts to recue or instigates, aides, or assists escape, or an attempt to escape, shall

## Chapter 55

be fined or imprisoned for not more than five years, or both. That's kind of the short version." A.J. leaned forward even further in his seat and rested his head on the back of the front passenger seat. "I can't let ya'll do this." Cecilia put her hand on his back. "You don't have a choice in the matter, Mr. Mack. We are civil rights attorneys and were assigned to your case long before General Patton's son sat in our passenger car."

Buddy shook his head. "Correction, ma'am, you all sat in my passenger car." She smiled and nodded. "I stand corrected, Mr. Patton. However, it was the colored section and we were quite surprised to see a white man and two small children in that section." She paused for a second. "We were on our way to file in the 15th circuit court when we got your telegram." She looked at Buddy with an intense look on her face. "When we were on the train and you said you were going to help a friend, I had no idea we had the same friend." A.J. interrupted and said, "Lady, I have never seen you before in my life! Don't get me wrong, I ain't complaining, but how can we be friends?"

Cecilia laughed again. "My dear man, you are living in my grandmother's house." She patted A.J. on the shoulder. "Your uncle and my grandmother kept each other happy for many years. Your uncle would even paint my grandmother's house for her." Now Buddy was getting a funny feeling he couldn't explain, but he knew it was some kind of weird karma that put him on the passenger car with these people. "You also don't know this, but your uncle helped put me through law school." A.J. couldn't help but be stunned. "The lady next door that passed way!" A.J. blurted it out then realized he didn't know her name.

Cecilia leaned back in her seat and for the first time since they met, Buddy could tell she was emotional. "She was a beautiful woman with the grit and determination to persevere through some of the hardest times; the loss of her children, her husband, and all but one sibling." Buddy spoke up and asked, "What was her name?" Cecilia paused for just a second before answering, "Her name was Barbara Jayda Brown."

# Chapter 56

SHERRILL EASED THE CAR INTO the front yard of what used to be Ms. Barbara Jayda Brown's front yard but was now Alvin Jerome Mack's front yard. He would have parked in the short driveway, but there were cars everywhere. Buddy opened the back door to their sedan and held it open for Cecilia. As she stepped out of the car, he held his hand out, which she quickly grabbed with her left hand. As she exited the car and stood up straight, she brushed her right hand against Buddy's stomach and let it drag across him as she walked by. She smiled at him. "Looks like we are missing a party."

Buddy looked down at her hand as she walked by. He tried to release her left hand, but she wouldn't release his. She pulled him along and as they made their way to the front porch, he saw the front door open and Janie and Jimmy bolted from the front door, ran down the steps, and practically knocked Buddy over as they hugged him. He knelt down so he could be on their level and where he knew the hugs felt the best. "Daddy! Mrs. Kari made us cookies and sang to us!" Janie was so excited to relay the news to him that she wouldn't let Jimmy get in a word, although he was trying. "That's so nice, Janie. Did you save some cookies for me? I

## Chapter 56

am mighty hungry." She laughed and hugged him very close. It was dark outside, so neither Janie nor Jimmy could see the marks and bruises on their daddy.

A.J. stepped through the front door of his small living room that was packed with people and the minute they knew A.J. was in the house, they all stopped and began to cheer, whoop, and holler. The clapping continued long enough for Buddy and the kids to enter the room. Buddy looked around and realized that he, Clancy, Janie, and Jimmy were the only white people in the room. When the applause stopped, A.J. was surprised to see Curtis Freehold, Jr. step right in the middle of the crowd and raise his hand and ask for quiet. "Listen, I am not much on words and we have to get these folks on a train very soon, but I need to say this."

He looked around the room and found his target, nodded, and a few people started handing out little cups to everyone in the room except the kids. "We don't have any champagne, but what we do have, thanks to my dad, is some of the best triple distilled sour mash in all of Alabama. Hell, probably the world." The crowd laughed. "I offer a toast to a man who broke my arm and the woman who broke my heart." The crowd giggled a little. "Hell, for that matter, she broke every single man's heart in the great state of Alabama the minute A.J. walked into the room!" He raised his glass. "We wish you well in Texas and leave our arms open for you when it comes time for your return." He lifted his glass higher and then to his mouth where he drank the mash contained in the cup, as did everyone that was holding a glass.

A.J. was confused. Why was he sending them off to Texas? He had no desire to move to Texas. He held Kari in his arms during the toast because the minute she saw him come in the door, she nearly knocked him over by jumping into his arms. His ribs still hurt from being kicked, but he never said a word. He was just happy to be holding her. Just a few short hours before, he believed he would never see her again. Kari could see the look on his face, she reached up and put her hand on his cheek

*Choice of Honor*

and kissed him on the chin. "We can't stay here, baby, we are going with Mr. Patton tonight, it has already been arranged." He looked around the room with a sadness in his eyes and then looked directly back at her. Before he could say anything, she continued and said, "It's time we started over, it is time we started a new life somewhere else. Besides, they will never leave you, us alone." He swallowed hard then said, "Are you sure? I am prepared to stay and fight. Honey, I have a company to run." She smiled the smile that melted him the first time he saw her. "Baby, I want to leave, I want to see Texas."

He was about to respond when Janie came up and put her arms around Mrs. Kari's leg and held on tight. Kari and A.J. looked down at Janie. "Janie, I want you to meet my husband, his name is Alvin Jerome Mack, but I call him A.J." Kari smiled as she said it. Janie looked up from the safety of Mrs. Kari's leg as Janie was always a little shy and stuck her hand out. "Nice to meet you, Mr. Mack" A.J. was impressed by the little girl's manners and was struck by her beauty. She was a little princess, for sure. Janie took a long look at A.J. as the two shook hands. "Were you in the same car wreck my daddy was in? His face hurts, too."

A.J. threw his head back and laughed. When he did, it caused pain in his ribs and he stopped laughing but made sure he continued to smile. "Yes, ma'am, I sure was, but we are okay. Don't you worry one bit." Kari placed her hand on the top of Janie's head and was about to kiss A.J. one more time when Buddy came up with Jimmy hanging on to his right hand and a mason jar in his left hand. "You up for shepherding this heard to the train station?" A.J. looked at Buddy like he didn't understand. "Corporal, I need you to get everyone to the train station. Thanks to Miss Adams and her friends, we have run our bluff, they bought the fake story and its time get the hell out of Dodge."

He looked down at Janie. "Honey, Mrs. Kari needs your help, she needs you to help her look after her boys, can you do that for me?" She let go of Kari's leg and reached for Buddy. He

# Chapter 56

knelt down to receive the hug she was trying to give him. "Are you leaving me, daddy?" Buddy choked back some emotions that he was not comfortable with. "I am, baby. Of course, I will catch up to you on the train and before you know it, we will be back in Texas." She hugged him tightly and as she was hugging him, he looked at Jimmy. "And I need you to help Mr. Mack get everyone to the train station. It's a man-sized job that only you are up for. Can you do it?" Jimmy smiled, he liked that his daddy was calling him a man. "Yes, daddy. I will."

Buddy released Janie and patted Jimmy on the head, then stood back up to face Kari and A.J. When he was eye-to-eye with A.J., he said, "What the hell are you doing, Sergeant, where the hell are you going?" Buddy grinned the same grin that A.J. saw when Japanese soldiers surrounded them both in the war. "I have a promise to keep. I will catch up to you on the train, you have my word. Just make sure everyone gets on the train headed West." A.J. shook his head as if he was about to disagree when Curtis Freehold, Sr. came up with Curtis Freehold, Jr. "We are ready when you are."

A.J. nodded and then looked back at A.J. and Kari. "I will see you shortly. Get moving, please." He was about to turn and leave when he turned back around, removed some papers from his pocket, and handed them to A.J., who took them without thinking, but then looked confused. "Don't look so confused. I just signed the bill of sale over to you, it's all official." Buddy let A.J. open the papers before he spoke again. "I had Ms. Adams sign as a witness, and she is going to deposit the draft in First National in D.C. when she gets back." Buddy smiled a crooked smile. "I trust her." A.J. looked up at Buddy and his eyes were as big as silver dollars. He started to speak, but he couldn't find the words. Buddy continued and said, "The amount is correct. Looks like you are a helluva business man." A.J. looked at Kari and back to Buddy, but he still couldn't speak. "See you on the train."

# Chapter 57

THE SEDAN THAT CURTIS FREEHOLD, JR. was driving rolled to a stop in the rundown neighborhood East of town. Freehold, Jr. shut off the lights and set the brake. "Are you sure this is the house?" Buddy looked around as if he spotted a different house, but it was more theatrical than anything. Freehold, Sr. had some questions of his own, but he kept it to a simple "Son, are you sure?" Freehold, Jr. continued to look at the targeted house. "Yes, sir, I been driving that old fool around for weeks now and he been coming here every so often." He paused and turned to look at Buddy sitting in the back seat. "Look here, they ain't but two doors and two windows in the whole house. Too cold to have the windows open and the front door has a porch light."

He looked back towards the house and then back to Buddy. "I guarantee you walk right in the back door if you want." Buddy nodded his head and then leaned forward so that his head was right between the two Freeholds. "If I ain't back in ten minutes, just ease on out of here. If you two get caught at this hour in this neighborhood, it won't be pretty." Freehold, Sr. turned completely sideways in his seat so that he could get a clear but darkened view of Buddy. "Son, we ain't goin' nowhere. Go do your thing."

## Chapter 57

Buddy walked with confidence towards the house as not to draw any suspicion, but when he got to the front porch, he veered to the side of the house and quietly made his way to the back. There was one little step leading up to the back door. He slowly put some weight on the step to prevent it from creaking, then reached for screen. Luckily, the screen was unlatched, and he slowly pulled it open. He was in luck, not one squeaking sound. He mumbled quietly knowing he couldn't be heard. "Good man, keep your house nice and oiled, nothing like a man who takes good care of his things."

He turned the knob of the door and just as he thought, it was unlocked. Once he was inside, he could hear a radio playing. It sounded a little like Tommy Dorsey, but he wasn't sure. He reached in his pocket and retrieved the switchblade knife he had retained from the war. He couldn't even remember how he ended up with it, but he liked it and he kept the springs in excellent condition so that all you had to do was push the little button and it would spring to life with a smooth and unmistakable sound.

He reached in his side coat pocket and retrieved the jar he borrowed from Kari. He eased down the hallway towards the light and peeped into the living area and he spotted his target. He was sitting in a worn-out easy chair with his head tilted back with what looked like a steak or some slab of meat pressed against the side of his face. Buddy almost laughed but contained himself until he decided it was time make his presence known. He stepped into the living room without hesitation, but the motion was obviously too quiet because his target was either asleep or he still hadn't heard his intruder. Buddy pressed the release on the switchblade, which had its intended effect.

The man pressing the meat against his swollen face nearly leapt out of the chair but froze when he saw his intruder. Buddy held up the jar and shook it with a smile on his face. "Hello, Frankie."

www.ingramcontent.com/pod-product-compliance
Lightning Source LLC
Chambersburg PA
CBHW070419010526
44118CB00014B/1816